Memoirs of a
SEX ADDICT

"Everything has beauty,
but not everyone sees it."
~ Confucius

Memoirs of a
SEX ADDICT

A Jersey Girls Bares All

Samantha Barrett

CHB Media
Publisher

ISBN 978-0-9886315-4-0

Library of Congress Control Number: 2013940140

CHB Media, Publisher
725 Laurel Bay Circle
New Smyrna Beach, Florida 32169
(386) 314-0871

chbmedia@gmail.com

www.chbmediaonline.com

First Edition
Printed in the USA

Dedication

To my brother, I love you, and I blame you for nothing. We were still babies when we believed this lie. You had no way of knowing I was in pain; I never let you know.

To my parents, I thank you for your love. If there was one thing I always knew for sure, no matter how angry or disappointed you were in my actions, I always knew that you loved me. To PB and KDM, you stuck by me through everything. I've always known I could tell you anything, without judgment or criticism and no matter how many miles came between us, I always knew, that if you loved me, I couldn't be all bad. I thank you and I love you.

Finally, my husband, the Love of my Life, I thank you for your kindness, your caring, your ability to make me feel like, "Everything is gonna be alright." But most of all, I thank you for your unconditional love; I honestly believe it saved my life. I don't know where I would be if I had lost you. I love you so much ... forever.

Initially, this book was written to help heal myself. It is my sincere hope that it will also benefit others who have suffered as I have with Body Dysmorphic Disorder. For me, BDD was a very rough ride, so some of the language and emotions in these pages are also rough. It had to be that way in order to tell the true story.

— Samantha Barrett

Introduction

We all know someone who has cheated or who has been cheated on. Unfortunately, the frequency of infidelity in our country is a hot topic. It breaks some couples up, some get through it, but let's face it, it's not really that rare. Then there is another type of infidelity. The kind where we gasp and ask, "What's wrong with her?" or "Something must have happened to that girl for her to do something like that!" We are talking about women who have sex with other men while their husband is sleeping upstairs, or someone who makes out with another man with her husband in the same club. We think, "She's gotta be sick; how could she do that?" Well, that's exactly it. Most of us who commit this type of adultery are sick and the disease is Sex Addiction. People roll their eyes and don't believe it's a real disease. They think these people just like sex too much and can't be monogamous. Well, I'm one of those women, and I'd like to show you how it certainly *is* a real disease. Just like alcoholism and drug addiction, sex addiction is also a disease of the mind that inhibits our decision making skills and takes control of our lives. It destroys relationships and tears families apart. There are many different reasons why a man or a woman will develop this disease; I know that mine started as a child, and will explain how, by the age of just twelve years, I was a Sex Addict. I'm going to share my memoirs with you, even though it may be humiliating for me and shocking for my family. I believe we learn from our mistakes. Perhaps what I have learned through my trauma will teach you how to save your child from those same experiences and the suffering that went along with it.

Chapter One

We dressed up like the Bionic Woman. My cousin Tiffany and I wore the same costume for Halloween that year. It was around 1978, a time when it was safe for two seven-year-old girls to go "trick or treating" without an adult, and a year that the Bionic Woman was a popular Halloween costume. We approached the white house on the corner, across the street from the woods near my house. I remember it like it was yesterday. By this time the plastic masks had become unbearably hot and we flipped them up on top of our heads. We rang the doorbell and a woman—looking back it was probably a teenaged girl, but to a seven-year-old, it was still a "grown-up"—opened the door. Another woman, older than the first, came over with the bowl of candy and put a piece of candy in each of our bags.

The younger woman pointed to Tiffany and said, "Oh mom, look how cute *she* is. Give her another one!"

The woman reached into the bowl and put more candy into Tiffany's bag. I can't really describe to you how I felt at the time. I'm sure I was more humiliated than hurt; my face felt flushed and my stomach queasy. I didn't say a word. We headed down the hill toward home. We were almost done. I remember not wanting to trick or treat anymore, but I also didn't want to bring attention to what just happened. If Tiffany noticed anything, she didn't say. I didn't care about being hot anymore, I just pulled the mask back down over my face and continued trick or treating until we got home. I wasn't gonna let *that* happen again!

Looking back, I believe that this experience was pivotal for me because it confirmed what my big brother had always told me ... I wasn't pretty. There must have been some hope, somewhere in the back of my mind, that he could be wrong. After all, he was the only one who said it, and he was just a kid like me; but now an adult confirmed it, and all hope was gone. In the mind of a seven-year-old, adults are right about *everything*! I actually felt sick to my stomach, and had no one to turn to. It was too humiliating. After all, my parents had heard the things my brother would say and never once yelled at him or punished him for being mean to me. What if they didn't think I was pretty either? I couldn't ask them. What if they agreed with him? I may have been young, but I knew for sure I wouldn't be able to handle that! So I never asked. I don't know, some of you may be thinking I was too sensitive.

You may think "that's what big brothers do, they pick on their little sisters and we accept it and go on." Well I didn't, I couldn't. It hurt me really deep down. It changed my mood. Whenever he said those things, it took the fun out of playing with my brother. I wanted so badly to be pretty. Even if I couldn't change the way I looked, I wanted so badly to change the way *he* thought of me. I wanted *him* to think I was pretty. I actually felt guilty, I felt sorry for *him* that he didn't have a sister to be proud of and it was my fault for looking this way—*crazy right*? I thought so too. And I was actually right; I have since learned that I had *Body Dysmorphic Disorder* (BDD).

According to the *Diagnostic and Statistical Manual of Mental Disorders* Body Dysmorphic Disorder is a "... disorder marked by a preoccupation with an *imagined* defect in appearance that causes clinically significant distress or impairment in social, occupational, or other important areas of functioning," a mental disease of the mind that causes people to obsess about their perception of themselves. For me it was my facial features, I had a bump on the bridge of my nose, but it could be any physical trait. It could be a birth mark or freckles, thinking they're too tall or too short, under or over weight, for girls it could be the size of their breasts and for boys the size of their penis. People with BDD often become so obsessed with a part or parts of their physical appearance (whether it's visible to others or not) that they become unable to live a normal life. My time became consumed by looking in, OR avoiding mirrors, trying to correct or change, hide or cover this "defect."

One of the BDD symptoms is relentless skin "picking." I would constantly scratch or squeeze bumps, pimples and any lesions on my skin. BDD sufferers often pick until they've created an obvious wound. This I will *never* understand. This worsens and draws attention to an appearance we are already unhappy with. But, sure enough, every time I would get the littlest pimple, bite or bump on my skin, I would pick at it until I created this huge wound; then would try to cover it with make-up which *never* worked.

Many people with BDD, myself included, also suffer Obsessive Compulsive Disorder (OCD). The similarities between the two diseases according to the OCD center of Los Angeles, are: "While the specific thoughts and behaviors may vary with each of these disorders, this cyclical process is identical." To make it clear, "the cyclical process is identical" means we can't stop doing either. We can't stop the rituals of the OCD, like hand washing, tapping or touching things a certain number of times; and we can't stop focusing on our defect from the BDD.

When I was young, I didn't know I had OCD. I never even heard of it so I deduced that my OCD "rituals" were "messages from God." As a church-going Catholic child, with strong faith, it was the only thing I could think was responsible for my odd behavior. I would pay close attention to the steps I would take as I walked home from school. If I got to some point, a quarter of the way home, half way, it didn't matter, there were some days that I would get this "uneasy feeling" that something wasn't right. I would then walk back to school and re-walk, the same route home again and again until it "felt right." It always had to be the *exact same route*. It was God talking to me, right? He was keeping me out of harm's way. I thought maybe there were burglars robbing my house, since my mom worked and wasn't home yet; or a child predator was hiding in the woods, near my house. I didn't know what it was; I just *knew* I had to go back and do it again. It's the same disease that the people who we sometimes refer to as "germaphobes" have, just different "rituals." But the "repetition" is the same. They may repeatedly wash their hands while I repeat the walk home from school.

I also played a "counting game," or at least that's what I call it now that I know it isn't "my deal with God" which is what I used to call it. I would flip light switches on and off seven times when I would enter or leave a room alone. I would also flip the shampoo and conditioner flip-top caps open and closed eleven times before I'd use them in the shower.

Things had to be in a certain order. I would adjust decorations around the house, that may not sound weird, but remember, *I was eight years old*, like a vase, a candy dish, a wall hanging, until it "felt right." Now realize, I didn't actually move anything, or clean, I would pick them up and put them right back down, sometimes several times, until I was able to stop; until, again, it "felt right". I didn't know why; I just believed God was watching over me and he had control, so everything was going to be okay. After all, that was what I learned that faith was, 'always believing even if I may not always understand.'

As I advanced into my adolescence, my disease advanced with me. My room had to be set up a certain way. If a friend came over and a chair was moved, I wouldn't be able to leave the house, or go to sleep until the chair was put back. I also had to always wear bra and panty *sets*, or at least the exact same color. I would not be able to leave the house, *even worse*, I wouldn't even be able to put clothes on if I had a miss-match, like a white bra and pink panties. Before I was actually diagnosed, friends used to make fun of me all the time. The silly things OCD would force me to do, would just be "funny" to them. My closet was like a military exercise; shoes were all in the boxes on shelves in one closet and my clothes, tops and bottoms separate, both in length and color order in another; and *all* the hangers had to match.

I have needed to learn to laugh at myself when my friends would say, "Uh-oh, the OCD is kicking in," as soon as they saw me straightening something out. Which is ironic, because at the time, we were all joking about it. We had heard about it, seen it on t.v., but none of them thought that I actually did have the disease. They mostly thought I was a "neat freak" because that was the only ritual I let them see. I never did the light switches, or the counting in front of any one. It was sometimes very scary, I knew it was not "normal," behavior, but I didn't how to fix it. I was certainly too embarrassed to tell anyone because nobody wants to feel like a freak, *especially* during the adolescent years!

So I just kept on flicking switches, matching panties, and retracing steps where nobody could see me.

Even now that I have it under control with medication, the "counting game" will still creep up on me once in a while. I'll still do it, whether it's the lid to a shampoo bottle or a light switch, or even something new may pop up. I've learned that it's quicker to just play the game, rather than try to work out what has brought the ritual on. Another thing that still happens for me is once I start something, whether it's a big job, like decorating for Christmas or just doing a crossword puzzle, I have trouble stopping in the middle. I can't just put it down till later, like most.

The medication I take for OCD, Luvox, also called Fluvoxamine, really does help. It has given me back so much control over the "rituals". People who have this disease, usually aren't totally cured or symptom free, I would, however, say I am ninety percent better since starting the pills nine years ago. They are non-narcotic and I've had no side effects. For me at least, there will always be traces of the disease left over and that's just fine! I say this because many of you reading have this disease, most of you have been hiding it as I did and may be ready to seek treatment after hearing how life-changing it can be. I don't want you to become upset or discouraged if the doctor or pharmacist tells you that the medication will only give you around a sixty percent improvement. You may have more improvement, you may have less, or you may need to try a different medication. I've tried many! I was thirty-three years old when my doctor finally gave me the medication that worked. Once you find the right medication, it's like being 'reborn' into a life that's more peaceful, more enjoyable and a life that you have more control of. As some of you may know, the disease is like a "puppet-master and we are the puppet" is the best way to describe it.

Ever since I first became aware of BDD and OCD, I have researched the connection between them. I don't remember where I heard it, but people with BDD are so consumed and frustrated with the "defect" we cannot change or control, that we compensate by attempting to control other things around us. I remember the feeling of relief when I was able to forget my defective nose by obsessing about everything externally, like the light switch, or the bras and panties, these were things I *could* control, and in doing so, make me forget about my looks, even if just for a short time. Some people become compulsive about germs, focusing all of their attention on keeping themselves "germ-free." I'm sure you recognize these people? Those who repeatedly wash their hands and refuse to shake hands with other people? The obsessive cleaners?

These are just a few examples, but since many people with BDD will develop OCD, we have developed many ways to camouflage ourselves and our unusual patterns of behavior. This behavior then appears "normal" so it can now *shield the underlying issues.* This is important for *you,* all of you moms and dads that are reading this. The *underlying issues* can be dangerous and may need some form of treatment. If your child has learned to shield it, you may have no idea your child is suffering.

For me, "the bump on my nose made me ugly." I was told that lie initially by my brother. It was then confirmed by the woman while trick or treating. I believed it; I reinforced it; and for the next twenty-two years, it was my obsession. This lie, not only became a truth in my mind, it consumed my thoughts. This is why plastic surgery couldn't cure me. I didn't need to change the physical "defect," I needed a "psychic change" This is very important in changing behavior that is out of control, including addictions. Remember this term, as it comes up later when my sex addiction becomes out of control, but at this point, I needed a "psychic change" to control the BDD, meaning I needed to change the way I felt about myself and erase this lie that I had believed. I needed to take control back. I, of course, didn't know this at the time. The only thing I knew was that I hated the way I looked and I wanted to change it.

Tiffany and I are cousins on my mother's side. Our mothers are sisters, they're Scottish and Dutch. Both are very beautiful, everyone always said so, even as they were growing up, and they looked very much alike. Tiffany looked just like them. I, however, did not. Tiffany's father is Irish. She had big blue eyes, freckles, dimples, and a tiny little turned up nose. My father is a handsome, Italian man, the kind you see in movies. I had brown eyes, a wider more ethnic nose with a bump I later realize is the same exact nose my grandmother, his mother had, no freckles, and no dimples.

We spent a lot of time together; my brother, Tiffany and me. Tiffany's parents divorced when she was two and she became like another sibling to us. She and her mom got an apartment in the next town over, and since she was an only child, my aunt brought her over often to play with us.

My feelings of self loathing began to develop when we started school. Living in the next town Tiffany went to a different school, but we started Kindergarten at the same time. My brother was only eighteen months older, but started school two years ahead of us. Learning came very easily for me, but for Tiffany, it was more difficult. Looking back, it was probably because her mom had to work nights and was unable to help her with her homework. I didn't feel like I was any smarter than she was. I would come home with A's on my tests and report cards and everyone would make a big fuss about how smart I was. At the same time, everyone would make as big a fuss over how pretty Tiffany was. Even strangers would compliment how pretty she was. One time, our moms took us to a flea market. Tiffany and I were walking around when two old men who were sitting at the end of a row noticed us; well, they noticed Tiffany. One old man leaned forward and grabbed her arm, he looked at her face, pushed her hair off her face, then turned her toward his friend and said, "*This* is a *beautiful* girl!" and then let her go. People can be so ignorant. You know the saying, "older but wiser," well, not everybody!

It was around this time that we—Tiffany, my brother and I—learned that I was the smart one and Tiffany was the pretty one. She is pretty; I have all of the opposite features, so I must be ugly. It became a fact in our minds, no doubt whatsoever. Over time, it infected my entire personality; it consumed my thoughts; it controlled my life. I would often think of my future, and how it was going to be. It made me sad. While other little girls were probably day dreaming about who they were going to marry, or what kind of house they would live in, I was not. I was sure that no one would ever marry me. I didn't even think I would have a boyfriend when I got older; I would wonder what happens to girls like me ... ugly girls. Before I learned that *I* was ugly, I actually didn't know any "ugly" girls; I thought *everyone* was so beautiful.

What happens to ugly women, I feared? What do women, who don't marry, actually end up like? What kind of life do they have? I was not only sad, I was scared.

Being the ugly one hurt, but I was too embarrassed to let people know that I was hurting. I didn't want to draw attention to myself, fearing that more people might confirm it out loud, or my ugliness will become apparent to the few who hadn't noticed yet. There I was, this sad, embarrassed, guilty little girl who has to act like every thing's all right; when, in fact, I wanted to die. I knew I was going to heaven, and looks don't matter there, just spirit, and I knew I had a beautiful spirit.

My brother would draw pictures of my nose and show them to me; *like it's not bad enough that I have to look at it everyday in the mirror!* If the sun shone through the window on my face, he would point to my shadow to show me what an ugly profile I had. And finally, we used to play this game that my mother taught us where we would draw a picture on each other's back using just our fingertip. The other had to guess what it was a drawing of. When my mom taught us the game, she would draw hearts, flowers, four-leaf clovers; you know, pretty, happy things. I remember this one time when we were on a long car ride with my parents. My brother and I were in the back seat playing this game. It was my brothers' turn to draw and, of course, go ahead,

you can guess: Yes, he drew my nose. I knew what it was immediately, even before he finished, but I couldn't say it. Isn't that
fucked up! I was so mortified that I lay there quiet while he kept
on drawing it over and over again saying, "Come on, it's easy,"
and then he'd draw it real slow trying to get me to feel the out-
line. You know, it's about thirty years later and I remember praying while he kept drawing. I was praying that he would change
his mind and draw something else, anything else, my brother
is an artist, he could draw anything in the world and he had to
draw that! So finally, he yells out, "It's your nose!" and he drew
it again slowly, describing it as he drew it. "I can't believe you
didn't guess that one!"

I didn't say a word. Remember, I acted like it didn't bother
me. I felt sick inside and so humiliated. We had just spent what
felt like an eternity on the one thing I hated so much, that I
couldn't even talk about. That's right, that's why I didn't guess.
I'd rather lose the silly game than just say "my nose." How crazy
is that? I don't know if I was delusional or if it was a result of
the BDD or both, but for some reason, I guess I was so sick back
then, I thought if I didn't talk about it, ever, something would
change. I knew my appearance wouldn't change, but maybe if I
didn't say the word, no one would see it. I knew if I said it, if ever
I said the words, "my nose" I would bring attention to it, which
was the worst thing that could happen, in my world. Wow, looking back, I was a very sick little girl. Here's my brother drawing a
picture of my nose over and over again on my back and I am unable to guess because I had conditioned myself not to say these
two little words, "my nose!" It's not even a case where not saying
it will keep the attention away. The attention is already on it. He
had drawn "my nose." If I had said it, he wouldn't have had to
keep on drawing it. It would have ended the misery much quicker. But physically, I was unable to say those two little words. I
can even remember how I felt. Just thinking back, recalling the
humiliation—my heart was beating loudly in my ears; my face
was flushed and burning, and again, my stomach was queasy.
This pain affected all of my body systems, I, literally, would rather have been punched or kicked. The pain would stay in just one

area, and go away much quicker. *This* ruined my entire trip.

I could never be mad at him though; I loved him. I thought he was the greatest and wanted to be just like him. I mean one side of my brain is thinking, "You mean little *fucker*, you knew how I felt about my nose, you knew I hated it and the way I looked; my God, it's you who caused me to hate myself" But then the adult in me knows that he was just a little boy, nine years old, and had no *idea* how bad he was hurting me. How could he? I *never* told him. Many people, including therapists, psychiatrists and family members would tell me that that's normal. Once again, they'd say, "that's what big brothers do, they tease their little sisters." But it wasn't teasing; he was never laughing, he was "telling me like it is." There was no silliness or making fun. When we were little, we were so close. We played together all the time. I adored him. But as I got older, I felt he became embarrassed of me, and embarrassed for me, because he loved me so much. He wanted to make sure that when I entered the "real" world, I would know who I really was, what "category" I was going to fit into—ironically in a caring sympathetic way. Unfortunately there was no way of letting me know this without hurting my feelings.

Both of us learning that lie, that I wasn't pretty, is actually what tore us apart when we were young. Like I said, we were very close when we were little, but then, I believe, when he was in fourth or fifth grade things changed. I think it was when he became interested in girls, and they him, that he felt so much pity for me, he couldn't even look at me.

I can remember mornings, actually feeling intimidated by him, almost frightened by him. Each morning before school for about six years. We would get ready for school while my parents slept. I guess it probably started when I was in first or second grade because I would get dressed, brush my teeth, and then make a bowl of cereal. My brother and I would sit at our small kitchen table, eating our cereal, just three feet apart, and he would never talk to me, not a word. You've all heard of "uncomfortable silence," this would have been called "fearful silence" for me. He would stare at the side of the cereal box, you know, where all the ingredients and nutrition is written.

You may be thinking, "Give him a break, he was reading it while he was eating." We ate Cheerios every morning throughout all the years we went to grammar and middle school together;. there is *not* five years worth of literature written on the side of the cereal box. He just wouldn't look at me. It was so quiet; I was so afraid to make any noise at all. I would let my cereal sit as long as I could so it would get soggy and not be too loud and crunchy when I ate it. Even now, I cannot tolerate the sound of someone eating cereal. Not only cereal, *any* chewing or crunching. I learned recently—from Kelly Ripa on *Live with Kelly and Michael*—that this is actually a real disease called "misophonia." It's a real thing! It makes me feel very uncomfortable, brings back the anxiety of those mornings I guess. You might be thinking it, "Why didn't I just eat first and get dressed while he ate?" I know why; it's gonna sound crazy, but it was because I loved him so much. I always wanted to be with him; I wanted to talk like him, watch the same shows as him. I wanted to be just like him. You know, if we didn't eat out of the same cereal box, I'd probably pretend to read the side of my cereal box too. Just to be like him!

The lie that my brother, Tiffany, and I had learned, was confirmed and reinforced. It was now a "fact" to us and it had taken over my mind, my life. Far too many people don't realize that these lies that children are told while their personalities are being developed contribute to a large part of who they eventually become. In my case, it shaped the way I felt about myself, my priorities, my confidence, even the way I viewed the people around me. As I grew older, I was no longer able to define myself. Yes, when I looked in the mirror or at pictures I would see the ugly face that I had grown to hate; but when I was in a social setting, I would use the people, most importantly, the boys or men, to determine how I felt about myself each day. If they showed negative attention, like if they were rude or mean, I felt very ugly and unattractive, and I would lose what little confidence I had for that day. Unless they changed their feelings or attitude towards me, I stayed that way. I was unable to change the way I felt about myself. On the other hand, if they gave me positive attention, if they were complimentary or kind, even if it was just to get me into bed as I got older—and by older I mean eleven years old—I felt pretty and happy, confident. I would be in a great mood. It wasn't just a mood either. Of course, everyone feels better when they get compliments, and hurt if they're insulted, but with me, and others who have BDD, it will ruin your day or your night. It even ruined some entire weekends for me. If I wasn't able to find another man to re-define the way I felt about myself, the feeling stuck. Self-love, the whole attitude of, "Forget him, I'm great and I know it!" didn't exist with me back then.

That is one of the main reasons why I am telling you all this. For you parents, you can *never* tell your child they are beautiful, brilliant, spectacular too often. That is where they will develop that attitude of self love and self worth from. That attitude is a *must* in order to have a happy life. You can't allow others to have the power to "make" or "break" your spirit. Unfortunately, more often than not, they will break your spirit. You can't depend on other people for *your* happiness. You cannot let other people define you. Self-love and self-confidence are as important in life as food and water are. Yes, the lack of food and water will kill you quicker, but living without self-love and self-confidence *will* eventually kill you. Whether you commit suicide, over- or under-eat yourself to death, accidentally overdose on drugs or alcohol, eventually it will kill you.

For me, sex was my "drug of choice." I became addicted to sex by age twelve; it was the only thing that made me feel good because it was the only time I ever felt "pretty." Obviously, by the Grace of God, it didn't kill me, that's one of the reasons why I feel I have to tell my story. Nobody calls girls like me "sick," or feels sorry for us for having low self-esteem, they call us "sluts" or "whores" and I hope I can help change that for young girls suffering with this disease.

I often wondered if others felt this way about themselves. For me, it was my nose, but did other people have things about themselves that they didn't like? No—I knew the answer to that. People always complain about something they don't like about themselves. But did other people have things about themselves that they *obsessed* about, things that they hated so much that they couldn't even speak about it? Like did people with weight issues hate the word fat or chubby? Did people with bad skin hate the word pimple or acne? Were they also not only unable to say it themselves, but did they become uncomfortable when people around them were talking about it? It wasn't until I heard about Body Dysmorphic Disorder (BDD) in my late twenties that I realized I was *not* the only one.

"Why didn't you just get a nose job?" Isn't that what most of you are thinking? And it seems like a great solution; so I did. I had *four* nose jobs. That's the problem with BDD; it's a disease of the mind not the body. You need the "psychic change." That is *very* important for everyone to understand and to remember. After each nose surgery, whether they broke the bone or just removed cartilage, I would look in the mirror and my reflection never changed, I still saw the same face that I hated so much. This is why I stress the need for a "psychic change." You need to change the way the mind has been programmed. It's like when you break a bone; they don't just put a cast on it and it heals back to the way it was. The bone needs to be re-set before the cast is put on. If it isn't, when you take that cast off, the bone will still be broken. Plastic surgery did get rid of the bump on my nose, but my mind was still broken. I still believed all of the lies that had been, told, confirmed, and repeated for so many years. Those beliefs also needed to change, not just the shape of my nose.

Chapter Two

My father thought I was crazy having so many surgeries. It had even gotten to the point that I would sneak and have a friend take me. I wouldn't tell my family about it because I was so embarrassed. They thought I was crazy already. My dad would say it after each surgery, "You're sick, you're out of your mind." He was right, I was sick, although at the time neither of us knew how sick I really was. I couldn't stop. That was very hard for me too, upsetting my father.

I said earlier that I felt guilty because I thought my brother wished he had a pretty sister; I felt the same way about my dad. I knew my parents loved me. I knew they would do anything for their children, but I don't think that they thought I was pretty either. They never said I was pretty. Well, for school pictures and times like that when they had to say it, but you can tell when parents think their child is beautiful, and mine didn't. But again, I did know they loved me, they did tell me that, often. They also complimented and encouraged all of my good qualities, like how smart I was, what a good athlete I was, so if they thought I was pretty they would have said it, right? That's what I thought. Also, if I was fresh or talked back or something my mom would say, "Shut your *ugly* little mouth!"

One time in fifth grade, I think fifth—fifth or earlier—my mom and my aunt Olivia, Tiffany's mom, were going to teach

23

me how to wear make-up. I had asked them for their help. They ended up arguing about it! My aunt put the eyeliner outside on the bottom lid and my mom said, "What are you doing, put it on the inside! My aunt said, "No, when you put it on the outside it makes the eyes look so much bigger." To which my mom replied sternly, "Her eyes are big enough!" So now, not only did I hate my nose, but I knew my mother thought my eyes were too big and both my mother and my aunt agreed that I needed to start wearing makeup at just ten years old!

I know, I sound like a shit, blaming my family for my ugliness, but I promise you I never did. I knew God had blessed me with parents who love their children and each other, unconditionally. I learned at a young age that was rare and have always been very thankful. I figured I just wasn't born with the looks "card," and I don't think there is anything any one of them could have said or done to make me think differently about myself.

No, that's not true! I'll bet that if my brother ever heard my father say I looked pretty, even just one fucking time, he wouldn't have been so cruel all those years!! I mean my brother wanted to be just like my dad, so even if my dad lied to me and said, "Look how pretty my little girl is!" or "You were the prettiest girl there!" my brother would have changed the way he felt about me, whether he believed it or not. I swear—if my father said that the sky was orange my brother would go around trying to convince people the sky was orange! That's the influence my father's opinion had on my brother.

I don't know, maybe I'm being somewhat of a hypocrite. I have always said that those families of the people on *American Idol* were the worst. I always said they weren't doing their children any favors by saying, "Oh you have such a beautiful voice!" and letting them find out on TV, in front of millions of people that they really suck! I think that was the reason that my dad didn't try to convince me or my brother that I was beautiful. He knew how beautiful people were treated. He knew that beautiful people were treated just a little bit differently and was afraid if they convinced me at home that I was beautiful, I would be hurt when people in my adult life told me or treated me otherwise. You see, again, I knew the love was there; they were protecting me from being hurt. I just wanted so badly to be a "pretty girl." Even though some people would tell me I was pretty, I never believed them. I figured they were family and friends just being nice because they had to. I guess that unless my father or brother told me I was pretty, I would never think so.

Even as I got older and kept getting plastic surgery and cosmetic treatments, my father just said, "What are you going to do, go to Hollywood? You look fine." I didn't want to be fine, I wanted to be pretty. What I heard, each time he said that was, "If I wanted to be in movies I would need to have work done, but being unattractive was acceptable for living in the suburbs of New Jersey." I know many fathers have done much worse to their daughters. My dad never physically abused me in any way, but when he would say that, it hurt so much. I would have rather been told I was pretty, and been smacked around once in awhile. I'm sure it's easy to say, because I was never hit by him. Again, it just seems that the physical pain goes away quicker, and my life outside the home would've been easier.

I know many of you will disagree, but it's just what I think. I can't help it. And if you think that's bad, you're really gonna think I'm fucking crazy after this. One of my closest friends was molested by her father. The kind of molesting where he would give her special attention, buy her gifts for no reason and then seduce her so that, like many molestations, it felt "normal." It started when she was eight years old and continued on until she was fourteen. When she started dating he hated it; he was jealous. You think that's fucked up, right? Here's something a little more fucked up: I was jealous! Not of the molestation, but that he thought she was so *beautiful* and so *irresistible* that even though he knew it was wrong, he said he fell in love with her and couldn't keep his hands off her. He was even jealous and didn't want anyone else to have her. While here I was thinking my father was afraid that *no one* would ever want me. I'm not saying I would change his *love* for me—I wouldn't trade that for the world.

I'm sure it sounds worse than it was. My parents were

young. They had my brother at seventeen and me at nineteen. As an adult, I came to the conclusion that I just wasn't my father's type, you know what I mean, right? My mother looked like Tiffany; in fact, people often asked if they were mother and daughter. Remember, I was the opposite of Tiffany and my mother, so I just wasn't the "type" my father found attractive.

Who knows, I looked more like him, and maybe he saw in me what he didn't like in himself. Perhaps he just expected his daughter to look like her mother and not her father and was unpleasantly surprised by the outcome. I had told this to my mother once, when I was in my early twenties, and she, of course, said I was wrong on all counts. I even told her this story, but made her promise not to get mad or tell my dad. It was twenty years ago; I had forgiven him already, so she couldn't get mad at him and she promised she wouldn't. I explained to her how that Sunday afternoon my dad and my uncle were sitting on the couch watching football. My dad asked me to get them each a beer, so I did. I handed my uncle his, but opened my dad's—it was a screw top. I was so proud, I said, "Here Dad. Look, I even opened it for you!" He started by saying, "Yes, I see that, thank you." He then went on to say, jokingly, "You're going to make someone a wonderful *husband* some day!"

My uncle's eyes grew wide in disbelief, but he burst out laughing, slapping my father's knee. My dad just laughed as well, proudly because my uncle was laughing hysterically at his joke. I was nervous to hear my mother's reaction to the story. When I finished telling her, my mother just looked at me and said, "I don't get it." I said, "Neither did I," even though I kind of did. It was confirmation that no man would ever marry me and I would never be any one's wife. I also remembered how it made me feel, but I didn't tell my mother that. I even remembered the details. I was long gone by the time they contained themselves and went back to watching the game. I just walked away embarrassed, yes, but a little bit confused too. I knew the joke was on me, and how I wasn't a "pretty" girl, but I didn't know what the punch line actually meant. I didn't know if he meant my facial features were so masculine that I looked like a boy and no man would ever want to marry me; or, was it because I was such a tomboy? I had short hair; I always wore jeans, never dresses, and I played in sports so maybe he thought I would grow up to become a lesbian. No matter which was right, none of it was funny to me.

I guess when my dad was nine or ten, girls were wearing dresses to school with bows in their hair. None of the girls in my class wore dresses and most of us played sports. My mother went on to say, "I don't even get it, he was probably drunk with your uncle. What I do know is that Daddy always thought you were beautiful; he was so proud of you." That did make me feel better, true or not. She then explained that my father didn't want to put any importance on looks because brains were so much more important for success than looks were. She continued, "That's why he did always compliment you on how smart you were!" He really did too. He would also reward good grades. He would give us five dollars for every "A" on our report cards and in the '70s that was a *lot* of money to give a child. I think my allowance was five dollars a week, and that was more than most! Who knows, maybe she's right. Believe me, if it is true, and I knew that back then, I would have felt a lot better about myself. I wouldn't even have had to hear *him* say it, I'm sure just knowing it would have made a difference.

Now, after talking to my mother about it, I'm going to assume that was the reason why he never said I was pretty. I'll tell you though, I swear, finally letting it out, just out of my head and onto paper, what I have believed and kept inside my entire life, has been more therapeutic than any therapist I've paid thousands of dollars to talk to.

For the *first* time in my life I'm looking back at everything so clearly without worrying about embarrassment, or judgment, saying exactly how I felt without being a martyr or trying to protect any one's feelings and it feels *really* good! I suggest it to all of you, any of you that are holding feelings in. Whether you stole a pack of gum when you were eight or had sex with your husband's brother, write it down! Write what happened, why it happened, how you felt, and what you can do about it. Even if there is nothing you can, or want to do about it, let it out because it feels good. Let it out because once you bring a secret into the light, it shrinks. Let it out because shame, guilt, lies, when held inside, can cause cancer. It's true. So often we make mistakes and there is nothing we can do about it besides getting it out. So do it, take action, either by telling someone you can trust or writing it down. Make sure you include that it's over now and you're forgiven. You made a mistake, we all do. Life is too short to spend feeling guilty all the time. Make sure you mean it too. Haven't you forgiven people for mistakes they've made?

Love and forgive yourself the same way. Then either destroy it, or make a book out of it if you think it will help others. That's the reason I'm telling my story. I've wasted twenty-five years of my life feeling either guilty, self loathing, or wasted. I never knew I was actually sick. I hope I can prevent others from the guilt and the suffering, specifically, children. My childhood ended at eleven years old. This book is obviously not written for children, but if just one parent recognizes this behavior in their child. If they then realize that their child is not a "bad" kid, or a "weird" kid, but potentially a very sick child who is suffering; and that child gets help, it will all be worth it.

Life is beautiful and precious, don't waste it. My mother told me, when she bought me a diary I had asked for, "Don't ever write down what you don't want read by others." That is some very good advice, so make sure you destroy what you write if it could hurt someone. Its best too, if you destroy it symbolically, like it's done and gone out of your life. I've heard a few clever ways that work. One way is to throw the pages into the burning fireplace watching them burn away, never to be thought of again. In the past I have written things in the sand and then watched the waves come and wipe it clear away. It really works; you just have to focus on what you're doing.

I do hope, though, around all this criticism you can hear how great my parents really were. We can't give what we don't have. My dad was one of four boys with an alcoholic, abusive father. I'm sure he *never* heard his father tell his mother she was beautiful, and there were no other girls in the family. I just want everyone to realize, including my mother, because she used to come down on my dad really hard for not complimenting us or her. I hope she knows that he didn't withhold it; he didn't have it to give.

He is a loving, old-fashioned man. The kind of man you can't find anymore, who opens doors for you and drops you off while he parks the car when it's cold or raining. He worked three jobs and went to night school when we were babies, but he would always bring us home a surprise when he was done with a long shift; like candy or gum, or a little toy. He was the best provider I'll ever know, even when he graduated college, I can still remember him working two jobs. Can you imagine how tired he must have been? But he would still take us to the Jersey Shore for an entire week's vacation each summer, go on rides with us at the boardwalk, and made sure he took us to Six Flags amusement park each year. When we started playing sports he would coach our teams; and on Christmas morning, under the tree and all our stockings were filled with gifts—everything we asked Santa for and more!

But most importantly, he was always there for me. If I ever went to him with a problem, he'd fix it. I wish I realized this then. If I had just told him how I felt, not only would he have told me how beautiful I was, but when he realized how sick I was he would have gotten me help. So before writing anyone out of your life permanently, remember people can't give what they don't have. Think why did they do or not do whatever it was that upset you so much. Were they aware they were hurting you? Was it taught or not taught to them? Be very careful. Very good people make very big mistakes.

My mother, I swear on my life, I have never known a mother who loved her children more. She would give her life for her kids. The only thing she ever wanted to be was a mother, nothing else, just a wife and mother. Like I said, my parents were young, but as we all know, no matter how old you are when you have your children, no baby comes with an instruction book. You never really know if what you are doing will help or hurt your child. It's not taught in school, and I will never understand why. Parenting is the most important job in the world and only some schools offer "child care" or "family living" as electives. In my mind these should be mandatory, and in every school! They are just as important as math or reading—they are skills that will improve the quality of life.

I am not saying schools should replace any other classes with classes that teach parenting, or single living. I remember, my junior year I had one elective and one free period where my friends and I sat in the cafeteria and did nothing but talk and go smoke in the bathroom. Kids have lunch time and after school to spend time with their friends. We are trying to prepare them for life as an adult. I have never worked at a job where I worked a seven-hour day, had a one-hour lunch, and a forty-minute free period to sit and do nothing. Kids hate being bored; if we are trying to prevent drop outs, lose the free period and add some classes that will teach them how to live. Make mandatory classes that will show them the cost of living. Teach them if they earn three hundred dollars a week, and have a seven hundred dollar rent each month, that they will have *no* money for fun or clothes. Show them how much food and water and gas and electric are. That may encourage college or trade school. Kids need to have name brand clothes and shoes, and once they see that they are only going to be able to afford a thrift store wardrobe, they might think twice about dropping out.

Use sex education classes to teach the things they'll need to know after the baby is here—it takes only five minutes to explain how a baby is made. Teach them how much diapers and formula, pediatricians, and medicine cost. Finally, we have to teach these future moms and dads how important it is to love this baby, and how to send that message of love to the baby. Remember, babies don't understand the language, the word "love" doesn't mean anything to them. You need to show them. Tell them that the way they look at their child or the tone of voice they use when speaking to the child is more important than what they actually say.

The one thing that is almost taboo to even say, is something I believe *needs* to be taught. We must teach, convince kids that having a child is *not* mandatory. Just because your sister and your best friend and your sister-in-law have babies doesn't mean you have to have one. You can still stay at home and be a wife and take care of the house if finances allow it. I only say that because I have met women who got pregnant because they didn't want to work anymore. They ended up miserable, and divorced. You will still get into heaven, or whatever the afterlife is according to your higher power. Whatever your belief system may be, if you're a kind person, your higher power, whether it's God, the Universe, whoever, whatever it is will smile down on you whether you decide to become a parent or not. Life is a gift we have been blessed with; we just need to do our best to enjoy it and try to leave the planet better than it was when we arrived. If a person chooses not to have children, they cannot let religion, family, guilt or society change their mind; both the child and the parents will suffer.

I think every couple, no matter what age, should get a puppy before they decide to have a baby. Then, after a year of loving their puppy and being patient with it, having potty training accidents on your bed or your couch, realizing they didn't know better than to chew your new shoes; after a year of getting up early to walk them and feed them, and a year of rushing home from work in time to let them out and feed them; after a year of trying to get family or friends to move into your house to watch your puppy if you want to go out overnight, or away for a weekend; after you add up the cost of one year of pet food, vet appointments, leashes and toys; after *all* that, multiply the stress, the work and the cost by at least a hundred, then decide when to have your baby.

My mother read all the books and parenting magazines available. She even wrote little notes to us when we were born in our baby books telling us that she loved us and promised she would do the best she could to keep us safe and happy. I remember after getting a booster shot—that shot you get before you start kindergarten—my mom held a cold cloth on my arm and sat with me all day. She sat and watched *The Magic Garden*, which was my favorite show; she watched *Woody Woodpecker*, *The Jetsons*, and all the rest of my favorite shows without complaining, or even falling asleep! So you can see why I believe that my parents were the best no matter how I turned out, and it took awhile, but eventually I turn out pretty good. Living with BDD is tough; as many of you know, there are obstacles that other people not only don't have, but don't see us having either, because of the secrecy of the disease.

Somewhere along the way my mother's unconditional love caused her to become an enabler. I only know that from looking back as an adult. She should have reprimanded my brother when he would insult me, but like many, she just figured brothers tease their sisters. I don't know, was it really damaging what he was doing or was it the BDD I had? Maybe other girls just went right back at their brothers? Maybe she wasn't wrong; she didn't know I was sick or how bad it hurt me; she didn't have any brothers; she was one of four girls, how would she know?

One Friday night, freshman year of high school, I was sitting on the side of a corner grocery store throwing up from all the vodka I had been drinking, when I heard, "Samantha, is that you?" It was my mother walking up to get milk or something. I quickly yelled, "Yes Mom, hi!" She asked, "Are you *okay*?" which was a good question! Here is her thirteen-year-old daughter sitting at the side of a grocery all alone on a Friday night! She didn't see that I had been sick so I said, "Yes mom, I'm fine, just go back home," and she did. She never even asked me about it, like where were my friends, who were hiding because they didn't want my mother to call their mothers once she realized I was drunk—which she never did. Little did they know, she had so much respect for me and my privacy that she would never do that. Can you believe that? She respected the privacy of her little, lying, burn out, slut of a daughter. Love is blind in all situations. Even respecting my decision to date a seventeen-year-old when I was twelve; she thought he was nice and he was, but come on, she had to know we were having sex but didn't dare ask.

I think she just got some bad information somewhere about letting your children express themselves. I looked ridiculous with tons of make-up on my face, but she figured I was expressing myself. I now know I was hiding my face, what I thought to be my "ugly" face, behind tons of thick make-up. When I look back at pictures, I can't believe she would let me wear make-up that way. But I wouldn't have left the house without it. I wouldn't have even gone to school. I guess she knew that. Even my grandfather, on my father's side, at a Mother's Day dinner when I was about fourteen said, "I just want you to know, if I was a young man, I wouldn't give you a second look!" I know he was drunk, but it still tore me apart inside. Everyone at the table, all sixteen of them—I have a huge family—pretended like they didn't hear it, but I was still humiliated. My dad saw me come back from the ladies room where I cried my eyes out and asked if I wanted to leave. I just shook my head yes, I knew speaking would make me cry again. He handed me the keys so I could just go to the car and wouldn't have to say good bye to everyone. He knew I was humiliated and on the ride home he didn't bring it up. I remember I got so wasted that night. I ended up getting sick and passing out at the park.

No wonder why I felt like my parents agreed with me about being ugly; their actions were saying, "Do whatever you can to hide that face." I guess I just felt somewhere deep down that whether they believed it or not they should have said, "You're so beautiful, you don't need all that make-up!" I think my mother actually did say that one time, but she never made me take it off, so I guess I didn't think she really meant it.

Chapter Three

I went to a public grammar school, walking distance from my home, kindergarten through the fifth grade and here's a surprise, it was some of the happiest times of my life. I know it sounds contradictory. I've bitched and moaned about my brother the whole time, how sad I was being compared to my cousin Tiffany, and now I'm saying it's the happiest time of my life. It was though, such a time of innocence; no responsibilities, no worries. It may have been different if Tiffany had also gone to this school but she didn't, and as a child you live in the moment, so I didn't think about her or our looks.

I think even for a adults the world was simpler in the '70s. There was a lot less social media back then. No computers or cellphones, we had three channels on our 36-inch TV. If you didn't read the paper or watch the news, the world seemed like a perfect place. During those grammar school years, looks weren't all that important. The things that were important were sports and grades. It didn't matter if I wasn't pretty; I was a straight "A" student and a good athlete. When I started softball I got a Rookie-of-the-Year trophy and I was an all-star basketball player. I won the Spelling Bee contest in our town and was friends with almost everyone in the class; I was even dating one of the cutest boys. How could this girl be ugly? She couldn't, she wasn't. She was *beautiful* and I love her now. I owe her an apology for not only taking away her childhood, but for *everything* else she had to go through because I believed this "lie." I am also *so* proud of her for being so strong. Not many people could go through all the things she has and turn out so kind and loving to everything—family, friends, animals, the planet. It may sound conceited to some of you, but most of you know there is so much self-loathing in this country right now, that self-love is rare, and necessary for happiness. Whether we don't like our physical appearance or are feeling guilty and filled with anxiety it doesn't matter, the symptoms are all the same and happiness isn't one of them. Looks, both good and bad, are temporary. Guilt is living in the past, and anxiety is worrying about the future. Learning to stay focused on the present moment is really the key to happiness.

Besides the trick or treat and flea market incidents, there is another from those grammar school years that stands out in my memory. After having discussions with friends and family about things that had hurt them in their lives, it seems most people remember life's traumas more vividly than other past experiences. I had thought, perhaps it was my BDD that made me more sensitive, but it seems to happen with everyone. As I describe these experiences, big or small, *every* detail comes back so clearly—the words, the faces the feelings. But one in particular has stayed with me. I can almost feel the pain again as I'm writing. I was in fifth grade and about five or six of us girls went to smoke behind the shed in Donna's backyard. Diane had stolen some Parliament cigarettes from her mom. I'm standing there smoking my cigarette and the tall girl next to me, Donna, is staring down at me. I look up and ask, "What's the matter?"

She answers, "Your nose." My whole body gets nervous, I don't want to, but I have to ask, "Why?" I put my hand over it and ask, "Is there something on it?" She answers, "No, it's just so big." For no reason! No laughing, no kidding around. I was mortified. Could you believe that? I wanted to leave. I have never understood people like that. Why be so mean? It's not even like she was a beauty or anything herself. She should watch out too, someone else, anyone else who didn't have BDD, would have said, "Well your ass is so big." But I wouldn't do that; I know more than anyone how much insults can hurt. I just finished my cigarette and went home.

Karma is a funny thing though; nine years later, I fucked her boyfriend. Not even out of revenge or anything, at the time I partied so much I probably couldn't recall the fifth grade. After high school she and I actually became like "best" friends; I would later realize we were more like drinking buddies who spent a lot of time together. Friends wouldn't treat each other the way we did. One night after a party at her house, she kicked her boyfriend and me out for no reason, or at least no reason either of us knew about. Now by that time, I had been a sex addict almost nine years. Not someone who just loved having sex all the time either—an out of control sex addict. Nobody knew about the addiction, not even me. I just figured I liked sex. So without explanation, she kicked her drunken boyfriend out of her house with a wasted sex addict. Can you guess what happened next? Right, we went to his house and we fucked.

Anyway, this was early in our "friendship" and I thought we were friends. I felt so guilty the next day, I called her to apologize. I didn't apologize for having sex with him, I was too afraid of ending our "friendship" and felt too ashamed to admit what I had done, but I wanted to find out why and apologize for the reason she threw us out in the first place.

You see, a few days prior to this party, the three of us went away together. Her parents had a lake house and I didn't have a boyfriend at the time so she and I were going to meet him up there to party for the weekend. On the ride up, she told me she didn't know if she liked him or not. They only met four or five days earlier; she hadn't even had sex with him yet. So I said, "Hey, if you're not interested in him long-term we could have a threesome or something!" Now I know I said it somewhat jokingly but remember, I had a sex addiction and no date—for an entire weekend at a lake house. If at that time she had said "OK" then that would be the plan for the weekend. I'm sure he would have gone along with it, what guy wouldn't?

She didn't say OK; she just laughed it off and said, "I don't think so" or "yeah right." But I knew she didn't seriously consider it.

Fast forward about four hours. We're at the lake house, we're playing drinking games, and we're loaded. She leaves to go to the bathroom and while she's gone he kissed me; without thinking, I kissed him back. I don't remember exactly what happened; she didn't see us but I think she knew something was up by the look on our faces when she returned. I remember going into the kitchen with her and telling her that he kissed me, and I didn't stop him. She was pissed. I tried to explain to her, "But you weren't even interested!?" And that's true; I wouldn't have let him kiss me if I thought she liked him. To which I think she said something like, "I said I wasn't sure." She then left the room and went to bed pissed at both of us.

I told him, "You better go in there; she won't stay mad at you." He did and she even had sex with him. Remember, she told me that she wasn't sure if she even liked him, and she wasn't as much a whore as I was who would fuck just anyone. I think him kissing me made her like him a whole lot more and the sex was a way of marking her territory.

Fast-forward three days to her party. There's like ten to fifteen people there, more like a gathering of friends than a party. Some girls in our loop were there, seven or eight of us, and a few of our boyfriends, sitting around playing drinking games. I was sitting next to him—Charlie was his name by the way—we were laughing, getting louder as the night went on. We would pick each other to drink, but innocently. Now that I knew she liked him, I had no interest whatsoever.

The party started thinning out. Donna came down in her pajamas and said, "Could you two leave? I'm tired." I remember being surprised because I didn't know what we had done wrong, but when I asked she just insisted, "Will you just leave, please?" So drunk me got all insulted while he stayed quiet. I grabbed my purse and stormed out. I didn't have my car so she knew we left together. Now before you hate me, I need to clear up a few things. I'm being loose and fast with the words "boyfriend" and "friend". When you hook up with a guy one weekend, and hang out two more times with friends, admit you're not even sure if you like him, is he really a "boyfriend" yet? Besides not fucking yet, they hadn't even been alone together on a date or anything. Secondly, if she and I were "friends," wouldn't she have spoken to me about what was bothering her before kicking me out of her house? Remember, this night nothing did happen; no kiss, nothing, and the night he did kiss me I told her right away. Like I said, I later realized we were never "friends;" we hung out, a lot, but nights like this don't happen between two *real* friends. I know, I have real friends and nothing close to this would *ever* happen.

When I called to apologize I asked, "What happened last night, what were you so mad at?"

She said, "I would think after what happened at the lake house that you would keep a little bit more distance between the two of you."

I apologized. I felt so guilty. She asked where he and I went, I just said, "He drove me home." I don't know at this point if she believed me or not, but she soon found out for sure that *something* happened. A few days passed and their "relationship" just ended; neither one called the other and I never asked about it. Then, like three days later, she was at my house, the phone rang, she answered it and it was him! Now he and I hadn't been talking or anything. That morning after, when he had driven me home, he kept on asking if we could see each other again. I felt so guilty, I told him, "No way, I feel horrible about what we did." I wouldn't even give him my number, but I guess he got it from the phone book! When he asked for me, she asked, "Who is it?" He said, "Charlie." Now he was the only Charlie either of us knows. Then she handed me the phone she said, "It's Charlie," with a very stoic face on.

I put the phone to my ear and before I even say, "Hello," he hangs up, knowing I guess that it was her! I told her, "Nobody's there." And I handed her the phone back. She hung it up and that was it. I couldn't believe it. We just never mentioned his name again. But she definitely knew something happened.

You may be thinking that I'm an asshole, but I'm not. Let me explain how bad this other disease, sex addiction developed from BDD and took over what little control I had left in my life. The addiction was so bad that I never said no to anyone who wanted sex from me. Any sex: blow jobs, anal sex, intercourse, I didn't care. I felt pretty when men wanted me and I loved feeling pretty. I had never felt it until I started fucking around, so I never stopped. It would start with that initial chemistry; so I guess it wasn't just *anybody*—the chemistry, the initial "spark" had to be there. After that, it didn't matter. Age, nationality, occupation, didn't matter. Having a man want me made me feel beautiful, and I loved that feeling. I never had it until the first time I had sex at age twelve; that's a nice story which comes up later.

Believe it or not, Donna and I remained friends for about fifteen more years! Ten years after Charlie, it happened again. Donna's steady boyfriend, who she lived with and later married, begged me to let him go down on me while she was sleeping upstairs. I said, "No," and went upstairs. We had been drinking all night and who knows what could have happened. I know, big deal, that doesn't make me a saint, but it was a big deal. I was like an alcoholic refusing a free drink. But by then I had met my later-to-be husband, who was asleep in our bedroom, and I wasn't about to risk losing him. If I needed sex I could go right in there and make hot love with him.

Her boyfriend called me on Monday at work and thanked me for having the willpower to say no. He said ever since he met Donna he never even looked at another girl and didn't know what came over him. I believed him and figured he made a mistake. I didn't think it was necessary to tell her; it didn't mean anything.

As a grown-up now and knowing all that I do about our "friendship," I feel sorry for Donna. She was jealous of me. She had no idea how I saw myself. To her, in grammar school I was smart, skinny and popular, so she thought she had to make sure I knew I wasn't perfect. Yea, right, like I need to be told that. How funny it is how things can look to other people on the outside. That wasn't the only time either. I remember one time when we had become friends we went to the mall shopping for clothes. Now my aunt Olivia had warned me as a child, "Never go clothes shopping with your girl friends; they don't want you to look better than they do so they will lie when you ask their opinion." As a child, of course, I didn't take her seriously. Especially because I had, and still have a loving and beautiful true best friend, Jennifer, that always told me how beautiful I was even when I didn't think so.

But Olivia was right, at least in this case. I remember trying on a pair of jeans and they looked great! They made my ass look so beautiful I forgot for a second that I didn't like myself! I knew I was gonna buy these jeans, and I knew when I wore them I would have my pick of men to fuck—after all, that's why I wanted to look good, right? But I stepped out to get her opinion because that's what you do when you shop with a friend. When I asked her what she thought she took a long time, I guess trying to think how she's gonna talk me out of these. Then she finally answered, "They're not very flattering; I wouldn't get them." I couldn't believe it. Olivia was right! Maybe you're thinking that that's her opinion, she could've not liked the fit. But that's not true. When you hang out with someone a lot, and we did, you can tell when they're lying. She would clear her throat and her eyes would shift back and forth, not looking me in the eye, and she did all that! This girl was not my friend.

It wasn't just me either. One day, right after my other close friend of thirty years now, Nicole, had her baby, Donna and I went to see them to say congratulations and see the baby. Now Nicole has always had an awesome body, so right after she had the baby, she looked like she was back to her size four that she was before. Donna wasn't fat, but she was tall and a little overweight. As soon as Nicole, who was only home from the hospital for a week, answered the door, Donna had enough nerve to look at Nicole's body and the first words out of her mouth are, "You bitch, you just had a baby and look how skinny you are." I felt embarrassed for even bringing her with me. Nicole is a very close friend of mine; we had been friends, at the time, for at least fifteen years, and I bring someone like this to visit her right after she has her first baby. I know, it's not really an insult, it's a compliment but she said it with a harsh tone; she didn't say it laughingly, or affectionately—the two of them weren't close enough for that. I thought it was inappropriate and later apologized to Nicole.

In case you're thinking, "Why did you keep hanging out with this girl if you knew what a bitch she was?" The answer is, "I don't know." I'm sure everyone around us thought we were best friends, maybe even she thought so, but I knew we couldn't be. I had a best friend and the way I felt when I was with Donna was nothing like the way I felt when I was around Jennifer. Jennifer and I loved and supported each other no matter what. Donna, on the other hand, was more of a "what have you done for me lately" kind of person. She really wouldn't go out of her way for another person unless she would somehow benefit. We became friends because we hung out at the same places to drink—down the meadows or on the tracks; we weren't twenty-one yet and couldn't go to bars. We were both going to college, which a lot of our friends weren't, and we both broke up with our high school boyfriends, so we had a lot in common. Personality wasn't one of them.

Another reason I kept hanging out with Donna might be the self-loathing brought on by BDD. That might sound ass-backwards, but when I'm done explaining how it worked with Donna, I'll give you another example of it. I knew, subconsciously, that this girl would keep me down, and she did. If ever I started to feel good about myself, she would make sure, in some way, to bring me back down to where I thought I belonged.

The second example of this was when I was fifteen. My friend, Nicole and I went to her boyfriend's house. I think we had been drinking. If not, we drank when we got there. He was eighteen or nineteen. The three of us were drinking together for a little while, but finally, "three was a crowd," and they introduced me to his good-looking twenty-five-year-old cousin, Mike, who also lived there, and left me with him.

At this point I was very wasted but I remember him pulling my clothes off and bending me over the bed. He started fucking me from behind and proceeded to flip me around into all different positions. I was a skinny 15-year-old girl who weighed about

105 pounds and he was a twenty-five-year-old man, so I was like a plastic fuck doll for him. All the energy I had left was used trying not to pass out from being so wasted. I don't even remember how he finished. If he came inside me, or even if he used a condom. I don't even know how Nicole and I got home.

What I do remember is three days later I was at a phone booth with Nicole. She called her boyfriend and the cousin answered. When she asked for her boyfriend, Mike asked, "Why don't you bring your friend back over?" Nicole frankly answered, "I don't think so." To which he replied, "Her loss." Again, it hurt so much. Not just because he said it, but because in my mind, I agreed with him.

Looking back, I should have had that mother-fucker arrested for statutory rape. But I didn't, instead, four years later, I dated him. Donna and I were at a Halloween party, getting drunk, and he was there. I didn't notice him but when I went into the bathroom near the kitchen he spotted me.

Now I don't remember if Donna overheard him or if he told Donna that he thought I was so beautiful and he wanted to meet me. I just remember Donna saying in a very surprised voice, "There's a really hot guy over there that saw you and thinks you're beautiful." That's what I mean about her keeping me down—showing she was surprised that a hot guy was interested.

Somehow we hooked up and I went home with him that night. He lived somewhere else by then, and I didn't recognize him or make the connection. When I finally did make the connection that he was that asshole cousin, Mike, from four years back I didn't want to remind him that I was that ugly little girl with no self-respect. And I loved the fact that this hot, twenty-nine-year-old was now thinking I was so beautiful. As we dated I realized that he was "dumb as a box of rocks" and no way would he recall that afternoon when I was fifteen.

Remember, I was an intelligent girl, just sick with OCD and BDD, or what I called at that time, "brain disease." It was a chemical imbalance, a form of mental illness. I didn't know this yet; I always thought that mental illness meant I would be eating checkers or collecting the heads of Barbie dolls—ya know, *crazy*! It wasn't until I became a registered nurse that I realized some mental illness was just as serious and deadly a disease as cancer.

Anyway, after about three months he started talking about what kind of engagement ring I would like. I was bored with him at that point and mostly still around because the sex was so good. He would go down on me until I said stop. Really, thirty minutes, forty-five minutes, an hour, of head; that's hard to break up with! He also had a huge cock, and I know, believe me I've been with enough men to really *know*, that size doesn't matter, but he had the skill to go along with it. I guess God gave him extra cock instead of brains, ya know. It took me about a year or more to finally break up with him. Each time I tried, he would say something and I would feel bad. I hated breaking up with people; it's one of the hardest things to do because I knew how bad being dumped feels—it sucks!

It finally got to the point where I told him we would see other people. I didn't want to cheat on him, but I guess that would be a step closer to breaking up. Then one night he followed me when I went out with my friends and made a huge scene. I was fucking someone upstairs at a party when my friend knocked on the door and said, "Sammy, Mike's here." I said, "Oh shit, I better go downstairs!" to the guy on top of me He was a friend of mine and I didn't want him to get in the middle of this craziness. I was so embarrassed; I just got in Mike's car and left with him.

When we got back to his apartment, we were still arguing. I took a beer out of the refrigerator and took a sip. I walked back into the messy bedroom, clothes all over the place, dirty sheets, where he had already gotten into bed. We continued to argue. As I sat on the bed, my bottle of beer tipped and a little spilled out. He saw this, and smacked me across the face, hard. That was it. I drove home, and never went back. He would still call me begging me to come back to him, and when I refused he would threaten that if he ever saw me with another guy he would kill us both. I taped one of the calls and was able to take him to court to get a permanent restraining order. I don't want to look a gift horse in the mouth, but the judge that gave him a restraining order actually *apologized* to him. He said, "I'm sorry, I don't think you were actually going to hurt her, but it is on tape." What an asshole. I found out two weeks later that this same judge wouldn't give a restraining order to a woman who filed for one that summer, and her husband ended up killing her in their house a month later. This judge probably makes decisions that affect so many people's lives each day. How scary is that?!

As you can see, I didn't re-find these two people, Donna and Mike, to get revenge. Perhaps my sick mind needed to try and change the way they felt about me. Looking back from where I am now, I just have to believe that for some reason, those things had to happen to get me where I am today. I knew enough to pray for God's will to be done, not my own. If I am asking God for something I want to happen or for a change in my life, but am not getting it, it just may not be right for me, or not right for me at this time. God has something better planned for me. If there's one thing I know to be true, it's that God has always been with me, protecting me. Whether I refer to him as God, the Source, or the Energy that brings us all together, whatever it is, it is love and if we follow, without resistance, it will guide us to our true happiness.

I no longer believe in a "religion" because no one *really* knows for sure. I left the Catholic church because according to that church, my gay friends and family members who are caring, loving people aren't going to heaven, but the Priests who have molested and destroyed the lives of little boys are? I couldn't be a part of that. What I do believe is that I didn't get through all these hard times on my own! My faith and my prayers kept God, my higher power, close at all times watching over me. Not to mention, I had so many other things to be thankful for. Besides my faith, being most important, I had a home; I had healthy parents and siblings that loved me and each other, and I had intelligence. Whether I used it or not, it was a gift that had been given to me, a gift that no other person could take away.

As I've grown up, I've seen how so many people live. I've realized that those gifts alone are enough to be grateful for.

These were the things that confirmed my faith so easily. There is no other way to obtain these gifts. You can't buy them, you can't make them; they are gifts from a Higher Power. They are luxuries that shouldn't be taken for granted. I don't anymore.

Chapter Four

Elementary school ended after fifth grade. These really were my "Wonder Years," but I was now ready to transfer to my middle school, which was sixth, seventh, and eighth grade. It was a little farther, but still walking distance. I was nervous, of course, but excited too. I figured, how different could it be? That was until my brother Paulie explained exactly how different it was. He was starting his third year there, so I figured he knew what he was talking about.

First, keep in mind, he and I did and still do, love each other very much. Nothing he ever said was meant to hurt me. He had no idea that telling me I wasn't pretty was hurtful to me. I never let on. He was a child; how would he know? So he told me about middle school. Wrong or right, this was his perception and he was a thirteen-year-old trying to protect and prepare his little sister, who he loves very much. I remember, so clearly. He sat me down at the kitchen table. He was very serious, I knew he hated having to tell me this but thought is was best I hear it from him. He said, "I know you're excited about changing schools, but things are different in middle school. You're popular now because you're good at sports and get good grades, but those things don't matter for girls in middle school. The only thing that's important is looks, so you're probably not going to be as popular as you are now." I felt a lump in my throat and got nauseous. I didn't let him know, I just said, "Oh, I don't care." He replied, "Good, I just didn't want you to think things were going to be the same."

I got up, went to my room, closed the door and cried my eyes out. I wanted to die. From that day forward, I would ask God every night to let me die in my sleep. I felt I couldn't face another day; I was afraid. I would beg him to take me while I slept. I really *did* want to die. I knew I was going to heaven, and looks don't matter there, just spirit, and I knew I had a beautiful spirit. I would have taken my own life—I was more afraid of living than of dying—but again, I was a Catholic girl. If I did commit suicide I would go to hell. As bad as my life felt, it would end some day. Hell was for all eternity. I was *more* afraid of that.

When I started sixth grade, I became a different person. I became one of the "bad" kids, or as bad as an eleven-year-old girl in middle class suburbia can be. I quit playing sports. I had this terrible need for the boys to like me. It's funny, I wouldn't even have cared if none of the girls liked me as long as the boys did. Of course, looking back, I know I was feeling that need for positive attention from boys because I felt like I had let my father and my brother down. I felt like I wasn't the daughter or the sister they would have chosen if they had been given the choice. The only thing that mattered to me, I realize now, was pleasing the boys and/or men around me—getting "positive attention" from them. Boys then and men later, that was the only time I felt good about myself. That's what was missing from my life, and kept me from feeling like a whole person—validation from the men in my life.

Anyway, I quit sports because I didn't think being a tomboy was very sexy. Can you imagine, I'm eleven years old and I want to be sexy? I also started smoking out in the open, so people could see how "cool" I was, and I cursed like a trucker. I hated school; I was no longer straight "A" for two reasons: somewhere I had learned that acting "dumb" was more attractive to boys so I kept my intelligence a secret. By the way to all you girls out there, the opposite is true. Smart is sexier than stupid at any age! Dumb guys may be intimidated by your intelligence, but you don't want them anyway; you won't be compatible and you'll soon be bored.

Never hide your intelligence. Second reason my grades fell was because some classes require you to get up in front of the class to read, and the last thing I was gonna do was let everyone in the class look at my face. As it was, I would sit against either side wall so I only had to hide my profile on one side.

As if I didn't think I was bad-looking enough, this was when I started using tons of makeup to try and hide my face, and when I look back, like I said, the way I wore it would have made any-one look bad. I would do anything to make the boys like me. I started making out with boys, French kissing, which I hadn't done in fifth grade, and I let boys get to second base. I'll bet I would've let them even get to third base but they were eleven too, and not only afraid, but wouldn't have known what to do once they got down there.

My first big "make-out experience" was at a party in the beginning of sixth grade. Me and my boyfriend at the time, a two- or three-week romance, were making out on the floor be-hind the bar at a friends' house. It was weird, not like you see in movies with couples making out all over the place. He and I were making out and everyone else was watching! He was on top of me with his hand up my shirt. We were French kissing, and he had my shirt all the way up so everyone was looking at my boobs. I didn't get aroused or anything. I didn't like everyone standing around. Who knows, maybe we were too young. May-be that's why nobody else was making out. Maybe that's why I wasn't aroused. Who knows? But things would change, and very soon. I used a razor to carve the boys' names that I liked into my skin, usually on my arms. Either boys' names, or names of a band I liked. I guess it was for similar reasons that you hear about kids "cutting." It actually felt good, but probably the same way OCD worked; it took my mind off the thought of how much I hated myself and tried to replace the emotional pain with physi-cal pain. It didn't last for long. Someone told my principal, and she told my parents. They didn't understand so I didn't get pun-ished, but I felt embarrassed to show them so I never did it again.

As you can hear, I'm different alright; I'm a "slut," a "whore," the other kids even said I shake my ass too much when I walk. I hated it! I hated me! I tried to change the way I walked, which apparently ruined my lower back and now I need to get injections into my spine for the damage it caused. I just recently found out from my aunt Olivia, as I was telling her about this, that the kids in school used to make fun of both her and my mother because of the way they walked. When they got older, men would tell them that they knew "they wanted it," meaning sex, by the way they walked. That was just the way I was built, and the way I learned to walk. Don't ever try to change yourself people; if others don't like something about you, tough shit! They need to change, they need to be more accepting. If you're not hurting anyone, including yourself, don't ever let others convince you to change something about yourself.

I was in sixth grade, but allowed out at night if I asked. We used to go hang out in the park and smoke cigarettes or pot if someone had it. One night, a boy in the seventh grade asked me if I wanted to take a walk. Of course I did. He said, "I hear them making fun of your walk, I think it's sexy. Don't change it."

I was so happy. I told him, "Thank you; you are the only person that ever said that, you've made me feel really good." We were sitting on the steps of the school at this time and he leaned over and kissed me. Tongue kissed me so I figured he really liked me. He grabbed my hand and led me to the top behind one of the pillars. He asked, "Have you ever given anyone head before?"

I told him, "No, I'm not even sure I know how to do it." He said, "From the way you just kissed me I'm sure you're gonna be great at it."

I was so excited, I couldn't wait! He told me to get down on my knees as he unzipped his jeans. I was so excited, my heart was beating so fast. He pulled out his cock and I opened my mouth. He said, "Now just try and get it as deep down your throat as you can and keep your lips wet and tightly around it letting it slide in and out."

And that's what I did. I first licked my lips making sure they were nice and wet, I sucked his cock so it slid into my throat but made sure I kept a tight seal with my lips so it stayed in my mouth as it slid in and out of my throat. I tried to get it deeper each time it slid in, until finally, I felt his cum shoot down my throat. I almost gagged but I knew I did so good I didn't want to ruin the moment so I just kept swallowing.

He asked, "So what'd ya think?" Looking back, I should have said, "You dumbass, what did you think? Are you fucking crazy? That was an expert fucking blowjob for a first timer eleven-year-old!! He obviously liked it cause it didn't take but a minute. Of course what I actually said was, "I liked it." He grabbed my hand and we went back to the park. He didn't speak to me the rest of the night.

Two days later, I was called to the guidance counselor's office. She asked, as if she didn't know, "How come all the boys keep calling you BJ?"

I said, "I don't know, maybe because I always wear Bonjour jeans." (Bonjour was a popular brand of jeans back then; I don't know if it still exists) I don't know where I came up with that but I didn't want to admit the humiliating truth.

She didn't believe me; she just tilted her head and raised her eyebrows and said, "If you ever want to talk, you know where I am." I went right to the ladies room and cried for about ten minutes. Once again, I was humiliated by a guy.

I felt very guilty. My brother was in the eighth grade and I felt sure, once again, that he's gonna be ashamed of me. Only this time, I could have prevented it. It was one thing when we were little, him wishing that he had a pretty sister; that wasn't up to me. But now, I am responsible for my behavior, or at least I thought so.

I now know that I was a child, my God, eleven years old, I was practically a baby! I was *not* responsible for my actions, I was *re*-acting to a lie, a lie that had been playing over and over in my head for eleven years. I take *no* responsibility for my actions, Paul! You didn't like having to listen to what people said about me, how did you think I felt!

I remember one time he told me a story about this girl in his class named "Jill." He said she was the nicest person he ever met. He said there is this boy in the class that sits in front of her and is so mean to her, but each morning as she passes him by to get to her desk, she says, "Good Morning James," and he doesn't even acknowledge her, but she doesn't get angry; she just sits down at her desk and starts her day.

I told my brother, "That's how I want to be. I want people to think of me as one of the nicest people they ever met," to which he replied calmly and expressionless, "It's too late, you've already made your reputation."

Well, listen up you fuckin' jerk-off! Not only was I eleven, and it's not too late for anything in life at eleven years old, but now, at thirty-six, I know that throughout my life many people have said I am the nicest person they ever met!

Seventh grade started. Nothing changed in the beginning but don't forget, my brother was two grades ahead of me, so he started high school. After we got pictures back from picture day at school, which was the worst day of the year for me because not feeling ugly enough, I thought I looked even worse in pictures. My brother came home and told me that he had shown my picture to his classmates. He chose to go to a private, all-boy high school, probably so he wouldn't have to go to the same high school as me, but I never asked why; I didn't want to hear it, thinking it felt bad enough. Turned out all his friends thought I was hot. I was very happy to hear that, more than you can even imagine. Yes, I was happy that a bunch of boys thought I was pretty, and thinking maybe this would change the way my brother sees me. After all, that was what I really wanted. I didn't have to live with the shame and be a disappointment to those other boys.

Again, I'm probably giving you the wrong idea. My brother and I were pretty close growing up. He's a good guy. It was just this nasty lie that he learned and passed on to me. I'm sure if I had told him how bad it made me feel and how important his opinion was of me, he would have stopped. I think he thought he was helping me. Like one time, it was Friday night and he was going to a party. I asked if I could come and he answered, "There's going to be a lot of good-looking people there, mostly the girls from the all-girls' school, I don't know if you'll feel comfortable." Ironically, this was after his classmates' response to my picture. I didn't understand. Nevertheless, I stayed home. That wasn't the only party though; often my friends and I would party with Paulie and his friends. I guess his friends had heard somewhere that I was "easy," either that or you could tell by just looking at me. Besides the "walk" and all the clown make- up, I would wear really tight clothes; I figured God was apologiz- ing for my face by giving me a good body. All the boys loved my ass and even though I had small breasts, every boyfriend told me they were perfect and never to get implants.

Anyway, on two occasions after I got really drunk, two boys—my brother's classmates—tried to double team me. The first time, we were in my brother's room. Paulie had left the room to get some more beers or something and when he came back, the three of us were in his bed. Looking back, I feel so sorry for the position I put my brother in. He called to me, "Sammy, come here, what are you doing?" I got up and went over to him. He asked with a very uncomfortable look on his face, "Are you OK with this?" Of course I was, I said, "I'm fine, don't worry about it." "You're sure?" he asked again, I think hoping I would change my answer. I said, "Yea, go in the other room." Imagine, this poor kid, just started high school. He has his new friends over double teaming his sister. Should he be an asshole and tell his friends to "get the fuck off her" even though she's willing. Or does he leave the room as his two friends have their way with his sister, who by the way, was a whore anyway. I let the boys resume, nothing big, one sucking my nipples and the other with my pants slid down fingering me. But then I stopped them. As young as I was, I figured my brother went to private school to escape gossip about me, and this would kill him.

Then, about a few months later, these same two guys were at my girlfriend's party. I got so wasted, they approached me again when I went to go pass out in her bed. I was still some- what conscious, so I said, "OK," but once they started I began to feel so sick that I ran to the bathroom, puked my brains out and slept on the bathroom floor all night. Sorry you fuckin' los- ers, but it seems like this threesome ain't in the stars for you. By the way, if you have any daughters now, and I hope you do, I pray that you lose sleep at night thinking she may meet two guys just like you! Don't misunderstand, I don't want her to pay for your Karmic debt. I hope she has the courage to tell them to go fuck themselves just like I should have told you.

Then one day, my brother came home with his friend. It was one of the assholes who tried to double team me, twice! Good friend, right? Anyhow, he brought his older brother over with him. He was two years ahead of them and I got the biggest crush on him. He was nice, cute, funny, and smart, but he had a girl-friend. I didn't even know if that mattered because I was now twelve and he was seventeen. Girlfriend or not, I could have been too young for him, but I didn't think so.

Apparently I wasn't too young for him. It all started when he would call on the phone for Paulie. I would talk to him, we would flirt, and our conversations kept getting longer and lon-ger. Like I said, he had a girlfriend, and they were having sex. I was a virgin, so sex was usually the topic of conversation. I was so curious. Remember there was never any talk about sex in my house. No conversations, no books, no movies with sex scenes or even sex talk. Maybe that's why I was so curious, you know the story, the "Forbidden Fruit."

We used to talk late at night. We were calling each other now; I was no longer intercepting my brother's calls. He taught me about phone sex, like what to do with my fingers. He told me to rub my clit first to get myself wet and relaxed, and then once I felt wet he told me to slide my finger inside. He knew I felt uncomfortable, so he told me to imagine it was his finger and that he was there with me licking my nipples. He told me that he was stroking his cock as he was giving me instructions. As I got more and more excited I could hear that he was jerking off faster and faster. I could hear his voice was shaking with his body. He talked me through my first orgasm while he got himself off at the same time. It's *crazy*, looking back that I have always told people I was mature enough to have that type of relationship and they agreed. They would even say, "You were very mature for your age." Even my mother and aunts would say it. I felt like I was. Nothing seemed wrong or uncomfortable, but I now have a Goddaughter who is eleven. I was just six months older than she is now when all this was happening. She's a little girl; there is no way a child that age could handle a sexual relationship like that—not even me, no matter how "mature" I was.

I loved this guy. I would rush home from school just to watch out my front window for his car to pull up. He came over every day because he drove my brother home. It worked out nice, too; his brother came over with them, so he hung out with Paulie. My mom worked, so I was able to spend time with Joey alone. We hadn't kissed or anything at this point. We just talked about it. I did tell him I wanted him to be my "first." I loved him and he was experienced; he was perfect. He told me he would love that. He told me he thinks about it all the time. He knew I loved him and he told me he was falling in love with me too. His birthday was coming up so I said I would give him my virginity for his birthday. He was all for it.

His birthday was on a Saturday. He came over to my house. My dad was working and my mom was out. My brother was gone too, I remember there was no chance we would be interrupted. I was wearing a sexy babydoll set. We were standing next to my bed. He started kissing me and then he took off my top and started kissing and licking my nipples. He continued to undress me. He slid down the bottoms slowly kissing and licking my belly, my hips, and my inner thighs until they were off. I was completely naked and trembling with anxiety or excitement, I didn't know why. My body may have been shaking, but I knew for sure I wanted this. He guided me to lie on the bed. I was lying on my back watching as he undressed. His cock was so hard and so big. He got on the bed and laid on his side next to me. He looked into my eyes and started kissing me. His soft tongue and full lips actually relaxed me. He softly caressed my breasts, my nipples and then his hand slid down my belly as he moved his lips and tongue off mine and onto my nipples. My nipples got so hard and I felt myself getting wet. He slid his hand down further between my legs to my inner thigh, then up to my clit. He started rubbing my clit softly and slowly. I couldn't believe how much better it felt when he did it. I was so wet. He kissed me again on the mouth, then got on top of me. He had his hands next to my shoulders in push-up position. Then, slowly he slid the tip of his cock about a half-inch inside me and then stopped. Remember now, I'm a virgin and he had a big cock, bigger than average I know now! He kneeled back on his heels and gently grabbed my ankles. He spread my legs wider apart and bent my knees a bit. I had no idea what to do, but I wasn't embarrassed or anything. I was loving it and I never wanted it to end.

He was able to slip his cock in a little further, and then asked, "Is that OK?" I nodded. I don't know why but I felt like I couldn't speak. He kept inching in a little further like every ten seconds. He was so hard and breathing so heavy it isn't till now that I realize he was holding back. He had to go slow for both of us! Finally, after like, I have no idea how long it was, he was all the way in.

I'm not gonna lie to you, it did hurt, but I didn't say a word because I didn't want him to stop. He was so caring towards me, I know that if he knew how much pain I was in, he would have stopped and I would be devastated. He slowly slid it in and out for I don't know how long. Even with the pain, I didn't want it to end. Then, he let out this moan that was so hot and gently laid down on top of me. This was lovemaking to me. I didn't care how old either of us were, but I heard love making was the best feeling in the world and there couldn't be anything better than that!

For all of you wondering, yes, he did have a condom on. I was in another world, a perfect world and whether there was a condom or not was the last thing on my mind. But he remembered. I didn't have an orgasm, but I loved it. I realize now I loved it because, again, I felt beautiful. But on top of that, this hot guy could have been with his girlfriend—yea, they were still together—or any other girl, but he chose to be with me instead! Having sex filled all that was missing in my life. I finally found "it." Sex was the cure to my sadness. This was the one thing that filled those two black holes in my spirit: I never felt pretty, and I always thought I was a disappointment to the men in my life.

Twenty years later, after I got out of rehab for sex addiction, my sexologist told me that the experience was a form of molestation. I argued that I asked him to do it, and was all for it. She said,

"That doesn't matter. He was seventeen and you were twelve. At twelve years old, nobody is emotionally developed enough to consent to a sexual relationship, and that is why you became addicted to sex so quickly." Not only that, it turns out this is the same reason why, as I grew up, I was never able to truly love someone I was having sex with. Sure, at twelve I thought I loved Joey, but it was just a crush, infatuation. At twelve, the only men I knew how to love were my dad and brother, uncles and grand-fathers. Even though as I'm venting they may not seem lovable, they really were.

Looking back I can see how growing up like this made long-term relationships more than just impossible; they were pretty much "doomed" from the start. I would be dating someone, having sex, thinking that because the sex was good, I was in love, but then, when I would really start falling in love, I would become skeeved, you know "turned off," when we were about to have sex, because I would have the same feelings for them, that I felt for the men in my family—YUK! I had no idea what was going on, but I would just have to end it for what appeared to them to be no good reason.

Joey and I had sex all the time. He showed me everything about sex—foreplay, toys, different positions, how oral sex is great for girls too! He even took me to Planned Parenthood to get birth control pills. I was infatuated with him, and becoming more and more addicted to the sex. I started using alcohol and pot when I would hang out with friends from school. But when-ever I was with Joey, I didn't need to get drunk or high. Sex was a better "high" for me than any substance. It made me feel beauti-ful, desired, and sexy. I loved the orgasms too, but honestly, if I had to give up one of those things I was getting from sex, I'd give up the orgasm in a heartbeat!

Orgasms, he taught me, I could get on my own. I could never feel beautiful, sexy or desired on my own. I loved how he wanted me and needed me. I wanted him all the time. I remember going on a week's vacation to Florida with Jennifer, my best friend. My parents paid for the plane ticket. After just two days, I wanted to come home. I couldn't stand the thought of being away from

Joey for that long. Especially because I knew he was probably with his girlfriend, giving her all the sex that I wanted. I was obsessed. I couldn't think about anything else. I called my parents and told them I wanted to come home. They bought the ticket for me, and I took the first flight I could to get home. Poor Jennifer. I felt so horrible; I was picking a boy over my best friend. She forgave me; never even showed any anger towards me. That's a best friend!

I've since told Jennifer all about the addictions and thanked her again for being so wonderful. It's funny, looking back as an adult, that I really didn't need to beg my parents or give them a good explanation why I had to come home so urgently. Like I said, they gave me so much privacy that they didn't interrogate me or ask me why I want to come home so quickly. I thought, maybe, my mom was a little bit afraid of what the answer might be if she had asked. Kind of like a "don't ask, don't tell" for fear I would tell her what I was actually doing. We both knew she wouldn't know how to handle a discussion about my "sex life" at twelve years old. Shit, she wasn't even able to give me the "sex talk;" forget about having a conversation about me having all kinds of sex at eleven and twelve years old. I'm tellin' ya, it was like taboo in my family; it may have killed her! But I wasn't complaining. I used to sleep over his house and go on trips with him. I have no idea where they thought I was, and I didn't care, as long as I was with Joey.

A month after he turned seventeen, I turned thirteen. We were in love, or as in love as a seventeen-year-old and a thirteen-year-old can be. He eventually broke up with his girlfriend, and I was his girlfriend. I was so happy again, it felt great! I hadn't been this happy in what felt like forever. Each day I would bring my lunch to school. We had the option to go home, but I lived too far and didn't want to walk that walk an extra two times a day. I would sit with a few of my girlfriends and tell them all about the sex I was having and what it was like, while we smoked cigarettes, sometimes pot and a few times we did a little cocaine that one of the girl's father used to sell. This is seventh grade in middle class America, and this was twenty years ago. I can only imagine what the kids are doing at lunch now. I guess that's why so many kids are "home schooled."

One time during recess, while we were playing kickball, Joey pulled up to the field to see me and say hi. How fucked up is that? Needless to say, that afternoon I got called to the principal's office where she asked me, "Does your mother know that you are "car-dating"? I said, "Yes," and that was it. A few months later, I did tell my mom we were dating and she was OK with it. She liked Joey and felt he was responsible. I didn't tell her about the sex part of it. It still was never discussed, not even now when she knew I was dating a "sexually active" seventeen-year-old. I say he was "sexually active" because when he was still with his girlfriend, my mom wouldn't allow her in the house with him when she wasn't home. I guess because they were seventeen she figured they would have sex wherever they were. My poor, paranoid mother!

Hey, I was happy; it worked out great for me because I got to have sex with him instead! The girlfriend must have hated my mother. Oh well. I'm not blaming my mother, I'm not blaming anyone. Twelve years old may be early to lose your virginity, but there were better conditions than many girls had. We weren't drunk, we loved each other, and it was in my own bed. If it hadn't led to sexual addiction, I would have no regrets about starting so young. So many of my girlfriends who lost their virginity didn't have the beautiful experience I had. They were either drunk, had a one-night stand, did it in a car or in the woods. One of my friends actually traded her virginity for a cigarette! But worst of all was Nicole; her father took her virginity.

Joey was a senior in high school when I reached eighth grade. What does every senior have? A senior prom, I was his girlfriend so obviously I had to go. Not only was I so nervous because I was going to be the youngest one there, I was sure I would also be the ugliest girl there. By this time, I had found the solution to situations like this: alcohol, and lots of it. Kind of a spin on what the guys say, "The more I drank, the prettier I got." Not really though, what did happen, which is how I became dependent on alcohol, was that as long as I kept drinking, at some point I would forget I hated the way I looked.

I went to Jennifer's house for moral support and help getting ready. I told her I was so nervous that I needed to have a few drinks before he picked me up. Her parents were out so I went into her parents' liquor cabinet. I don't know what the heck I drank, but I drank a lot of it! He picked me up and could tell I was a little buzzed, which I was at that point because it didn't all hit me yet. It took about twenty minutes to get to the school. On the way I puked in my purse and was totally passed out by the time we got there. As soon as he parked, I opened my door and threw up for about twenty minutes. He asked me if I wanted to go home, but I told him to go in and leave me out there, which is what he did. I laid there on the front seat with my head hanging out of the opened passenger side door, passed out for four hours; he did come to check on me a few times. I felt bad, I must have apologized a hundred times, but he was so good to me, he wasn't mad. He said I should have told him I was that nervous; I didn't have to go, but, as usual, I kept my feelings to myself.

Joey was a great guy, but after eighth grade comes high school. I went to the public high school in town. I remember all the girls talking about this hot sophomore named "Kevin." I was still with Joey, but I wanted to see what all the talk was about. Joey lived in another town, so I really didn't know a lot of local people outside of my middle school. Kevin and I were introduced; we flirted a little bit, and I knew I wanted to see what sex was like with him. It sounds like I'm cheating, but at this point, I'm a fourteen-year-old sex addict and a big-time drinker. I was done with pot; it made me paranoid and tired, and I never did like the feeling cocaine gave me, but I still drank alcohol because besides making me forget that I hated the way I looked, it decreased any inhibitions and took away the humiliation for me to have random sex, with anyone. Until the next morning, when I would hate myself. I would even bring alcohol to school and have "liquid lunches." Without the alcohol I couldn't handle the humiliation. I knew everyone thought I was a slut, and let's face it, I was.

I broke up with Joey, which was very hard. We had been

together for over two years, and he was very upset. He couldn't understand what changed. I was infatuated with him for so long, and now I didn't want anything to do with him? I felt terrible too, but we started dating when I was twelve, and so far he was the only "real" boyfriend I ever had. He started college when I started high school. Our worlds were very different now. So I started dating Kevin. Looking back, I never felt nearly as close to Kevin as I did Joey. I was young; I guess I just got bored. High school seemed exciting; I think I just wanted a change.

Six months later, I broke up with Kevin. We had very little in common. I still had BDD, but I drank so much, I rarely cared. In my town, in the '80s, we would party, but nothing like the kids do today. When we partied, it was mostly beer. I liked vodka though and would steal it from my parent's liquor cabinet if nobody was available to buy it for me. Sometimes we would "trip" on mesc. or acid, but alcohol was the drug of choice for most of us; it was also the easiest to get. We usually stayed outside to party. We'd hang out in parks, behind schools, empty parking lots, and at the end of the night couples would just "hook up." Sometimes relationships would form but, for me anyway, most were just "fuck friends." There was no one I knew that I really wanted a relationship with, but I wanted the sex.

I think these days, "fuck friends" is called "friends with benefits." It sounds a little nicer, but it is still very damaging to the girls and guys that are in these relationships, girls more so because the guys are usually in control. Girls are teaching themselves two lies in these little "friendships." One lie is not only do you have to have sex to keep your boyfriend happy, but if you want to maintain your friendships with boys you have to give some of them sex too. Whether it's a blow job on the school bus or actual fucking, girls are learning that without offering sex, they won't be any use to a boy. They can't even be a good friend.

The second lie some of you are telling yourselves is that maybe this will bring the friendship to another level. Maybe once he sees how sexual you are, he will want you for his girlfriend. This will never happen because he is already getting the benefits of having a girlfriend, without the responsibility. It's just another version of, "Why buy the cow when you're getting the milk for free?"

I had mostly guy friends. Yeah, some of them I fucked, but some I didn't. I was actually very close to a couple of them; I was like one of the guys. Think about it, at the end of the night everyone hooks up. Most of the guys and me of course, are just looking for sex; the other girls, most of them anyway, were virgins. It's freshman year and we're fourteen; they should be virgins, I should be a virgin too! So the other girls don't want a one night stand, even if they just give a guy head or something; they want to be called the next day; they want to know "where is this gonna lead to?" "Am I your girlfriend now?" I was sick and had no self-respect; I didn't care; I didn't need any of that from those guys; I just needed sex. I didn't care if they called me; I didn't want to call them. I didn't have anything to say and I hated those awkward phone calls. I knew I'd either see them in school or the following weekend. We were friends.

One night I was at a party. One of my guy "friends" asked me if one of my girlfriends and I wanted to join him and his friend down in the basement. I was drunk but I knew what it meant and so did she, but we both agreed. Once we got down there, the guys were already naked lying on the floor and they told us to undress, you know "strip" for them.

So I started, but my friend didn't. She pulled me to the side and said, "I don't want to do this." I pulled her back and said, "come on, it's no big deal." She then said, "No really, I'm totally flat," meaning her chest. She didn't have a problem with the sex! She was just self conscious because she didn't have breasts yet and was too embarrassed to strip. We were still in our freshman year, but how screwed up is this country about appearances. This poor girl had no problem giving her virginity to one of two random guys, but she didn't want them to know she had a flat chest.

I think this is a prime example that we have a big problem with priorities, and that was twenty years ago! It's only gotten worse! Parents are getting their daughters breast implants as high school graduation presents now. How fucked up is that?

Anyway, she slipped out so I ended up having sex with both of them. I remember the one who was my friend walked me home, and I cried the whole way. I didn't have a problem having sex, but afterwards I always hated myself. The other guy died about ten years later. I heard it was from an overdose but don't know for sure. It was rumored that he had AIDS when he died—talk about "There but by the Grace of God go I."

There was one other horrible night, much worse than that even. An older boy—didn't know his name, not a regular in our party crowd. Looking back now, I can say raped me, or molested me; it doesn't really matter what ya call it? He lived on the same side of town as I did and offered to walk me home; I was very drunk. As we passed the school he grabbed my hand and said, "Let's hang out for a little while," or something like that. The next thing I remember was him laying me down on my back on the blacktop, forcing his cock into my mouth, and doing push-ups on my face until he shot his load down my throat, got up, and left.

I don't remember anything after that, the walk home, nothing. I don't think I told a single person when it happened, not even Jennifer. This year, I told my husband. It felt really good telling him. Remember, once you bring a secret out into the light, it becomes much smaller.

Chapter Five

Then one weekend, after a house party, I woke up in a sleeping bag with Anthony. Anthony and I were friends. He was so beautiful. He had long brown hair, dark almond shaped eyes. A killer smile too, white, thick, straight teeth; and his body, thin, but cut, sexy as hell. It wasn't just me who thought so either. Before we started dating, one of his friend's mothers would hit on him when he would sleep over. This is a woman in her thirties hitting on a 15-year-old boy! She would crawl into bed and jerk him off, telling him how much she loved him. Damn, people are screwed up.

He had dropped out of high school, but would have been a year ahead of me. I usually saw him on the weekends and we got along great. We would laugh at the other drunk people and the crazy things they did. He would sing Jimi Hendrix to me; he was awesome. I can't remember if we had sex that night, but we definitely hooked up because that was the beginning of our relationship that lasted over three years, during which we had incredible sex, often. We'd have sex at my house whether my parents were home or not. If they were, I'd just close the door and do it quietly. We'd do it at his house too, anywhere we could. Some nights we would drive to bars with our friends, but we would just stay in the car and have sex until they came out. I never cared about getting caught; having sex was the most important thing to me. I remember one time riding him on my water bed while my parents were home. I remember because I got off eight times, the most I ever had at that time. I can't believe my parents didn't hear either of us, or the water bed splashing around.

He proposed to me my senior year. I said yes, and we went and got tattoos of each other's names, on his arm and my hip. I didn't want my dad to see it. He hated tattoos. I really thought this was it, and so did everyone else, except my father. He didn't take us seriously. After all, Anthony was a high school drop out with long hair and tattoos. How was he going to support me? Then one time while Anthony I were dating, he went away to a detention center for getting caught with drugs or something. He wasn't a drug addict or anything; I can't even remember the details why he had to go away. All he and I would do is drink; I always preferred alcohol to pot. He would sometimes smoke a little pot, but not with me, and we were always together.

While he was away, I received mail from "Planned Parenthood." I had gone off the pill after Joey. The office was in another town, and I had no way to get there. Anthony would just "pull out" and that was our birth control. This was before anyone in our town either had or even knew about AIDS. I remember coming home drunk one evening during the week, like eight o'clock, and my mother, after getting the mail asked in an angry voice, "Are you having sex with this 'Anthony' who's in a detention center?" I was making a peanut butter and jelly sandwich so I kept my head down to hide my drunkenness, but answered, "Yeah, so?"

She then said, "I think you're too young!" The alcohol then gave me the confidence to say, "Oh yeah, well I was having sex with Joey when I was twelve!" Finally, she stuttered, "Well you were more mature then," I stayed quiet and just thought to myself, "Yeah, good come back mom." She ran to her room and slammed the door. I was probably fifteen then, and that was the only conversation we had ever had about sex until I was like twenty-seven years old. She never brought it up again, so I figured I wouldn't either. She obviously wasn't comfortable with the conversation. I wanted my parents to take my relationship with Anthony seriously. Looks can be deceiving. They did like him once they got to know him. He even let my dad cut his hair after we were dating like two years. I just think every father wants to be sure their daughters will be taken care of.

As far as that birth control "method" we were using; it didn't work. I did get pregnant when I was sixteen. We were so in love and so young we initially planned on keeping it. We thought he had a good job, was making $300 a week, and had great benefits. As soon as we got married, I would be covered too, and that would pay the hospital bills once I had the baby. We thought we could find somewhere nice to live with both of us working.

We started looking for places to live and as it turned out, $300 wasn't really that much a week. After taxes were taken out, rent, car insurance, food what money would we have left? If I continued working, all my money would pay a babysitter. We started thinking, "maybe we should find a trailer." Some were really nice, but no trailer parks were nearby, and I knew I would need to be close to my family. Nothing we thought of seemed to work, not to mention, I knew my parents would be so upset, to say the least. I had only completed up to sophomore year in high school. There didn't seem to be any way we could do it; I had to get an abortion. It was such a difficult decision for two *kids* to make, but it was really the only option we thought we had. We were so sad after that. I can't believe that some parents still have a problem with birth control being available at high schools. How many kids have to go through what we did before these parents open their eyes and realize that kids are going to have sex whether we give them birth control or not?

As smart as I had been in grammar school, I just got by in high school. I didn't care about it. I would often have a "liquid lunch," for any of you parents who don't know what that is, it's when kids drink alcohol during the lunch hour instead of eating; usually hard liquor like vodka because they can't smell it on you like they can beer. I remember, well I remember my friend, Diane, telling me that I passed out during a history test. She sat next to me and was able to fill in the answers for me. I guess the teacher didn't notice; or maybe she did but didn't know what to do. She was a hick, maybe she was afraid. Anyway, I was so wasted that day that I hid my purse in the cabinet next to my desk. There was still half a quart of vodka left from lunch and I guess I was afraid she might trip on it as she walked up and down the rows.

After class, when my friend woke me up, I went to grab my purse and couldn't find it. I had no idea that I put it in the cabinet. I freaked out! I was so afraid someone found it and brought it to the principal's office. The purse wasn't that big. You could obviously see and feel a bottle that size was in there without even opening it. I remember being so upset and begging my poor father for money to replace not only the purse, but *all* my make-up that was in it as well. Remember I told you I wore tons of make-up, I also had it with me *at all times*, that's also part of my BDD. I was scared to death that someone would see me without make-up on.

Another time, in high school, my friend Rita and I took a hit of acid at lunch time. Now the first period after lunch was typing. I remember just sitting there listening to all twenty something students typing. It sounded so much louder than usual. Rita typed the lyrics to the song "Comfortably Numb" and handed it to me. I remember as I was reading the words, the sound of the typewriters sounded like the music to the song. It was mesmerizing. I just sat there and listened the entire class.

I don't know how, but I graduated. I went to the Community College for Dental Hygiene but after taking some of the same liberal arts classes that were required for nursing, I realized I would like that better.

Anthony and I broke up when I started college. I only found out in my early thirties about this broken connection I had between love and sex. I hadn't realized at the time that the deeper in love I fell with someone; the closer we were to breaking up. I was madly in love with Anthony, and we had great sex, but I remember one time we were having sex, and when he was on top of me, I got that feeling, you know I started to feel like brotherly, fatherly "*icky*" type love for him. I told him to stop, I said "You have to get off, I can't do this!" He stopped and got really pissed!

I don't blame him; he probably thought he was doing something wrong, which never happened. He was great, but that was the first sign of us breaking up. I think another reason was that he had stopped drinking and wanted me to stop also, but I wouldn't. It was difficult for Anthony and me for a while after we broke up. Remember, we were engaged and had each other's names tattooed on our bodies. He even came to my house in the middle of the night one time and knocked on my window. When I went outside to talk to him, he said he missed me and he wanted me back, but we had fought so much towards the end about drinking and how much our sex had changed. I told him we couldn't get back together even though we still loved each other so much. He didn't understand why, if I loved him, why we couldn't make it work. I didn't understand either; I just knew we couldn't.

Twenty years later, with my sexologist, I found out why. My love for him had changed from a passionate love, to a familial love, like I loved my father. Again, this was happening because what I thought was having sex with my first true love was actually a form of molestation. It's important to me that you know I am not blaming Joey. He was a 17-year-old kid. If he, for one second, thought he was damaging me in any way, he *never* would have pursued me.

That's what I mean when I say I'm writing this to protect the children who are nine through fifteen and having or contemplating sex. Mom and Dad, tell them they aren't just ruining their reputation, they are ruining *all* future relationships! We all think, as Simon and Garfunkle tell us, that we'd "rather be the hammer than the nail." But breaking the heart, of someone you love and you know still loves you is one of the most painful things I've ever had to do.

He was so hurt that I wouldn't stop drinking for him. Little did he know, little did I know, I *couldn't* stop drinking for him or for anybody else. I *wasn't* an alcoholic like so many people said I was, I know now that I was self-medicating with alcohol. I didn't like myself, and when I drank, it didn't make me like myself better; I just didn't think about it so much. As soon as I learned to love myself, almost twenty years later, in my early thirties, I realized that I had been so self-destructive over a lie, a miscommunication between me, my brother and my parents, I couldn't even imagine taking a drink. I go to bars and restaurants with family and friends who all party, some pretty heavily, I'm not even tempted. No AA, no twelve-step program; once I found out *why* I was drinking so much, I was able to realize that I didn't need to self medicate anymore. I was a pretty good person and I was able to love myself just the way I was. Now I'm not saying AA or twelve-step programs aren't necessary for people to quit drinking; they have helped so many people I love stop their addictions. I'm only talking about my situation and everyone is different.

After Anthony and I broke up I started going out with my girlfriends, drinking, of course. About a week or two after Anthony and I were over, not even speaking anymore, I went out to a bar with two of my friends. We were loaded but there were no hook-ups so we went back to crash at my friend's married sister's apartment. On the way home we saw a guy walking; we were in an open jeep, so we could see he was hot and offered him a ride. He jumped in, and I got on his lap. By the time we got to the apartment, we were making out. My friends went to sleep; he and I stayed on the couch making out. When my friend came out to bring me a blanket and pillow, I was lying naked on the couch and he was going down on me. She said, "Oops," and started laughing. She wasn't surprised, I don't think; after all, it was me, what else would I be doing, the slut that I was.

She started laughing and said, "I brought you a blanket and pillow." I looked up at her, she and I both laughing. I said "Thank you; you can just throw them down anywhere." She went back to bed and I went back to enjoying myself. I remember being so pleased with him. I was a bit wasted and still came so hard, just from oral. He was good, slipped his finger inside while he was licking me on the outside, but different than other guys. He had a rhythm going or something. I don't know, maybe I wasn't that wasted. I remember the night so clearly.

The next morning we woke up and he had to go to work. He called his brother to pick him up; he worked with his brother laying carpet or something—that I do forget. Anyway, I remember him telling his brother, "I need you to pick me up. I met the girl of my dreams last night." That was it, I was hooked. My BDD ate that right up; what a fucking player he was, but I bought it.

We started seeing each other. He had an apartment in that same town so only about ten minutes from home for me. It was a nice town, mostly middle class, but his apartment was nasty. It was an old brick apartment house, like you see in the projects. The elevator was always broken and the hallways smelled like piss, you know the type, but it was probably cheap to live there and I don't think he made a lot of money, who knows. Oh, his name was Tim, by the way.

He had no education after high school; I guess his brother gave him work as a favor. He was not only a player, but a real shit. After like two weeks of us seeing each other, he said, "You want to have your friends over, we'll have like a party, it'll be fun." So we did, only he didn't have any of his friends over. He even hit on one of my friends, and she told me that night as soon as it happened. I waited till everyone left and asked him about it. He, of course, denied it, said she was a pig and would never go near her. He said, "I'll bet guys are never even nice to her so when I offered to get her a beer she thought I was hitting on her."

I bought it. I didn't really believe it; she was beautiful and always had a boyfriend, but it worked for my ego to believe it, so I did. Not to mention, she wouldn't lie to me and knows when a guy is hitting on her. He would put me down, treated me pretty much like shit; but I stayed with him. Remember, that's what I do. Oprah and Dr. Phil both say, "You teach people how to treat you." That's exactly what I did. I wasn't kind to myself; why would this loser be kind to me. When you don't love yourself, it's impossible for anyone else to love you.

I was in my last semester of the nursing program, taking over eighteen credits, so my parents allowed me to stop working. If I wasn't out partying, I was studying, that was it. So I had no cash and he paid for everything when we went out. He didn't have a car, so we used my car and he paid—that's why I stayed; and the sex was good. Also, he didn't drink as much as I did, so he was able to drive to and from Hoboken every weekend. I would just stay at his place.

He was originally from Hoboken, so all his friends still lived there. We would go there every weekend; that's another reason I stayed, I was going to all new bars, meeting new people, a nice change of pace. I was pathetic to stay with him as long as I did— about eight months. One time, on the way home from Hoboken, he got on the highway going towards the city. I asked him what he was doing. He said, "I have a friend in Harlem who's got the best weed; I want to go pick some up." I said, "No fucking way, I am not going to Harlem at one in the morning." He just kept driving and said, "Don't worry about it. It will take like two minutes. I'll be in and out; he knows I'm coming." I was in the passenger side of my own car, wasted; what was I gonna do?

So we get to Harlem. Everything was dark and quiet on this street. I couldn't believe it; I had never even been to Harlem, only heard about all the bad shit that happens there on the news. He pulled over in front of an apartment, in what looked to me like the projects. He was so hyper, who knows, maybe he did some cocaine that I didn't know about and needed some more. I wouldn't have cared if he hadn't dragged me into the projects at two in the morning. His adrenaline was racing, and I thought he was probably scared too but had enough alcohol for the courage.

Ya know, I'll bet I'm right! He was so full of shit *all* the time. I didn't think it was a friend, he never talked about any friend, I didn't even remember him smoking pot since we had met. Not that I would have cared; I just didn't smoke it anymore.

So he pulled over, turned off the lights, took the keys, jumped out of the car and ran into the building. Meanwhile, the windows were down cause we both smoked—my car was electric so I couldn't roll up the windows or lock the doors. I was more scared than I had ever been in my life. What he said would take two minutes took about fifteen minutes, fifteen of the longest minutes of my life. Here I was the whitest girl from Jersey, skinny little thing, what was I going to do if someone wanted to steal my purse, or my car? Honk the horn? What was my loser "boyfriend" gonna do? You know *he* isn't coming out to help me, he was chicken-shit; he would have watched from the window until it was over. I really thought to myself while he was up there, "What am I doing with this douche bag? I went from someone like Anthony to this? Something is severely wrong with me to accept being treated this way."

He finally came down and didn't even apologize for taking so long. I went off on him for leaving me there with no keys, and the doors and windows being open. He didn't care. He was a real loser.

At that point, after everything he had done, he didn't even look that hot anymore. He *looked* like a loser. Even his friends didn't seem to like him that much, never happy to see him. He was fuckin' pathetic. He even had one friend that was always happy to see me and asked me what I was doing with Tim. I even told him the truth. He told me, "Dump him then; you're way to good for him. I have money, I'll take care of you."

I thought about it. We always flirted with each other, but I didn't like his friend, Ronnie, enough to rock the boat. I would just hang out with him every time we went to Hoboken. Then one night, we were playing pool with some couple that came in who he didn't know. She was wearing fishnet stockings, a miniskirt, and the guy was in a jacket and tie. I guess it was a first date, or a blind date because Tim was flirting with her, which was normal, but she was flirting back. I even saw her slip him her number!

I said loudly, so her date would hear it too, "I saw that." He laughed and said, "Saw what?" as he shoved her number in his pocket. I grabbed my keys off the table and said, "I'm leaving." I wished Ronnie was there; I would have just started making out with him, but he wasn't.

That was it for me. I was done being humiliated. I got in the car; I only had a beer or two since we had just gotten there, so I was OK to drive. Tim came running out and got in the car. He was still laughing, that dick! He said, "What's wrong? So she gave me her number. I wasn't going to call her." I said, "That's not the point. You humiliated me! I'm done, I can't even believe I stayed with you this long."

Still laughing, he said, "So what, you're breaking up with me?" I said, "Yup, I'm done." He said, "OK then, but we can still hang out, can't we?" I don't remember if we stayed out that night. I don't think so 'cause I was really pissed off at him; but we did end up back there together as a convenience. Remember, I had no money and he had no car so we were just hanging out, not as a couple anymore. I don't know if he called that girl or not, but if he did, nothing ever came of it. Then one night at the usual bar, Ronnie asked why I wasn't sitting with Tim. I told him what happened and he said he was glad to hear it. He asked if he could kiss me even though Tim was there and, of course, I said yes. He leaned over and kissed me. Pretty long kiss too. I'm not gonna lie to you, my eyes were closed, but I was hoping Tim was watching.

I sat with Ronnie that whole night. He asked if he could take me home. I told him, "No, remember that's my car and I don't trust Tim to leave it with him." He, Ronnie, had to go to work the next day, so he was leaving.

I walked out with him to his car in the parking lot. We were making out and it got really hot. I was leaning against his car and he was grinding up against me. I could feel how hard he was and it got me so wet. His hand was up my shirt and he was stroking my nipple nice and softly, getting me even wetter. It was so hot. We must have been making out for like twenty minutes because I could tell by the way he was grinding up and down and how his breathing had changed that he was gonna cum. I squatted down in front of him, undid his pants right there between two cars in the back parking lot and slid his cock down my throat. He was right there. It only took like three strokes down my throat and I could feel his cock start pulsing as his hot cum shot down my throat. It was so good. He grabbed my arms and lifted me back up. Leaned me back up against the car and whispered in my ear, "My God you are so hot!" Of course *that* was the best part for me.

He said, "Forget Tim, if you want to come here, I'll pick you up each week. I don't want you to see him anymore; I want you to be my girl." I should have jumped right on his offer, but I could be so stupid sometimes. I forget what I said to him in response, but I know I didn't accept his offer.

The next thing I remember, I was in my car on the way home with Tim. I remember him asking, "So you and Ronnie are a thing now? Aren't you being a hypocrite? I can't get a number from a stranger, but you can make out with one of my friends right in front of me." See how stupid he was?

I said, "You really don't see the difference? You gave her your number while we were still seeing one another. We are just friends now, I can kiss anyone I want in front of you." We went back to his house; I still stayed there 'cause I was too wasted to drive. He even asked if we could still have sex, which I immediately answered, "No way." Then I passed out. I woke up in the morning and just left while he was still asleep.

The next week came. He called me and asked if I still wanted to go with him, or if I was going out with Ronnie. I told him I would pick him up and that I would see Ronnie when I got there. I don't know why I didn't get Ronnie's number or give him mine. No, actually I do. I wasn't really that into him. For some reason I would rather stay with the fucking idiot who didn't give a shit about me, instead of the nice guy who really liked me. I don't know if it was a case of wanting what we can't have, or just my low self esteem at the time. All I know is that on the ride in, Tim said to me, "I heard you gave Ronnie a blow job in the parking lot." I said, "So what, I fucked you the first night we met." He said, "Well, I don't like this. I didn't think I'd be jealous but I am. Why don't we go back to the way things were?"

I said, "No way. I won't be humiliated like that again, you made me feel like shit." He said, "No, this time you'll be my girlfriend. I won't do anything like that." Stupid me, of course, was happy. I didn't show it though, with someone like him you really can't or he'll treat you even worse. What a guy, right? Why the fuck was I so happy?

When we got to the bar, Ronnie was there waiting for me. He kissed me when I came in and I told him I had to talk to him. I told him Tim was upset that I was fooling around with him and wants us to get back together. I said, "I know he can be a real asshole, but if he made out with one of my friends in front of me, I'd be really pissed off too. We have been together six months and I don't know if I would have kissed you in front of him if he hadn't gotten that girl's number in front of me."

He understood, but said, "I think you're making a big mistake." I knew he was right, but I was sick. Some people have low self-esteem, but self-loathing really takes it to a different level of self-abuse, and you're not even aware of it.

Within a couple of days Tim was nasty to me. I don't know what he had done, but that weekend I was going out with my friends instead. We went to that Halloween party, remember, the one where Mike told Donna I was so beautiful four years after using me like a plastic fuck doll. Well, after a few nights, I became his "girlfriend." This was when our relationship began. Even though it ended with a restraining order, Mike, was so much hotter, so much better in bed, and treated me like gold. So one other benefit Mike had was getting me away from Tim.

Tim actually called me a week later and said, "I just want you to know that I realize I may not have treated you that great all the time and I'm sorry." Could you believe that? He *may not* have treated me so great! You fucking sociopath! I just said, "Too late Tim," and hung up the phone.

Chapter Six

I was partying a lot, just alcohol, but a lot of it. I was making decent money as a registered nurse, especially since I lived at home. My parents and I got along really well; I had my freedom and I would pay the phone bill as rent each month. I had offered to contribute to the house because all I had was a car payment and insurance, which totaled only about three hundred dollars a month.

I wanted to pay the phone bill. Two of my mother's sisters lived out of state, and her parents lived down the shore, so my parents would always fight about the phone bill. I hated it because when I was little my parents separated for a few months and, my goodness, it still makes me sad just thinking about it. Anyway, I always hated to hear them argue; it scared me, you know, it still does! But that's why I took over the phone bill. I told them that neither of them were allowed to open it; they had to just leave it on the counter and I would pay it. It worked out great. I didn't want to move out and they didn't want me to either, but I felt like a "mooch," working and not contributing. But my dad wouldn't take anything more. He would always say, "Save your money." He still does.

I loved being a nurse. I was on a Med-Surge floor, which meant I had patients who had surgeries like hip replacements, gallbladders removed, stuff like that. It came easy for me because I loved taking care of people who couldn't help themselves. I have to admit I am a very patient person and I think people could recognize that. You couldn't rush healing, and everybody heals differently. One patient may take overnight to heal from a surgery, and a different person having the same surgery might take three days. Some nurses, most doctors, and *all* insurance companies fail to understand that, but I did.

I loved my job, except for when my BDD would get in the way. If you think about it, as a nurse I had to wash my hands before leaving every patient's room, and what's above every sink? Right, a mirror! I hated it. Not to mention I worked with a gorgeous nurse, my age, who was also a swimsuit model! Even the doctors wanted to go out with her. Great, that was just what I needed. Even worse, she was nice, and we became friends. We used to rearrange our schedules so that we would work together.

I had a male patient. He was an older man, in his eighties or nineties; he had cancer in his penis. His family would come to visit often; we became friendly. It was very sad. Then one day, his daughter—she was about fifty years old and had a son my age—asked me if that "pretty nurse" had a boyfriend. She said she wanted to "fix up her son." This woman I barely knew, unintentionally, just ripped my heart right out. I told you we had become friendly, so she knew I was single, so in my dysmorphic mind, she just told me I was ugly; or at least not attractive enough for her son. I didn't want this man to be my patient anymore, I was too humiliated.

Faith, the pretty nurse, and the woman's son did go out, so it was easy for me to switch patients with her the next time we worked together. Do you see how powerful and consuming this BDD can be? Here is this poor man who is about to be castrated, and I can't take care of him because his daughter doesn't think I am pretty! I know it sounds superficial but it's just the opposite. This disease goes down so deep; it takes over the person that you are, the sibling that you are, the son or daughter that you are and when you grow up it controls your occupation. I self medicated all I could with alcohol and men, not even realizing that those two things were making me worse.

Donna, Carol and I continued to party. We were even looking forward to a long get-away weekend in Florida. It was March and New Jersey was freezing, we couldn't wait to get out of the snow and under the sun. Finally the day came. We packed the car and took turns driving straight through to Fort Lauderdale. We were only going be there for three nights, so the first night we started to party. We went to a big club that we heard was good; I don't remember the name. We all got pretty loaded, and from the pictures it looked like we had a good time at the club. I don't remember leaving the club, but I do remember having sex in a car at our hotel. I don't remember the guy, or his name—my friends would later tell me.

The next morning the three of us woke up in our hotel room and exchanged stories from the night before. Carol had gone back to one of the bartender's apartments where his bed was held by chains hanging from the ceiling. I don't remember Donna's story, but as you can hear, safety was not a priority at the time. While we exchanged stories and nursed our hangovers with Tylenol and Alka Seltzer, we put on our bathing suits.

There was a Tiki bar right by the pool outside our door, so we started drinking pretty early, I knew that a Bloody Mary was really all I needed to kill the lousy hangover I had. I don't really recall most of that day. To tell you the truth, I don't even remember the drive to Florida. We took a lot of pictures, and it looked like we had a blast. We took pictures at stops during the drive; we took pictures at the club, by the pool, even as we were getting ready to go out that night, we took pictures. I can see from the pictures we were drinking even when we were getting ready.

We were going back to the same club; it was right across the street so we could walk there. My friends tell me that I was supposed to meet "Lou" there—that was the guy I was having sex with, in the car, the night before. They said he came to our hotel room late that night to return my watch that fell off in his car, and he wanted to know why I stood him up. My friends explained to him that I planned on meeting him, but was hit by a car on the way to the club. I was in a coma and on life support.

My little sister got the call. It was a Friday night; my father was at a meeting at work, and my mother was in Atlantic City with her sisters for the weekend. My poor baby sister—the hospital needed consent to operate from one of my parents and she was unable to reach either of them. Carol made the call and tried her best not to make it sound so serious. Donna said she was great, she just let her know that I had been in an accident and said as soon as she heard from one of my parents, they needed to call the hospital. It was 1994; cell phones weren't popular yet.

Finally, my dad came home. He called the hospital and asked the doctor what my options were. The doctor said that brain surgery was the only chance I had and it wasn't definite that I would live through the surgery. My father then asked the doctor if he had a daughter. He did. He then asked, "What would you do," and the doctor said he would do the surgery. He said it's risky because it's new, but if we don't do anything she's going to die. My dad, of course, then told him to go ahead with the surgery. He was unable to reach my mother, so he just jumped on the next available plane to Ft. Lauderdale.

I had never asked my dad to tell me about that night in detail; but when I reached this part of my book I asked him if he could write down everything he remembered about that night. Sixteen years later, this is what he remembers in his own words:

> *Samantha, Donna and Carol had gone to Florida for spring break. The girls were at the end of a trip to Florida that had a dual purpose.*
>
> *Not only was it traditional spring break get-away but Samantha was actually contemplating moving to Florida. She had just begun her career as a nurse and was on her way.*
>
> *Early that Friday Ellen, Samantha's mom, left for Atlantic City with her sisters and I was in charge. Audry, my youngest, was home with her friends Lucy and Georgia when I arrived home from work and immediately was negotiating with three eleven year olds why I should allow then to have a sleep over.*
>
> *Actually it was a good idea since her mom would be away and I planned on grabbing a bite out with Pat.*
>
> *So I called Mama's pizzeria and picked up two pies and*

a bottle of coke; the girls were giddy their successful outcome of what turned out to be a carefully laid plan. A sleep over, pizza and no adults.

About 8 p.m. Pat picked me up and we headed for the sports bar for a roast beef sandwich and to watch an early season Yankee game on the new 42-inch screen.

Life was good. Everything seemed to be in it's rightful place.

Pat drove me home after the game and we sat in the car saying our good byes when the side door of our house flew open and Audry popped her head out and was looking for me. I didn't think she'd be asleep but this was an unusual welcome home from an eleven-year-old with guests. So I jumped out of the car to the terrified welcome of my little baby.

Sobbing and crying, she was struggling to tell me her sister Samantha was hit by a car in Florida and was in the hospital. She was holding onto me so tight as the dreadful, unfinished story started to sink in.

I didn't notice Ruth, Lucy's mom through all the panic shrill of the other girls as she handed me a note and told me to call "Dr. X" at the Broward City Medical Center.

The doctor answered the phone and explained how serious Samantha's injuries were. In addition to her broken leg was the more serious injuries to the head. Brain swelling was occurring and the doctor wanted to inject a new experimental drug that prevents the swelling, which most likely could prove fatal.

Shocked by the candid and unfamiliar but deadly serious conversation, I asked the doctor what he would do if it was his daughter and he promptly said he would administer the test drug, but it would have to be done soon since the accident occurred two hours ago and time was of the essence.

He further explained that Samantha was in a coma and not breathing on her own. When I asked how long the coma would last he couldn't tell me. He said it could be a few days or a few years. I told him I would take the next flight and see him in the morning to discuss this further.

I called Carol and Donna in Florida and could hear the dread in their voices. They couldn't even talk about what had happened to Samantha. So I told them I would see them in the a.m. and for them to pick me up at the airport. Then I urged them to get some sleep. It was now about 2 o'clock in the morning.

Audry woke at 5 a.m. hoping it had all been a bad dream. She helped me get ready and handed me a note which I opened and read before I left.

"Dad, Have a safe trip. I just wanted to say goodbye again before you left. Tell Samantha I said Hi and I love her and I want her home. She'll be OK! And be extra careful. I love you!

You're a GREAT Dad!

See you home again.

Love, Audry"

My brother Tony drove me to the airport, my flight was 7:10 a.m. but I had one more terrible chore before I left: to tell to Ellen what had transpired. I dreaded it. I knew how her life was about to change—the fear, the anguish about to transform her life at that moment, as mine had been the night before. The psychological scars inflicted by me on her—it was an awful task, but I had to do it before my plane took off.

I arrived on time in Florida at 9:30 a.m., greeted at the small Ft. Lauderdale airport by Carol and Donna. They had already been to the hospital and were still crying and upset by what they saw for the first time since Samantha was hit by the car. They weren't capable of driving and I took them back to the hotel on A1A in the crowded resort area so they could rest. Then I headed for the hospital which was 15 minutes from the hotel.

I walked in the hospital, numb, but anxious to see Samantha. I took the elevator to the ICU and the nurses seemed to know who I was and escorted me to the private room where my beautiful daughter lay. Tubes were emanating from all over her body, with a breathing machine with it's constant motion and the pressure gage protruding from her swollen head. It was all too surreal.

I approached her and laid my hands on her stomach and hip and asked God to restore my daughter to full health.

My dad was eventually able to get in touch with my mother, and she also flew to Florida. I had lived through the surgery but was still in a coma and on life support. After a few days my dad had to fly back for work. He said it was so hard to leave us, my mother and me. I was hooked up to machines that were doing my breathing for me, and dozens of tubes led in and out of my body. My eyes looked like plums; my face was purple, and with the tube for the respirator sticking out of my mouth, my mother was in no shape to be left alone.

So my aunt Olivia came to stay with my mother at an apartment the hospital used for family members of the patients. My mother had to give notice to work because they had no idea when I would be taken off life support or come out of the coma. I had smoked cigarettes, especially when I drank. I probably smoked a pack a night when I drank so one of my lungs had collapsed. They put in a chest tube, a tube that goes in the side of the body through the ribs and into the lung to re-inflated the lung, but I developed lung infections while this machine was trying to breathe for me. My poor mother, she and my aunt took turns staying at my bedside everyday. I was in intensive care so they couldn't stay with me over night, but they said they would pray to God to keep me safe and leave their guardian angels to protect me each night. After I recovered, they told me how I had armies of angels all around me because so many people were praying and sending their angels to me.

It brings tears to my eyes when I think about how blessed I am. When I look back, in my mind, I was literally resting in the hands of God. Even my very best friend Jennifer and her mom came all the way to Florida to visit me. This is very significant in the way that things we assume are just "a part of life" can actually have a *huge* influence on the way you feel and the person you become. Jennifer and her family didn't have a whole lot of money at the time. I think it was around the time her dad had lost his business, but they still came to visit me, knowing I wasn't responsive, realizing I may never know they made the trip, but still they came to see me, to support my mother.

I don't remember anything from those six weeks of hospitalization. When Jennifer came I was still in a coma, but my mother told me even when I woke up I didn't recognize anyone. Jennifer didn't care, my mother explained. She said, "There you were, in a coma, tubes and machines all around and Jennifer came running in the room with a big smile on her face, gave you a hug and a kiss, and spoke to you with love as she always had, as if nothing had changed."

It made me cry when I heard that. I felt, and feel so blessed to have a person like that close to me. That, you'll see as you read on, is the difference between a true friend, and a person you think is a friend. People will eventually show you who they really are; it is up to you when you want to open your eyes and see the truth. For me, it took nine years before I realized that Donna was not only "not" my friend; she was a person who, for some reason, encouraged the negative feelings I had for myself. She tried to keep my spirit broken. The worse I felt, the better she felt. I'll never understand it. Like I said, it doesn't take long before a person shows their true self. Eighteen years earlier, smoking cigarettes behind the shed, Donna showed me who she was.

It was not until now, as I kept this journal, that I realized having a friend like Jennifer is like having faith. Whatever's going on, whatever the situation is, if she's on my side and she still loves me, everything is gonna be alright. She's one of my favorite people in the whole world; she has strong faith; she's kind and smart, beautiful and fun. She married her high school sweetheart and never gave herself to any other man. I always knew, somewhere in the back of my mind, that since she loved me, and she thought I was a good person, even after knowing all the things I had done in the past, than it must be true.

After fourteen days, I woke up. I was still on the respirator, with that tube down my throat and a machine doing my breathing for me. I don't remember one day in the hospital, not even waking up out of the coma. My mother said it was terrible, though. She said I couldn't talk, but I looked at her wanting to know why this tube was down my throat, and why she wouldn't tell them to take it out for me. I kept trying to pull it out, along with all the intravenous lines I had in my neck and my arms, so the nurses had to put mittens on my hands, strapped to paddles. She was frightened that I was going to lose my mind. She told me she would cry to the nurses, begging to take the straps off my arms. The nurses told her, "She will pull her respirator out and her IVs out. Those paddles are saving her life." My mother would cry, "What good is saving her life if she loses her mind?"

Finally, about three days after I woke up, they weaned me off the respirator. My leg had also been shattered, but my father wanted me to have that surgery in the hospital in New Jersey where I had been working already for two years. He figured I would be close to home and be taken care of by people I knew. He had me flown back to Jersey in a little jet. Just us—my parents, me and paramedics; I don't remember a thing. My aunt Olivia kept a journal the whole time, which she wrote as sort of a long letter to me. She said she knew I was going to be OK and would have a lot of questions, and she wanted to have the answers. I am so happy she did. She was right; I did have a lot of questions. Her journal of those days and weeks was extensive, and the information was helpful. But what I really got from it was how lucky I am to have such a loving family. I feel their love coming through despite all the mistakes which helped lead to my problems. Here is a small excerpt from aunt Olivia's journal:

> *"Samantha,*
> *Jeanie, Caroline, your Mom and I all left for Atlantic City. Before long we were at the hotel and your mom got 'the call'. 'What could possibly make him call so early?' Then I heard your mom say, 'Oh no she was hit?!' Then, I started to wash my face and I heard your mom let out such a horrible, scary cry and gut sound that I'll never forget it. My knees went weak and I felt scared and thought I would vomit so I ran out to the room thinking for sure that something terrible had*

happened to Grandpa as you're mom was trembling uncontrollably and crying and praying all at once. I yelled, 'What's wrong, tell me?' Caroline and Jeanie were holding her and someone said, 'We think Samantha was hit by a car. Jimmy is leaving for Florida, she may need brain surgery.' I burst into hysterical tears; I sobbed; I couldn't get control of myself. I pictured your thin, perfect little body being hurt and scratched and the pain was unbearable. I wanted to scream. I wanted to turn into an airplane and be with you in seconds, but I saw your mother's condition and I got on my knees and prayed with her and we all prayed aloud and I told Ellen, 'I know she'll be okay.' You are too close to God, He won't let anything happen to her. I just knew it. We drove straight to my house talking and crying and wondering all the way how this could happen to someone as good and kind and wonderful as you.

It was such a sad, somber meeting at your house. Paul looked so sad, so worried and was holding everyone together, being strong, taking all the phone calls, etc. Everyone prayed for you. People you never met asked about you; you are on every one's prayer list and mind. It was touch and go. We'd get good news then bad news then good news and always we were thinking of you and your mom and dad and knowing and feeling their pain. It was a horrible week; no one could enjoy anything and yet we forced ourselves to do things to try to get our mind off of it, but then we felt guilty for trying to get our minds off of it.

I am very anxious to come down. I want to see you, talk to you, help your mother. I feel I can do some good. Somehow, I think I'll feel better when I see you for myself and see your eyes open. I feel a miracle will happen when I'm there.

So I'm on my way. I've written this on the plane. I left Easter, April 7, 1994 at 8 p.m."

Chapter Seven

My mother told me that the paramedics on that little jet were two young guys, and I asked her for my make-up. The accident left me brain damaged, but my BDD was as strong as ever. I'm not complaining though. I am really blessed. The little bit of brain damage that I have makes it hard for me to explain things; I have what's called "word-finding difficulties"— I'm unable to read and comprehend long text, like instructions and books, and my short term memory isn't too good. I have no sense of smell, which I really only think about around Christmas. My family always got a real tree; I loved the smell of it. Christmas has always been my favorite holiday and that, to me, was the smell of Christmas. Don't get me wrong, it's still my favorite holiday, love it just as much as ever.

I have a titanium rod in my leg, but I can walk and even do Yoga regularly. This accident was a *gift* from God. If you watch Oprah you've definitely heard that first God throws a pebble, then a rock and if you don't get it, a boulder. This was my boulder. I had to change my life, and now I didn't have a choice.

I was admitted to St. Joseph's Hospital in Passaic, New Jersey, to the floor that I had worked on. I don't know how many days I was there before I had surgery on my leg, but I remember hearing that I was there for a total of four weeks. The bone was shattered so they had to replace it with the titanium rod. My parents said it had taken much longer than the doctor had planned, but when it was over it was successful. I don't remember any suffering in either hospital at any time. Doctors try to explain that away with the medications, but I thank God. I think there was no reason for me to remember, so he removed it from my mind, just like when he forgives us of our sins, he erases our sins as if they never were.

The only thing I can remember is being wheeled out in a wheel chair by a nurses' aide named Cindy, my father walking beside us, wheeling me to his car, him lifting me into the car, and the ride home. I remember everything after leaving the hospital, even though they sent me home with the same medications they were giving me in the hospital. I think some doctors have trouble accepting that they and God are working together.

I was home now. I still didn't know what happened though. Remember, for the past four weeks I've been in a hospital, out of the coma, and I don't remember a thing. I had visitors; my mother was able to stay with me overnight, but I still didn't remember a thing. My leg was in a cast; one side of my head was shaved, but I had no idea what happened. I don't remember how long I had been home, but I know at some point I asked my mother, "What happened to me?" She told me I was on vacation with Carole and Donna and got hit by a car. She kindly left out all the gory details at that time.

She then started asking me questions about family to see how bad the memory loss was. They knew I had brain damage, but they didn't know the effects, or the extent of it. I recognized most of my relatives in pictures now; she told me that when I was in the hospital she would show me these same pictures and I didn't recognize anyone. She told me that in the hospital I didn't recognize many visitors like relatives and friends, so I was getting better quickly. I couldn't get out of bed, though, I was very lonely. I slept a lot.

As I began to recover at home, I was very lonely. I didn't understand why I had no visitors. My mother said that so many friends came to see me in the hospital. Not only that, there were boxes of cards and candies, prayer cards, and stuffed animals.

Where were all these people?

Believe me, I didn't expect everyone who sent a card to visit. I mean, *duh*, my mom's boss isn't gonna "pop-in" in the middle of a work day to see me. But my friends, where was everyone who came to see me in the hospital? You want to know why they didn't come to see me ... because they "saw" me already. That's what I was, the "freak" and everyone wanted to see the freak.

Think about it. People I *never* hung out with, people whose phone numbers I didn't even have in my address book came to see me in the hospital. Why? Because they wanted to see "Samantha," thin, sexy Samantha, with half of my head shaved and *no make-up*—no one had ever seen me without make-up. Seventy-eight pounds, that's right, when I say I was thin before the accident, I was 110 pounds and five-foot-three. After being in the hospital for six weeks, not eating real food, I had gotten down to seventy-eight pounds and looked like a skeleton. I was unshaven for six weeks—an Italian girl, unshaven for six weeks, so you can imagine the hair on my legs and under my arms ... sexy huh? And you know how well those hospital gowns hide everything; they came to see the freak.

I was so out of it that I didn't have any shame. Like when little girls are in bikinis and don't realize the top is up by their neck. I didn't think about not lifting my arms or keeping my legs under blankets. They saw me already. They were at the "freak show." They didn't want to see me now, at home with my sweat shirt on, all clean and covered in my own bed. All except Jennifer; she came over to hug me, and smile at me, and talk to me. That was another thing; I wasn't a very good conversationalist. I had lost most of my vocabulary, but she didn't care. She came over and talked to me!

Even Nicole would call every day to see how I was doing and cheer me up. I didn't expect my two friends I had gone away with to keep our "no boyfriend" pact; they each had found boyfriends—boyfriends that they are now married to, but looking back, they should have visited. Donna and I had seen each other every day for five years. We used to go walking each day and go out four nights a week. I was a registered nurse, I worked three twelve hour days, and she was in college so she never had to get up early. We did *everything* together. Other friends asked me if she and I had gotten into a fight in Florida or something, as if that was why she never came over. I would defend her by saying, "She has a new boyfriend; you know how it is when you meet someone you really like, you want to spend all your time together." And at the time, I meant it.

Two months passed and I had to go back to the hospital for one more procedure, just a same-day surgery to get the screws out and the cast off my leg. Everything went smoothly; I remember being in the hospital this time. I knew why I was there, and I was aware of everything that happened. While I was waiting for them to come take me, I balled my eyes out. I was lying on the gurney when the head nurse, my boss at the time, came over to wait with me. She saw I had been crying and asked if I was OK. I answered, "No, I'm so different. How can I go back to being the person I was before this happened? When will I be 'normal' again?" She grabbed some tissues from the nurses station because I was sobbing again as I asked the questions.

She was a caring but stern woman, always with straight answer, never pussy-footing around to be kind. She said, as she dried my tears, "You gotta give it a couple years, you have to be patient."

That was it; now I was hysterical. You know that kind of crying infants do where they don't breathe for a few seconds? That was me. And, of course, transport arrived to take me into surgery. I just couldn't believe it, *a couple of years*?! Remember, during this time I had the mentality of maybe a ten-year-old. A couple of years was a very long time for me to get my life back! How incredible hindsight is. Looking back now, I am *so happy* that I never got *that* life back. But if anyone had told me then, that my life was never going to be the same, I would have wanted to die.

The next day I finally got to take my first shower. My mother put a wooden stool in the tub because I still needed a walker to get around. I still couldn't stand on my own, but I was so happy I finally got to shave my own legs. Thank God I was "out of it" in

the hospital, and didn't know about all that "hair" on my body—
I was one of those girls who shaved every day. I would never
have let visitors come. After my shower, my mother brought me
back into my room to get dressed. I saw myself naked in the mirror. I almost fainted. I cried to my mother, "I look like a boy!"
I weighed seventy-eight pounds; my small but perky, beautiful
breasts were gone; my butt was gone. I had *no* curves and dark
hair on my face.

My mother explained that I was on tube feedings while I
was in the coma, and while I was in St. Joseph's I wouldn't eat
anything. As far as the hair on my face, my mother told me that
she even asked the doctor what was causing that and he explained it was the seizure medication. I told her to make an appointment with the neurologist as soon as possible to get me off
this drug. Remember, BDD, I hated my face even without hair!
How do you think I felt now? I went to the doctor and he tested
my brain function and found I was no longer at risk for seizures,
so he stopped the medication.

About a month later at a follow-up appointment I showed
him that the hair was still there on my face. He responded, taking you off the medication will stop more hair from growing, it
won't get rid of what's already there. If you didn't believe the
freak story before, you do now, right? I was "the Bearded Lady."
I couldn't believe it. I started waxing every three or four days.

One of the reasons why I called this accident a gift from God
was that my family had gotten very close. My father saw how my
mother was with taking care of me, how she stayed in Florida
the entire time, how she slept on my floor once I got home for
two months in case I needed anything during the night. He even
said, "Watching the way your mother took care of you, I fell in
love with her all over again."

My mom and I would watch "Mary Tyler Moore," and re-
runs of "Dallas" and "Knots Landing," and twice a week she
would have to take me to outpatient cognitive rehabilitation
to determine if I could continue working as a registered nurse.
They could have taken my license away.

We would talk about everything. It was then that she told

me that she used to get so upset because Donna wouldn't visit me, but she didn't want me to know how much it upset her. My mother was right to be upset, but I think that was one of the other gifts God sent me through this accident. Donna showed me, once again, the kind of person she really was. As you read on you'll see, I still wasn't ready to open my eyes and see her for what she really was. I kept denying the abuse. Just like an abused wife often does. I don't know why; I wasn't gaining anything by being her friend. She was very draining to me. Maybe if I finally opened my eyes and saw the person who she really was, I would have to take responsibility for choosing her to be a part of my life, therefore, responsible for all the abuse I put up with and had to witness in the way she treated others too.

Don't get me wrong; I know it's weird using the word abuse talking about a friend, but no matter who it is—a spouse, a parent, a child, a boss—someone who intentionally breaks your spirit daily is an abuser, whether it's by physical abuse, verbal abuse, or mental abuse. I believe this was mental abuse, and it was pretty much daily too. Even though I was the one putting myself down, she was confirming it and encouraging it.

If it were a "boy" friend that was treating me this way, there would be *no* problem using the word "abuse." I don't know why it seems so weird when it's a friend. Probably because I could have stopped hanging out with her, but then again, if it's a boy friend, you can just "stop" dating them. It really is the same situation, just a different relationship I guess.

My mother also told me that Anthony, the boy I got engaged to in high school, was such a big help to my parents and to me. She told me that he used to come to the hospital all the time in New Jersey. He used to sit with me so that my mother could go to lunch and run errands. He was going to school at the time, but even when I got home he would call me practically every day and talk to me for hours. I told you he was great. I hope he's happy; we lost touch years ago. My mom saw him in the mall and he was engaged; then my sister went to a drug store near her house and he was the pharmacist, so it sounds like he's doing great. That makes me so happy; if any one deserves a great life and true happiness it's Anthony. He worked so hard for it, and is one of the few truly good people out there.

Chapter Eight

My parents knew how lonely I was after my accident. I felt so guilty too. Right here's that Catholic guilt again, but I felt like God had really taken care of me and I had no right to feel anything but grateful. How silly! I was going to rehab for physical, mental and cognitive therapy.

In one of my therapy sessions, the psychologist asked me, "What do you do when you get angry about the accident? Do you ever think about or question why this happened to you? You were with two of your friends; do you ever ask yourself, why me?"

I told him, "No." I explained to him, "I have never questioned God's will relating to my life in the past, the way he blessed me with such a wonderful life. We lived in a beautiful home in a safe, quiet town in the suburbs. We all loved one another and were well taken care of. Daddy had a good job and worked hard. My mom stayed home and took care of the house, cooked dinner every night. In my parent's eyes, we, their children *always* came first. I always believed I had the best parents in the world. I would feel like a hypocrite if I questioned this accident after everything I had already been given. I trust it happened for a reason."

After that session, he diagnosed me as "In Denial" and "Poor Coping Skills." If I had been throwing things around and crying out, "*Why me God, why not them?*" like they do in the drama films on cable, he probably would have had a healthier diagnosis for me. I would probably fit closer to the example in his text book. Needless to say, my parents stopped my sessions with him. My parents would help me to re-learn basic activities of daily living, such as how to cook, and the hot and cold knobs on the sink and tub. I remember I kept burning myself. For some reason I couldn't get it straight, which side was hot and which was cold. If it isn't marked, I still don't know, years later—weird how the brain works! I knew where eyeliner and mascara went, but couldn't use the sink.

My mom even went and bought the video game SEGA because it had games like Jeopardy and Wheel of Fortune that would be a fun way to learn how to read again, and learn the definitions of everyday words. She was great, at night she would sleep on my floor in case I needed anything, and during the day she would sit there and play SEGA with me. She would buy me my favorite candy because she knew I wanted to gain my weight back.

It was hard gaining weight because I had no appetite. I later learned that I wasn't eating back then because the taste and the smell senses are connected. My brain injury took away my sense of smell, so I couldn't really taste the food I was eating. I remember my mother used to put peanut M&Ms on my lunch tray and in all different spots in my bedroom, hoping that if I got hungry I would snack on them. But you'd be surprised; when you have no sense of smell, not even chocolate tastes as good. For some reason, I was able to taste coffee. I would drink a pot of coffee a day, which I know now is very unhealthy, but thank God I didn't know that then because it was my only pleasure each day!

Then my dad took me out to re-teach me how to drive. I had forgotten that too. I was only allowed to drive during the day, so I would just drive around town. One day I got hungry, so I went to the Chinese restaurant and I was able to taste that too! Everyday I would drive to the Chinese restaurant and get "shrimp with lobster sauce and spare ribs," everyday, the same thing, so I did start to gain weight, and I started walking again. The only difference was now I would walk alone, I didn't bother calling Donna. My God, looking back, I *can't believe* I thought she was my best friend. What an evil bitch.

I can still remember times after the accident, lying in my bed trying not to feel lonely and sorry for myself, but I was so jealous that the two girls I used to hang out with found guys and were in love. I even remember thinking about that guy at the bar who said he thought I was so beautiful. I was so angry at myself. Why didn't I stay and talk to him longer that night? What if he was my "soul mate"? Why did I have to make that stupid pact with my friends?

I even wrote to the boy in Florida, the one who returned my watch the night of the accident. Both my friends and Aunt Olivia said he was so cute and so nice, and he had given Olivia his address for me to write him. She would beg me, "You have to write him, it's like *An Affair to Remember*. For those of you who haven't seen that movie, it's one of the best movies! It's an old movie, but if you don't like old movies it was re-done in 1994. It's about a woman and a man who are supposed to meet on the Empire State building and then get married, but she gets hit by a car on the way and becomes paralyzed, so he feels stood up. I'm not gonna tell you the rest, I'll ruin it for you, but definitely rent it.

Anyway, Olivia told me that he was there at the hospital in Florida each day and was so sure he would love to hear from me. So I finally got up the nerve and wrote him. I never heard back from him. I just kept crying and praying to God that I would find love; I wanted a boyfriend so badly but how was I going to find anyone now? I was twenty-three years old, an eighty-seven pound invalid with half shaved head, unemployed, and unable to complete a sentence. Even if there was some guy out there willing to humor me, or even just fuck me, I couldn't drive at night to go out and find him.

Some of the friends that were actually calling me would take me out with them on the weekends. I could tell they were uncomfortable with me. I was very quiet, so they never thought I was having fun. Also, they were all afraid of being "responsible" for me. What if something happened with "Samantha" in the car?

Like if someone got into an accident or a DWI with "Samantha" in the car, they knew they would catch a lot of shit from everyone.

One night we went out. I was going out with Renee and perhaps a couple of other girls; I don't really remember details. What I do remember is it was the first time I got fucked since the accident. I hadn't been touched by a guy for like seven months, *not* including the time in the hospital. I didn't even know what sex was while I was in there, which was very a long time in my world. Luckily I did remember I had a vibrator and how it worked. So here I was, all kinds of brain damage, but I still have BDD stronger than ever, which really sucked, because I looked worse than ever. And I'm still addicted to sex. Not just craving orgasms either; I had the vibrator for that. I still needed the cock and the man who went with it.

It was a mechanic that worked in town. We had been screwing on the weekends for like two weeks before the accident. He would call me; we would make plans to meet at the bar. Never alone, my friends would come with me; his friends were there. All of us just hanging out. I would talk to my friends; he would talk to his. We would all just be standing at the bar, or we'd push two tables together. Then, at closing time, I would leave with him instead of my friends, we'd go somewhere and fuck. I don't remember where. It was inside somewhere, but not an apartment. Who knows, maybe he lived with his parents still so we couldn't go to his place—he was around thirty I guess, so it's possible. That night, the same thing happened. The only difference was, I was nervous—just a little nervous 'cause I got pretty drunk that night for the first time since the accident. And here I had figured, not decided, that I probably wouldn't get drunk anymore. I wasn't very bright back then.

Anyhow, I remember another detail. Remember, my perky, beautiful, "B" cup boobs were gone. That little bit of fat that filled them up and kept them up was gone. It was not a pretty site. I had been wearing *two* padded bras so no one would notice the change and thank God I remembered that when we got to wherever it was that we screwed. I excused myself to the ladies room and being so loaded it took me awhile, so long that he came looking and scared the hell out of me. I didn't mind being a slut, but ugly boobs, I wasn't about to reveal that.

I think I ended up coming out in one bra, shoved the other in my purse, maybe ... it's still a blur, but I'm pretty sure we fucked that night. I was probably too drunk to get off, but I had to get it over with. And it's true what they say, "It's like riding a bike." I wasn't as confident or as wild as I had been in the past. Maybe that's why he didn't call me. Maybe he saw the ugly boobs. Who cares, he's thirty and still lives with his parents. That's worse, that's a personality flaw, he needs years of therapy for that. All I needed was implants!

Then, my cousin Tiffany got engaged. Yeah, I guess I was a little jealous because she was younger and getting married first, but again, I felt too guilty thinking any negative thoughts and felt I should just feel so thankful for how God had taken such good care of me. Not to mention, I had always known because she was the "pretty one" that she would marry first. Her wedding was in December. My accident had been in March, so I had nine months of rehabilitation, of weight gain, and time for some of my hair to grow back. I, of course, didn't have a date for the wedding, but I have a huge family and was looking forward to seeing everyone.

I went to the wedding with my parents. I weighed about ninety pounds and the way my hair had grown in, I looked like a punk rocker in a pretty, frilly dress—what a sight! I was sitting at the bar waiting to order a Bloody Mary. The bartender that came over to take my order looked familiar. At this point I was remembering family members and close friends, but that was it. The bartender looked about my age, and we were just one town over from the town I grew up in so I thought maybe I had gone to school with him or something. I didn't want to seem rude just in case we had been in the same homeroom all through high school or something, so I said to him, "You look familiar, do we know each other?" To which he replied, "Maybe, I'm not sure. I'm a bartender; I meet a lot of people."

I felt embarrassed because it must have sounded like a typical pick up line: "Don't I know you from somewhere." How stupid! I picked up my drink and started to walk away when I heard him call out, "No, Samantha, I do know you, we did meet one time." He said, "We met at Leo's Pub for a little while, you were playing pool."

I couldn't believe it. It was him. The one that said I was the most beautiful girl he'd ever seen. We spent the entire wedding talking at the bar and made plans to meet afterward at that same bar to play pool. I was with my entire family, so my cousins drove me to the bar and came in to play pool and keep drinking after the wedding was over.

Yeah, I have one of those families that never want the party to be over; they are a fun freakin' bunch! I think the wedding ended at like eleven o'clock. I was nervous that he wouldn't show but sure enough, there he was, just as cute as I remembered. We played pool and drank and talked. I totally ignored all my relatives, but I'm sure they understood. I was so happy. I thought, "I'm getting another chance, thank you, thank you, thank you God!" I hadn't been this happy in what felt like years. I never wanted the night to end. When the bar closed, he asked if he could take me home. I, of course, said, "Yes." I was not about to play hard-to-get, or anything stupid. Then again, I *never* used to played hard-to-get. I was quite easy. I just hated games. Never understood them; it was like starting a relationship as a fake. Life's too short for that shit. If you like someone, let them know it.

I remember the first time hooking up with the mechanic. We kept on making eye contact; I thought he was hot. Long dark hair, black leather jacket, faded jeans, but he just kept looking at me. Finally, I walked over to him and asked, "Hi are you shy, or are you just not interested? I remember my friends were dyin'; they couldn't believe I did that.

Anyhow, cut back to what felt like the happiest night of my life, Tiffany's wedding night. My new friend and I left the bar together, and I remember when he dropped me off at home he leaned over to kiss me good night. It was a pretty long kiss. I felt so comfortable with him and so happy that I found him again. After the kiss, I remember him saying, "I'm in trouble now, you're beautiful *and* a good kisser." He took my number and said he would call me from work the next day.

I woke up the next day and couldn't think about anything else but him. I would pray it would be him before I picked up the phone every time it would ring. I knew sometimes guys don't call, even when they say they're going to. But I had a feeling he wasn't going to play that with me. I really believed him when he said he would call. I was right!!! He called at 11 a.m. Thank you God ... my prayers were answered! We were gonna see each other again that night! No games, no bullshit. I was *so* happy.

We went out that night with another couple, a guy that he worked with and a waitress he was seeing. They all worked at a banquet hall in Hoboken, New Jersey. We went back to Leo's Pub to shoot pool, and of course drink.

I was up to my old bad habits again, drinking, and I started smoking again. I had sworn because of the collapsed lung and the scar I still have from the chest tube that I would never smoke again. No, I don't have a problem; why, you think I might? We talked most of the night. He joked how the first time we met I didn't even give him the time of day. See, so often people would assume I was "stuck up," or "conceited." If you learn anything from reading this book, please learn not to assume anything about a person. Get to know them before you decide whether you're going to like them or not and never judge anyone. It's really not your place; it's not your job, life is tough enough, why take on an extra task? God, the Universe, fate, whatever you believe in, has got everything under control and doesn't need any help from you.

The thing I first fell in love with about Mark, was his sense of humor. He made me laugh so much, and remember, I hadn't laughed in nine months. I wasn't working, and it was the slow season at the banquet hall where he worked, so we got to spend every night together. Even though I started drinking again, I was still a different person than before the accident. I was very timid. Besides being so small and skinny, my voice was very mousy from having the respirator in for so long, and don't forget, my word-finding skills were poor, so it took me forever to put a sentence together. He didn't seem to mind though. I think he kind of liked the protective role that he had over me. Not in a serious way—he would joke about it, make fun of me in a loving way, teaching me to laugh at myself, not mocking me or hurting my feelings, not yet.

Mark and I didn't have sex until two weeks after we met. It may not seem that long, but we spent every day and every night together. When it finally happened, it was so beautiful. He was gentle and loving. It began with us making out, like in high school. He had a small apartment two towns away from where I lived. He told me he had asked a waitress from work to clean the apartment and make it look nice before he had me over. I thought that was so sweet. He cared about me so much. What I thought of his apartment was so important to him, he had someone come to clean it! We were in his bed, he was on top of me, fully clothed. Grinding a little bit, just like in high school, we were so hot for each other.

His hand began to go up my shirt and I stopped him. Remember the boob issue? I wasn't still wearing two bras, just one padded one, but I knew I would let him go under the bra and I didn't want him to feel them how they were then. I didn't just push his hand away because I didn't want him to think I didn't want to go further. I just wanted to skip "second base." I said as I held his hand from going up, "I don't want you to do that, I lost a lot of weight from the accident and haven't gotten it back there yet." He was so wonderful; he just started kissing me again and put his hand up to my head and started stroking my hair— the side that had hair, but he didn't care about the way I looked. Again, he would kid around and call me his punk rocker.

After a couple of minutes, he moved his hand down to my pants. He started to unbutton and unzip my jeans, then kneeled up between my legs looking down at me and he asked me if I thought I was ready. I shook my head yes and he slid my pants off and tossed them on the floor. He then leaned forward and started kissing my belly; I could feel myself shivering. We were both totally sober. He slid my panties down and off, leaned back over and started licking my pussy. My God it felt so good. I loved him so much already, after only two weeks. He felt how wet I was getting, kneeled up and took off his shirt. He was so beautiful, broad shoulders, great chest. Even with that great body, I still couldn't stop looking at his face—his beautiful brown eyes, perfect nose and full lips, but most of all, I could see the love in his eyes. Believe it or not, I knew, even after just two weeks, he loved me. He took off his pants and then lay back on top of me and started kissing me again. His cock slid right inside me and it felt so good. I almost had an orgasm immediately.

When we finished, we laid there with his arm around me, my head on his chest. The entire experience was better than I had ever remembered. Then he asked me how I felt. I told him, "I don't remember sex ever being that good." It felt like the very first time. This was my Prince Charming. He really was my soul mate! We just stayed there, quietly holding each other. I was just listening to his heart beating, thinking, hoping, praying that I was in there, that he really did love me, that he was feeling the same thing I was.

When he asked me, "What are you thinking about?" I told him, I'm thinking how much I want this to last forever. How much I want you to love me.

I then asked him, "What are you thinking about?"

He said, "I'm thinking you know I already do." I couldn't believe it! Not only did he love me, but he could read my mind. We were this close in two weeks. I knew it was the real thing.

We went Christmas shopping together. We went to the mall. It was so great, the Christmas spirit all around, the mall was decorated, Santa was there, and Christmas music was playing in every store. Then we stopped in a coat store. None of last year's fit because I had gotten so skinny. I found this beautiful coat; I even tried it on but it was over $200. I never spent that kind of money on coats. For one, I never really had that kind of money, nor would I ever think to spend that much on a coat. I had a savings account when I was working, and most of my spending money was on alcohol and cigarettes. I went to the other racks in the store, looking around but now none compared to that first coat I loved.

After a couple of minutes, he put his arm around me and said, "Come on, let's get out of here."

I said, "I'm sorry. You must be bored, I didn't even realize how long we were in here."

He said no, "I wasn't bored." As we walked out of the store he handed me a bag and said, "I was busy getting this." It was the coat! I couldn't believe it; he bought me that beautiful coat! I was so excited; I hugged him and kissed him and told him I couldn't believe he did that. I just kept repeating, "I love you so much, I love you, I love you, I love you!" He was smiling and laughing a little bit at how giddy I was.

Again, he put his arm around me and said, "OK, we're done here." And we went home. When we got into the apartment, he put his keys on the table and not a second later, I grabbed his arm and pulled him into the bedroom for some love making! That's all I ever wanted to do; I was hooked on Mark, to his body, to the sex. The addiction was awakened.

We would spend our nights together renting movies, or going out to bars, playing pool. My birthday came in March, so Mark got that same couple that we had first gone out with to celebrate with us. We went to the usual bar, but to celebrate, everyone was buying me shots of tequila. Now I know you have all gotten to know me as a party girl, but I really had never done shots, or drank tequila, but of course, I got them down. Especially because Mark was doing them and each time I tried to stop, he'd say, "Come on, you can do it!" and the last thing I wanted to do was let him down. No, I'm not blaming him; he didn't tie me down and funnel them into my mouth. I accept all responsibility for every fucked up thing I did in my life; I'm just letting you know how "pleasing" I wanted to be for him. He brought me out of hell and into this heaven on earth, happier than I ever thought I'd be, so I would do anything for him!

Needless to say, I blacked out. I remember sitting at the bar at the beginning of the night, but I don't remember leaving, or going back to Mark's. The next morning I woke up with a hangover from hell! I got up to get a drink of water and Mark woke up. He asked, "How ya feeling?" I said, of course, "like death." He asked, "Do you remember anything after we got home?" I said, "No, I don't even remember leaving the bar." He said he carried me upstairs, all five flights up to his apartment, and put me to bed. He said, "After about five minutes you didn't look too good. You got very pale, and I couldn't tell if you were even breathing. So I flipped you over with your head hanging off the bed and stuck my fingers down your throat to get you to puke all the alcohol out." He said I started to come around and finally woke up. I didn't remember a thing, except telling them, "I don't do shots!"

He did say it was gross, and that he left it for me to clean up, which I did. It wasn't that gross, it was just tequila, but then again, I can't smell, so it probably was, I mean puke usually is. Yuk!

I wasn't working, but I was getting disability, so I was able to contribute to the dinners and the drinking. I felt very comfortable with him; he told me that when he had heard about the accident it really upset him. He said, "I had only met you that one time but I didn't understand why something like that would happen to somebody so nice and so beautiful." He also thought I was still beautiful and didn't think I was too thin at all. Oh yeah, I *loved* him! We were telling each other we loved each other after only two weeks. I just knew we were meant to be together. Mark did too. After only about four months together, I was practically living at his apartment and seducing him every opportunity I got.

Then it happened; I was late and afraid I might be pregnant. We weren't using birth control, I didn't even think of it. I had forgotten all about the fact that having sex can get you pregnant, didn't remember, or think about, where babies came from. I was really like a child in a woman's body after the accident, a child with all these demons hidden away. We would go out drinking and he would drive home. I still couldn't drive at night, but if I could, I would drink and drive. I wasn't thinking about a potential DWI, or killing ourselves, or God forbid, someone else. Again, I was like a child—very irresponsible.

I was still going to rehab for speech and cognitive therapy, so it wasn't like everyone thought I was all better. I just hadn't realized how far from "all better" I really was. When I told Mark I thought I might be pregnant, he was fine with it and said, "It will just speed my plans up a little bit." He made me so happy. I even kind of hoped I was pregnant after he said that, but I wasn't. I figured that God had put us together now and that first time we met was an introduction; it just wasn't time yet. He was two years younger than me, so maybe at that time he was too young. I needed to have that accident, and if he and I were together, I wouldn't have been in Ft. Lauderdale with my two girlfriends. I knew it! It was God's plan to get us together. Even our families knew each other. My mother and Aunt Olivia used to work for Mark's father, and Olivia even used to baby sit for Mark when he was a baby. My family was thrilled to finally see me so happy.

Chapter Nine

After we were dating six months, the lease for his apartment was up. He said we should move in together. I wanted to so badly. In six months, we had only one argument. I don't remember what it was about, but I do remember me crying, and him storming out of the apartment. He took my car and left for three hours. We always used my car; he didn't have one and he lived so close to work he would just walk there. I just sat in his apartment crying. If we ever broke up, I was sure I would die.

He finally came home. I guess whatever the fight was about, it was his fault. The reason I know this is because the first thing he said to me when he got back was, "I want you to know, I will never say I'm sorry. I'm not saying I'll never be wrong, but even if I'm wrong, and feel bad, I'll never apologize. I just want you to know that." Then he hugged me and wiped my tears away. I was fine with that. I didn't need an apology; I just needed him.

I remember seeing an Oprah show where she said, "When someone shows you who they are, believe them the first time." Before the accident if someone said that to me, I'd have told them to go fuck themselves. I would not have accepted that shit. But I had just come out of the darkest place in my life, a sad and lonely place, and Mark was my light. I would have accepted anything he said not to have to go back there.

I was still collecting disability, but it was about to run out. I was concerned about money and wanted to go back to work. We wanted to get a nicer apartment and needed another income to make that possible. I was still going to rehab every week and did not yet get the "OK" to go back working as a registered nurse. Mark had told me that he thought I was fine and didn't think I even needed to go to rehab any more. So I stopped going. He was a bartender; he should be able to judge, right? How stupid are we when we are in love! He could have told me the sky was purple and I would have agreed. He wasn't lying; he really didn't see anything wrong with me, but he didn't know me before. I was still very mousy, spoke very softly, never cursed—that was one of the things he loved about me, that I didn't curse!

I guess you all realize that I was *so* not myself yet. I'm not proud of it, but I have a pretty foul mouth at times. No matter who I'm around, if I'm pissed off, I don't filter my vocabulary. If I think someone should "shut the fuck up," I'm going to tell them to "shut the fuck up." Don't care who it is. Again, I'm not proud because I've embarrassed my friends and my parents; I disgust my sister, but I won't change for anybody, ever again. Mark fell in love with an entirely different person. He had no idea who the real me was.

My last session of rehab, I told them I didn't think I needed to come any more, and asked what they thought about me going back to work as an RN. They said at this point, I had come so far that it was up to me. If I felt confident going back to work, I should. I was shocked, but I was happy. I called the hospital and told them I was ready to come back; to which they replied, "Oh, I'm sorry, the census has been down and we had to close down the floor you worked on. We don't have any openings anywhere else but will call you as soon as something opens up."

Now, if that had happened today, I would take it as a sign that I was not ready to go back to work. But not back then; I started sending out resumes to hospitals, nursing homes and doctors' offices all over the county.

I was twenty-four years old, but I still asked my mother if she thought I should move in with Mark. She said, "No." She knew I wanted to marry him and thought if we lived together he would never ask me. I applied for a job working nights at a nursing home. I figured nights were slower because patients are sleeping much of the time, so I could ease back into nursing. I got the job and was excited to go back to work.

I was a damn good nurse before the accident; patients loved me. After the accident I was even better. Along with being caring and sympathetic, I now had empathy for the patients. I understood that when you are in the hospital, your illness or injury isn't your only problem. I really enjoyed the one-on-one, and nights were slower, so I was able to spend more time with the patients who needed it.

Despite Mom's advice, we found a nice apartment in the spring. I loved the apartment; I loved living with Mark, but it was difficult for me to change my sleep schedule. I thought working all night would make me so tired that I would sleep with no problem during the day, but that wasn't the case. I was also working five days now instead of three. Before the accident, I worked 7 a.m. to 7 p.m., three 12-hour shifts. It was so awesome and I hadn't even realized it. But that's how it goes, right? You don't realize how good something is until it's gone. Now I was working 11 p.m. till 7 a.m., only eight hours, five days.

Everything in the hospital did come right back to me— starting IVs, taking vital signs. It was a "step-down center" more than a nursing home, a place people went when they leave the hospital but aren't well enough to go home yet, mostly elderly people.

Everything was still great with Mark and me. I overheard him on the phone one night while I was getting ready to go to work. He was on the phone with a friend and said, "I won't be out until later, Samantha works nights now and I want to stay home until she leaves." I remember tears of happiness pouring down my face when I heard that. That was one of the nicest things I had ever heard. It's sixteen years later and I still remember exactly what he said.

It was now July, and we were in our new apartment. We were like two children in this big, beautiful playhouse. The bedroom, kitchen and living room were downstairs, and there was an attic upstairs. The landlord had told us most people used the attic for storage, but not us. We turned it into a party room. Since he was a bartender and I was a nurse we had opposite schedules, which sucked, because we never got to see each other. Remember, he worked at a banquet hall so he had to work weekends. If he wanted to have people over after work, or on his nights off, which he usually did, he couldn't use the living room because it was downstairs, right next to the bedroom, where I would be sleeping. Not having parties wasn't an option for him; he was a die-hard partier. So, instead, he drilled a hole in the ceiling so we could have cable upstairs and threw together a small sleeping area for those who were loaded and couldn't drive home.

I hated us being apart so much, so I started looking for a day job. It didn't take long. I found a Dermatologist to work for and quit the nursing home. I thought this job was gonna be boring. Working in a hospital, you're very independent. No one is looking over your shoulder; it's hard work but very gratifying, and the day goes by so quickly. Since I had only worked in hospitals, I thought these were going to be long, boring days—following around a doctor as he treated acne patients, or people with poison ivy, or maybe a mother would bring in her baby who has a rash. Wow, what an exciting day that would be! I was wrong. I was working for a dermatologic surgeon who did mostly cosmetic facial surgeries.

To all you BDD patients out there, this is the worst job you could ever get. Working for a plastic surgeon would also be very dangerous for us. Both jobs enforce the myth that beauty looks a certain way, and whoever doesn't look that way is not attractive. Whatever flaws you already think you need to fix, patients come in giving you ideas about what else you should change. It's kind of like a person allergic to dogs getting a job in a vet's office. *Big mistake!*

At first I liked the job. I got to spend my nights with Mark again and at this point that was all I cared about. I was making pretty good money too, and Christmas time was just around the corner. I liked having extra money to buy decorations for our new home and "great gifts" for my "great guy."

My "great guy" and his brother brought home a Christmas tree, and I was so excited—our first Christmas tree together in our beautiful apartment. I thought it's going to be so festive, decorating the tree together listening to the classic carols sung by Bing Crosby and Nat King Cole. Then the weekend came; he was off and I was so excited to decorate the tree. Unfortunately, we weren't on the same page when it came to Christmas tree decorating. He thought it was the "woman's" thing to do—that's how it was in his house growing up. He and his brother sat there and watched me decorate the tree. A little weird, but I didn't care. It was Christmas time; not much can upset me during the Christmas season.

Christmas morning came. I had asked for a dust buster because it was a big apartment to vacuum weekly when you work full time, so I wanted a dust buster so I could pick up little messes as they happened, and for all the cigarette ashes that were left after Mark's parties. That too was the woman's job, cleaning the apartment, but again, I didn't mind. When we met, it was only seven months after I came out of the hospital. My personality had been erased along with all my opinions and beliefs. Mark was able to mold me into whatever he wanted me to be. I was like a "Stepford Wife." Whatever he told me was the woman's job, I would do.

I opened my first present, and he did get me my "hand held vacuum." He got me a deluxe wet/dry model. I was so happy. For real, it was even better than what I had asked him for. There was another big box wrapped up with my name on it. I had no idea what it was; I hadn't asked for anything big. I opened it; he had also bought me another winter coat, just like our first Christmas together, only this one was even nicer. I was so happy. He told me to try it on, so I did. I was afraid it was too small. I couldn't get my arm through. He said "just push," so I did. My arm came through and pushed out a velvet rose. I thought to myself, how romantic, I'm so lucky. He then said open it. I was confused; I asked, "Open what?" He said "the rose, it opens." I figured out that the rose bud was actually a ring box. I opened it up, and there it was, the most beautiful engagement ring. I hugged him and kissed him and cried. I was ecstatic, I was shaking with joy! He asked, "Does this mean yes?" I said, "Yes, yes of course!" Once again, my prayers were answered. I drove to my parent's house to show them; my mother cried. Nobody knew. He didn't tell my parents or his parents. Everyone was so happy.

We were going to be married in one year. Within the first month, Mark and his dad had everything picked out. The wedding hall, the DJ, the photographer; even the menus were set—how lucky I was, I thought. I didn't have to do a thing. They had worked in a banquet hall, which is pretty much the business of planning weddings, their entire lives, so they knew the best of everything. I was so excited; all I had to do was pick out my dress, and my mom and I picked that out within the first month of the engagement. Mark and I would talk about having children and what their names would be; we were definitely having children, at least two, and probably twins because twins ran in both our families!

As that year went by, besides planning a wedding, things started to change with us. I realize now that it had only been about a year and a half after my accident when we got engaged, and all my doctors told me it would take several years before my full recovery. I still had a lot of healing to do before I would have the confidence to think for myself, make my own decisions and recall the way I felt about certain issues relating to relationships, marriage and sex.

After the engagement, we started having sex less often. Mark's priorities shifted from spending time with me to going out with the guys. He would still go to the bars he and I had gone to, but I wasn't always invited. He would come home wasted after the bars and wake me up for sex about once a week, but there was no foreplay or anything. I, of course, assumed it was because he was tired of me.

We had often told people about that night, that first time he had seen me, two years earlier, before the accident, when he said I was the most beautiful girl he had ever seen. Only now he told it resentfully, saying "she" was so stuck up she wouldn't even give me the time of day. He would say, "She thought she was too good for me." I would defend myself, "He hadn't known we had people waiting for us at another bar."

I figured he was feeling about me like when people want what they think they can't have. When and if they finally get it, it's not all they imagined it would be. Now I was his; he got me. Now that he saw me with no make-up, I wasn't that pretty to him anymore, I thought. I would re-do my make-up when I left to come home from work. After I washed my face, I wouldn't leave the bathroom until I did my make-up. I tried to always look my best around him. Since I had no breasts because of all the weight loss, I asked him what he thought about me getting implants. He said I should. "All guys want a woman with large breasts," he said. So I got implants. This was twelve years ago when they weren't so popular; I was embarrassed, and tried to keep it a secret.

We were talking one day about the future, when we had children. He told me he wanted them to look just like me, except for their lips; he wanted them to have his lips. I don't know, some of you may think "what a nice thing for him to say, that he wants his children to look just like you." That's not at all what I thought; I never liked my nose, but didn't have a problem with my lips, until now. As soon as I got back to work, I asked my boss to give me collagen injections in my lips. Mark didn't even notice. He also told me that his favorite eye color was green eyes. He said that before me, he always dated girls with green eyes, so I went out and got green contacts. I don't even wear glasses. My eyes are fine; I just got the contacts for the color alone.

We were listening to Sheryl Crow one time and he said she was so hot, which she is, but he also said she was the only girl he'd ever leave me for, which was like a back-handed compliment, right? But with BDD, what I heard was that he liked brown-haired girls. I went out and died my blond hair brown. It turned orange; I looked like an ass. I tried everything I could to stay attractive in his eyes. He liked me skinny, so I stayed skinny. I had just the body he wanted, very thin, with large breasts. My finger nails were always manicured because if I had chipped nail polish, or God forbid, a broken nail, he wouldn't even hold my hands.

I thought, finally, I look just the way he wants me to. Until we were sitting on the couch watching a movie and I felt him looking at me. I looked back at him and he said to me, "You know you have large pores." I didn't know what to say. I worked for a dermatologic surgeon, and I never heard of anything being done for that. You know if there was something I could do to "fix" it, I would. That's how much control he had over me. I just went back to watching the movie and couldn't even pay attention because I realized I was never going to be beautiful in his eyes. He was always going to find something wrong with me, but that was OK, I survived this long not feeling pretty; he was going to love me anyway because with all my experience, I was so great in bed!

Then one day, we both had the day off, so I asked him if he felt like making love. We went into the bedroom, and after kissing and caressing, I opened his pants and attempted to go down on him. He stopped me, and pulled me back up. He started kissing me again and said, "You're going to be my wife now, I don't want you doing that anymore. That's not something a wife should do."

I thought that was so sweet; that he respected me so much, he didn't want me to give him head. What I didn't realize until about a year later was that I liked giving head, I missed it, and I liked getting head, too. This respect thing went both ways; he didn't think he should go down on me either, but I had no problem with him giving me head. I wanted it, very much! I could never tell him that though. He was very hard to speak to about sex. If I brought anything up about sex, he would either turn it into a joke or become disgusted with me.

I got myself a vibrator that came in a box called "The Body Massager" or something like that and told him it was because my back hurt from being on my feet all day. Imagine that, not being able to tell your husband you have a vibrator because he will think you're disgusting. As far as him jerking off, never saw it. He must have done it, all men do, I don't care what some might say, they all do it. But he would never do it in front of me. I didn't understand why he was so uptight about sex. I sure wasn't, and it was really becoming a problem for me.

As I started getting better, my "brain disease" (a term I made up for my OCD and BDD before I knew what they really were) started to get stronger and stronger. My sexual addiction started to show itself too, except at this time I didn't know I had the addiction. I thought I was thinking about other guys and getting myself off at least once a day because I wasn't having enough sex with Mark. The BDD was at its worst because sex made me feel beautiful, and I wasn't getting it much anymore. Not to mention, despite everything I tried, I didn't seem to be beautiful in Mark's eyes anymore.

I was feeling less and less attractive, and I started craving the wild sex I used to have with strangers. I craved not only the oral sex that we had stopped, but the anal sex that Mark didn't like at all. He tried it with me once, but that was it. I think a lot of American men are afraid to enjoy having anal sex because they feel like it's a "gay" thing. I missed having sex in crazy places like bathrooms in bars, and on pool tables after the bar closed. I had given head on subways and in cars. I guess prior to the accident I had defined myself as a "party girl," a slut, and when I wasn't, I didn't know what to be.

My single friends would tell me about their wild nights out on dates, the ones with boyfriends would tell me about all the crazy sex they were having, and I was jealous. I never said anything because I got just what I wanted, not to mention I had what many of them wanted: my boyfriend proposed to me. My friends had been with their boyfriends for a few years now, and Mark proposed after just one year of dating.

During the busy season at Mark's work, my single girlfriend, Michelle, got a really good deal on tickets to Florida. We went for a long weekend. I was so looking forward to it. I swore I thought once I started working again I would know how much better it is to go to work instead of just lying around like I had done for six months, but of course after eight months of working, I was sick of it. I needed to get away and this was perfect. It turned out to feel like the worst weekend of my life. Little did I know, in the next couple of years they were just going to get worse and worse.

I don't know how, but when you are a woman with sexual addiction, men can tell. I don't how, maybe pheromones or something, but it's just like how drug dealers know who to approach, which kids will buy and which will go running home and tell their parents. Men always knew, not only that I was approachable, but that I loved sex—everything about it. Just sitting at a bar next to some guy, he knew it was OK to talk dirty to me and that I would respond. It was more than just being an easy lay. I was never a flirt, because I didn't like the way I looked, so maybe there really are pheromones they can sense or something. Maybe sex addicts, which I was later diagnosed as by a sexologist, have extra hormones that increase their libido, and men can sense them like some dogs can sense if a person is going to hurt them or not; I don't know how, but somehow they knew.

Michelle and I went to Florida. The first night we were sitting at the bar by the pool outside our hotel. It was dusk; our hotel was on the beach, so the sunset was beautiful. We weren't drunk at all; we were having our first drink, just enjoying the view while deciding where we were gonna go for dinner. The pool area was empty, even the bar. There was one guy sitting across the bar from us talking to the bartender. The bartender was great. He was a kind, older man who was full of information. He had told us about all the restaurants within walking distance, which ones were good, what was overpriced, and the type of crowd that would be there. I felt very relaxed. I was so happy we decided on this trip; it was just what I needed.

The bartender came back over to us and asked if we decided where we were gonna go. We told him "not yet," and ordered a second drink. The guy sitting across from us looked younger than us; neither of us were interested in him, but he looked lonely. He was by himself having French fries for dinner at this little poolside bar. We felt sorry for him, so we sent him a drink. He accepted, picked up his drink, came over and sat next to me. The three of us were talking about who knows what. The only part of the conversation I remember was him pointing to my engagement ring, saying, "It seems all the beautiful girls have one of those."

That's all I remember about the beginning of the night. I don't remember where we went for dinner, or how he ended up with us at the end of the night, but I remember sitting around the pool with him. It was late, dark, so quiet and cold. I remember freezing while we sat on beach chairs around the pool, and him saying, "come sit on my lap," which I did. I became very turned on when I felt his erection as I sat down. He had a sweat shirt on, so he wrapped his arms around me clasping his hands in front of my chest, so we were very close. I can also remember being turned on by his breathing. His mouth was right by my ear; it's hard to describe, but his breathing was that of someone who was very aroused, like how a man breathes right before an orgasm, and it was hot breath going down my shivering spine.

I felt his cock getting harder with each breath he took. I was so wet. He slipped his hand down my pants and I couldn't do anything but let him. His finger slipped right up inside me, so he felt how badly I wanted him. He stood up, pushing me up too by my waist; he grabbed my hand and brought me inside the gym of the hotel. It was past midnight so the gym was closed, and all the lights were out. He started fucking me from behind as I knelt on all fours on a weight bench. He then moved me to the floor, on my back with my feet crossed around his neck, while he, in a kneeling position, pounded me until we both came.

I don't remember going back to my room, or where Michelle was. She may have been sleeping, I can't remember. I woke up the next day and wanted to kill myself. I felt so guilty. I didn't know how I could have done such a thing. I know I was promiscuous growing up, but I wasn't a cheat. I hated people who cheated. Olivia's husband cheated on her when I was young, and I remember thinking that was one of the cruelest things you could do to another person. Michelle was no help, I don't remember what she said, but she was never very sympathetic, not to me anyway. You know, my friends really sucked!

I felt sick all morning. I called Mark just to hear his voice and cried my eyes out when we hung up. Michelle and I went down to the pool. We got Bloody Marys to help with the horrible hangovers we had. I hoped I wouldn't see him again. We were there by the pool half sleeping, half recovering, for about forty-five minutes when I felt someone standing over us. I opened my eyes; it was him, with drinks for us. I had already had a few, so I accepted.

Michelle was disgusted and said, "No thanks, I'm going up to the room." I asked her, "Are you OK, do you want me to come?" She said very nastily, "no, you can stay here," picked up her towel and left.

He sat down in her chair next to me. I told him I felt like shit, and said, "I talked to my fiancé this morning and I feel very guilty. Last night was a big mistake." He said, "I'm sorry, I feel like it was my fault." I didn't say anything. He started talking about how beautiful it is in his country. He was from South Africa; it was obvious he had money too. He said he had pictures and asked if I wanted to see them. They were up in his room, but I was ready to go up to our room and take a nap, so I figured I could look at his pictures on the way. I wasn't scared, I wasn't drunk and I still did *not* find him attractive. It was broad daylight and he seemed to understand that I regretted the night before.

We got to his room and he did show me some pictures, I forget what. I saw someone, a heavy-set guy, out on the balcony. The curtain was pulled shut so I only saw his silhouette. All I remember is being pinned down on the bed, and him begging for sex. I kept saying "no" and asking, "who is that out there?" He kept on saying "there is nobody out there!" I was very scared; he was giving me the creeps. Finally, I guess he realized I wasn't gonna have sex with him, so he called out to the guy on the balcony, who he told me was his cousin, and said come inside. He did, and they were both laughing while he kept me pinned down.

He yelled to his cousin, "grab the camera," which was mine, "and take pictures of her!" I started to struggle to get up, I remember him keeping me down while his cousin took pictures of me. He would spread my legs and tell his cousin, "Take a picture of this!" He put the camera between my legs, and took pictures of my pussy, of my bare breasts and the two of them kept laughing while they were doing it. I got mad and yelled, "That's enough, let me go!" He let me up, was still laughing, and said, "Don't be mad; we're just playing." I picked up my towel and my hotel key. I asked him for my camera; he said, "OK, but let me keep the film." I realize only now that he must have been a psychopath or something.

Surprisingly, he handed me the camera back. I said, "No way, you can't have the film!"

He said, "OK, wait, let me write down my address and you keep your vacation pictures but send me these when you get them developed." I said, "Fine." He did, he wrote down an address, which I later tossed, and let me leave. I can only imagine that I had an angel right beside me in that room. He went through all that trouble getting those nasty pictures—I had been fighting him and scratching him to stop—and he just handed me the camera and let me go. They were two spoiled little rich kids, probably early twenties, who were out on "holiday" for three months. They had adjoining suites for three months in this nice hotel. He didn't work, and I'll bet everyone in the hotel catered to them. Remember he and I were in the gym after hours; how did he have the key? I remember him unlocking it with a key. I'm just wondering now, how come he didn't take me back to his room the night before? Why did he bring me to the gym? Was it because there were security cameras in there? I remember telling Michelle about the camera in there and she said I was being paranoid. He could easily buy the video from the security guard; just like he probably bought the key? They obviously had some kind of fetish or something for keeping pictures of the women they fucked, why not video too? What do you think? Am I being paranoid?

I didn't do a thing that night. Michelle had met some guy the night before who she went out with. They invited me out, but I just wanted to stay in the room. I was guilty; I was sad; I missed Mark; I just wanted to go home. I stayed in the room and cried and slept.

The next day, we flew home. I couldn't figure out how I let that happen. I felt like I had to tell Mark. I couldn't lie to him— even withholding the truth was a lie by omission, but I knew if I did, I would lose him. He was my whole life now. I remember how sad I was before I met him. I couldn't go back to that life; I was so lonely.

I thought maybe the guy in Florida had put something in my drink. I remembered the night by the pool, he kept going up to his room to get beers for us, and when he got back downstairs with the cans of beer, they were opened already. Why would he open them before coming down four flights of stairs? I know he didn't use the elevator because we were in the back and the elevators were in the lobby in the front. He could have slipped something in mine, some kind of date rape drug or something, but Michelle said "No, if he did that you wouldn't remember anything." I guess she was right, who the fuck knows?

I was so depressed when I got home I couldn't keep my head straight. I couldn't focus at work; I felt like crying every time I saw Mark. I told my mother what had happened and how fucked up I was. She said I should go see a therapist. She suggested that I go see hers, because she knew my family background; she knew all about my accident and it would save a lot of time catching someone else up to date, so I did.

The therapist agreed that I wouldn't remember as much as I did if I had been drugged. She thought it was a red flag sent up by my subconscious that maybe Mark wasn't the right one for me. He obviously wasn't satisfying me sexually. I hadn't known at this time about my sexual addiction. I disagreed with her, and didn't go back like I was supposed to. What did she mean "not the right one for me?" We were soul mates; we had a wedding planned, and I had the dress already. *That* was out of the question. She didn't know what she was talking about. Looking back it seems "someone" couldn't handle the truth!

It was very hard for me to forgive myself for what I did. What kind of person was I? I was happy for the first time in a very long time, and I almost blew it by fuckin' some stupid foreigner! I was in the process of buying a house, which helped to distract me a little bit, but I also continued to drink, a lot. Prior to the accident, I was working in the hospital and living at home for about two years, so I was able to save some money. I also received a check from the insurance company of the woman who ran me over.

There was never any lawsuit or anything; it was considered "no fault" because I was wasted and didn't cross in a crosswalk, so nobody got sued or anything.

I had enough money for a deposit on a two-family house that my dad had found for me. I had wanted to buy a house, and Mark and I had discussed how a two-family is a good investment because the tenants help to pay the mortgage. I fell in love with the house as soon as I saw it. It was in a town where my dad grew up; my grandmother and many of my relatives still lived there. My uncle was right next door, and still just a ten-minute ride from my parent's house. I was talking to my father one day about buying the house. He asked me if Mark was as excited as I was and I said, "No, not really, but after we move in I'm sure he will be." My dad said maybe his pride was a little hurt because he was going to be living in his wife's house. Mark hadn't had any money saved to contribute to the purchase of the house.

My dad and I were in the car on our way to the closing when I asked him, "Should I put Samantha Jones or Samantha *and* Mark Jones on the title?" My dad pulled over. He said sternly, "Samantha Barrett is the only name that should be on that title." My dad's brother was my lawyer, so he was able to stop it if he felt he needed to. Not to mention, I was still a little slow from the accident, and depended on my father's advice whenever it came to money. Thank God I did; that would have been a big mistake.

I was still very excited about the house. My very first house; I loved it, I was so proud of it. I had my friends over just to show them. Mark had already seen it, and I wanted to show it off. When I was walking Donna through, I said, "Isn't it the most beautiful house you've ever seen!?" To which she replied, "I don't know about that, but it's nice." Now, don't all of *you* know that when your friend is showing you her first house, and you know even her husband isn't excited for her, you say, "*Yes*, it is the most beautiful house I've ever seen, I'm so happy for you," when asked that question? It wasn't a literal question, Jesus, it was a two-family house near a highway in the suburbs, give me a fuckin' break here. She was just pissed because she wanted to move in with her boyfriend—of two years now—and he wasn't as in to it. Suck it up you jealous bitch, I'm finally happy ... or is that the problem?!

When I told Mark about not putting his name on the house, he wasn't surprised. It was a very big strain on our relationship. When we finally moved in, whenever I would talk about what color paint he thought would look nice, or what type of carpet would look best in the bedroom, he would always answer, "It's your house, do what you want." That used to get me so upset. We are in our first house together, and he won't get involved because his name wasn't on it? Male pride can be so fucking ignorant sometimes. Sorry guys, but even you know it's true.

His father had told him he wasn't going to have any control, and didn't think Mark should have moved into "my" house. He was just a miserable bastard because he had to borrow money from his in-laws to buy his first house, and had to work for his father-in-law his whole life. He was afraid his son was getting into the same situation and tried to prevent it. When really, dumb fuck, he could have prevented it by being a better father and spending more time with his son as he was growing up. Oh yeah, that was another rule that Mark had told me, that the wife takes care of the children. He said his father had no involvement in his life—never went to any of his games, never helped with homework, so all that was going to be my job once we had kids, in addition to working full time as an RN.

I can remember one time when I went to his parents' house for dinner. After dinner, his mother and I cleared the table while the men just sat there. Now that alone was *not* how I was raised; my father always helped out. I sat back down while his mother brought in the coffee. As she placed his father's mug down in front of him, he said to her, "What do you think you're doing?" She answered laughingly, "I'm serving coffee." He pointed down at the three or four grains of rice that must have fallen off his fork while he was eating—fucking slob—and said with a nasty tone, "You don't serve coffee to company without wiping off the table first."

Very lightly, still smiling, she answered, "Oh, I didn't see that, I'm sorry" and smiled at me while rolling her eyes. You can tell she was used to it, and realized that his ego was broken from having to work for her dad, so consoled him by allowing him to be the big bad boss at home.

I asked Mark about it on the car ride home. I said, "Did you see what happened at dinner? You're mother just cooked and served a beautiful dinner, cleared the table, and brought out the coffee and dessert. Then your father had the nerve to reprimand her for missing four grains of rice on the table." I told him that if he ever did that to me, he'd be wearing that coffee. He understood and was a little bit embarrassed by his father's behavior.

Summertime came. I still regretted what I had done, but was able to handle it with prayers and alcohol. You may laugh when I say prayers, but I have always had strong faith in God. Even if my actions told otherwise, I was a good person, and would never intentionally hurt the people I loved, or anyone for that matter.

I went out one night; one of Mark's friend's drove me. I invited him out since Mark was working. He had just moved into the area, and a bunch of my girlfriends were getting together at this local bar. One of my friends, my "fuck-friends" from high school was there. I told him I was engaged, showed him the ring and all; he seemed happy for me and saw how excited I was. We had stayed friends after high school. We were never really in a relationship; we'd just have sex when we were both single. He and I talked the entire night; we hadn't seen each other since way before the accident. He told me how upset he was when he heard and couldn't believe it. While we talked, Mark's friend asked me, "Do you think your friends could drive you home, I'm tired?" It was early and I said, "Yeah sure, you can leave."

Next thing I know, I guess an hour or so had passed, my friends had left. I remember them saying "goodbye," without thinking about it because we hadn't gone there together and we were all loaded by this time. The bar started to close, and when Jeremy noticed my friends were gone he asked, "Do you need a ride home? My friend drove me here; he could drop us off at my car and I'll take you home?" I accepted his offer, but instead of taking me home, we got in his car, went for more beer, and went to the park. We drank and talked at the park. We talked about how fun it used to be messing around. I used to sneak him in my window at night while my family was sleeping. We got all sentimental about what close friends we really were and that led to us hugging, which led to us kissing.

He was always such a good kisser and a real flirt; more than that, he didn't only flirt with every girl he talked to, but actually fooled around with and maybe fucked most of the girls in town. So kissing on the bleachers at the park led to his hand up my shirt and, remember, now I had implants and they were beautiful. My breasts were beautiful before the accident, just small. Now I had these big, beautiful breasts. I was getting so turned on, he lifted my shirt, and started kissing and licking my nipples, which by this time were so hard. I could feel how wet I was getting and when I leaned back and he got on top of me, I could also feel how hard his cock was. We only made out in that position for a few seconds when he grabbed my hand and said, "Come on, I know where we can go."

It's funny, I thought we were going to some secret place he knew, like a place we could park and no one would bother us. I was pretty wasted by now so I didn't even remember the ride, but after we parked, I looked up and we were at the "Days Inn." For those of you who don't know, it's a hotel chain. Too funny, this was the secret place. Don't get me wrong, I was pleasantly surprised. He checked in and we went up to a pretty nice room. I was so excited; it had been so long since anyone went down on me and after making out for a few minutes that was the first thing he did. Remember, I said he was a good kisser; he was great at this. He had soft full lips, a nice wide tongue; I don't know, I can't describe it, but he knew what he was doing. I realized then how much I missed that. Oral sex was at the top of my list when it came to sex, better than toys, better than any position. Then he got back on top of me and slid himself right inside me. I don't know how long we were doing it before we both passed out. We were *so* wasted.

When I woke up, you can imagine how I felt. I hated myself. The guilt was too much for me to handle. I was going to have to tell Mark this time. Jeremy dropped me off. As I came inside,

Mark was on his way to work. He said, "Rough night, huh?" and laughed. He had no reason to be suspicious; we used to party all night all the time, sometimes if we went out after he got out of work, we wouldn't even start partying until midnight. I was out with my girlfriends; he figured I slept at one of their houses.

He started to leave; I told him, "Wait, I have to tell you something" and started to cry. He got a shocked, but frightened look on his face and said, "What, don't tell me you fucked someone!?" I said, "No, but I did kiss someone—my friend Jeremy from high school; we were making out, and I passed out; that's where I was all night." He called me a "fucking whore," and left for work. I tried to call him at work, but he wouldn't take my calls.

I called my mother and explained what happened. I was hysterical; I didn't know what to do. My mother had known about the guy in Florida and asked me the same thing the counselor did, "Are you sure you want to marry Mark?" I lost it. I said yes, I love him, I can't live without him please call him, he'll talk to you."

She did call him, and when she called me back all she said to me was, "Let him cool off, he needs some time."

Mark called me at home that afternoon. He said that his father canceled the wedding, and he was sending his brother to our house to pick up some clothes for him. I became more hysterical. "You mean you're moving out? I'm sorry, I was so wasted. You can't leave me. It will never happen again, I promise!" He said, "I don't know if I'm moving out yet, I just need some time away from you." His brother came over but wouldn't speak to me; he just packed up some clothes and left. Mark went to stay at his parents' house.

Donna and I were friends at this time. She did give me a hard time when Mark and I first started dating. You're not gonna believe this, but she used to get pissed off because I would only go out with her when Mark had to work, but if he was off on the weekend, I would never go out with the girls. *Well yeah!* You Donna, of all people, should have known that new boyfriends come first, remember? That's why you didn't visit me for six months when I was bed ridden after my accident! Anyway, I digress. She came to sleep over the night Mark moved out. We talked all night. I told her everything, even about Florida. When I had told her that we weren't having oral or anal sex, she knew I loved both of those, understood my actions, and warned me that it may keep happening unless I tell Mark how important those sex acts are to me. I told her I couldn't; I didn't want Mark to lose what little respect he had left for me. Really though, looking back, I wasn't able to speak to Mark at all about sex. Imagine that, not being able to talk to your fiancé about sex! She then said exactly what both the therapist and my mother had said. "Maybe Mark's not the right one for you." She went on to say, "I never wanted to say anything because you were so in love with Mark, but I can't believe the way he speaks to you."

Donna and I had both moved to the same town and started walking together just like we did before the accident. We weren't as close as before, too much had happened, but we were friends. We used to talk as we walked about our relationships, sex, arguments—you know, girl stuff. She said, "When you tell me how he speaks to you, the names he calls you, like 'cunt' and 'whore', I can't believe it. Jerry never even called me bitch, in the three years we've been together. I don't understand why you put up with it." I was still defending him. Especially now, I felt like I deserved to be called all those names, even worse, if there was worse! I told her that he was so good to me, how he was my best friend and we have so much fun when we're together. I could tell, she still didn't understand.

Many people used to ask me why I put up with the way he treated me. I probably did because a lot of how I saw our relationship was created in my mind. I saw our relationship how I wanted it to be and not how it was. I didn't realize it then, but in hind sight it's very clear what I was doing.

I called Mark at least every hour the next day. His father had already canceled our wedding reception which was going to be at his banquet hall, so he was in control of that, but I didn't want him convincing Mark to leave me for good. Every time we spoke, I would ask him what I could do to make him come home. I had promised him I wasn't going to go out at night anymore unless it was with him. That wasn't just to get him back either, I knew now that I was out of control and didn't trust myself. I said I'd do anything to make him forgive me.

The third day, his friend, the one who drove that night, called me to see how I was doing and to apologize for leaving me at the bar. He had spoken to Mark already and heard what happened. I asked him if he knew of anything I could do that would make Mark want to come home. He said, "Mark just needs time; give him some time, stop calling him so much." So I did. About three hours later Mark called me. I told him what his friend had said and Mark told me, "Don't listen to him. You can call as much as you want." That made me happy.

The next day he came home. I promised him that he could trust me and that I wouldn't go out without him anymore. He did say that the wedding was still off, and took my engagement ring away from me until he was able to trust me again. I knew I could regain his trust, as long as I stayed home.

Now you see why I couldn't tell him about Florida, or about what really happened with Jeremy. He moved out, canceled the wedding and took my ring away because he thought I kissed a boy from high school. There was *no way* I could tell him what actually happened that night. I know I lied, and I hated having to lie to him, but now you see why I had to.

About two months passed. Mark came home from work and said, "I hear your friends are all getting together tomorrow night, why don't you go?" I said, "No, that's OK, I like only going out with you." He said, "No, that's no way for anyone to live; you can start going out again, I trust you." He went into the bedroom and got my engagement ring. He said, "The wedding is back on, our date had been filled, so my dad rescheduled it for September 10th." Originally we had picked February 14th, Valentines Day. He put the ring back on my finger and gave me a kiss. It felt like one of the happiest days of my life! I was so happy to hear that he trusted me again, but I didn't care about going out. To be honest I didn't want to go out anymore; I still didn't trust myself. As I was beginning to heal from the head injury, my sex addiction was trying to force itself through, after all, it was part of the person I was prior to the accident. Only at this time I still didn't know it was a disease I had, a real addiction. I thought maybe I loved sex so much I wasn't able to say "no" to anybody. Maybe it was because I wasn't getting as much as I wanted at home. I hated myself; I thought, "What's wrong with me, why can't I control my own behavior like everyone else can?" There was nothing I could do to stop it; my old habits were back and going ruin my new life. I was so afraid.

When I told my parents the good news they were annoyed. Don't misunderstand them, they were happy that I was happy again, but thought Mark's father had a little too much control over a wedding that my father was paying for! I begged them not to say anything, especially after what I had done. They finally agreed, but they knew I still wasn't healed from the accident and were afraid that I was being taken advantage of. They knew that the person I was before the accident would *never* let anyone else plan my wedding, and run my life. Looking back, they were right.

Mark was insecure. I think that's why he reacted so drastically to a kiss. Although he did say a few times that he didn't believe Jeremy and I just kissed that night, he never really pursued it. I don't think he wanted to hear the truth anymore than I wanted to tell it. I think it was his father who was putting ideas in his head anyway. My God, he was such an asshole. He used to put down his wife and kids so much, just for a laugh too. When they were at work his father would always make fun of his sons just to get laughs from his co-workers. His wife was very beautiful. I think he believed she was too good for him and that's why he would insult her and emotionally abuse her. He wanted to keep her confidence down because he was afraid she would leave him for someone better. Mark watched and learned this behavior growing up. As we got closer to the wedding, he started to treat me the same way.

Chapter Ten

With the date changed, I now had fourteen months before the wedding. It seemed like forever. I wanted to hurry up and get married because I knew once I was his wife, everything magically would be better. I was only going out on the weekends with Mark when he was off, which isn't very often in the restaurant business. I spent most weekends at my parents' house, watching movies, just spending time with my family, where I knew I couldn't get in trouble. I never went out during the week because work was busy and the hours were long. Mark used to say to me, "Why don't you go out anymore? You're at your mother's every weekend, what happened to the party girl I used to know? I hope you're not turning into a bore right before we're getting married." I would just blow it off; I would say something like "I want to be able to fit into my dress," or something like that. What was I going to say, "If I go out I know I'll end up fucking somebody?"

Neither Mark nor I realized that when he and I met, after the accident, I was just a small portion of the person I was before. As time passed, not only did my addiction and my BDD start to come through, but eventually, so did my personality. I began to recognize some of the abuse I had been tolerating, and it was becoming more and more difficult to put up with. I told you, in the past, Mark was able to mold me into this perfect little obedient wife. I was a weak, quiet, skinny little girl. I was like a puppy that he adopted from the pound. I was so grateful and dedicated. I was going to love him no matter how he treated me. Anything was better than the place I was before I met him, and I would tolerate anything. He became very abusive, and I don't even think he knew it. Again, I think this was behavior he learned, not realizing it was abuse because his mother always put up with it.

He would look at other girls and say, "You should wear your hair like that." There was this couple we used to go out with, Tommy and Gina, a high school friend of Mark's and his girlfriend. In their spare time they would go rock climbing or skiing; Mark used to say to me, "Why can't you be more like Gina?"

All you women know, and I hope you men know too, that *no* woman wants to be compared to other women. You men wouldn't even like that. I never would have gone back at him and said, "Oh yeah, well Tommy holds the door for Gina, and pulls her chair out for her. And you know what else he does, *honey*, he gives her oral and anal sex, that's what! I nearly got killed crossing the street, I doubt I'm gonna want to rappel down the side of a mountain any time soon—use your fucking head!!

I still remember some of the hurtful things he would say to me. Working as a nurse, you get to hear a lot of silly little jokes, but sometimes, these funny old men will tell you a real winner. If Mark and I were out with a group of people and by chance I would remember a good one, I would tell the joke. Everyone would laugh, even if it was just to be polite, except Mark. He would shake his head in disappointment and say, "You have to work on your delivery, your delivery sucks." Well you know what, Mark? For all those times, Fuck You!!! I'm a registered nurse trying to have a little fun, not a stand-up comedian, I will *never* work on my delivery, no matter how many times you say I need to; I'm too busy working to pay our mortgage. You, you nasty son of a bitch, need to work on your manners!

Another really weird thing he would do is this ... wait, before I tell you what it is, I first have to tell you that I have very white teeth. Remember, I had BDD and hated my face, so you know I'm not gonna let the only part of my face I have control over go to shit, so I kept my teeth very clean, even some of my patients used to comment on them. OK, here's the weird thing. I told you he was very funny, and used to make me laugh at a time I really needed it. I think it started as we got closer to the wedding, because I remember him doing it in the new house. If we were face-to-face and he made me laugh, as soon as I started to laugh, he would ask, "Did you brush your teeth today?" If you are reading this and thinking "maybe you had bad breath, or something in your teeth," but that wasn't it. I would immediately stop laughing and get very embarrassed, I would feel my face get red and put my hand over my mouth and say, "Yes, you know I brush my teeth every day. Do I have bad breath or something?" He would always answer, completely seriously, "No, you're fine, I was just asking." Isn't that weird? It was like he liked the control of changing my laughter to humiliation in a split second. It was never a joke, he never laughed or smiled afterwards. Again! I never said anything back at him. I had much whiter teeth than he did, but I would never go down to his level.

I told you earlier about my brain damage, that I have word-finding difficulties, so I often will become nervous if I try to tell a story. When I got nervous, I would look away or focus on an object in the room to stay focused and recall the word I was thinking of. If this would happen when I was speaking to Mark, he would say, "Look at me when you talk to me." As if he was my parent or something. So now I lose all track of what I'm even talking about. It was degrading, and I think that may have been the intent. But again, it wasn't Mark's fault, it was his father's. That's exactly how I saw him treat Mark's mother. Do you hear this all you men out there? Be very careful the way you treat women when your sons are around. Even if you don't care if they hurt women, you're ruining their chances of getting laid. And I know you all care about that!

The year goes by and it's getting closer to the wedding. I'm starting to panic. I fear that Mark knows what I did with Jeremy and is just going along with the wedding so my poor father has to shell out all that money. I had heard stories like that. Like husbands that know, or find out but still go through with the wedding to humiliate the bride in front of all her family and friends.

I was a mess; I really just wanted to get it over with. Can you imagine, not looking forward to your wedding, but wanting to get it over with?

It's August and I have one month before the wedding. Both the bachelor and bachelorette parties are over with, thank God. I was terrified of the bachelor party; so many guys were going, I was sure at least one found out what I had done. I was such a wreck. I was afraid the guy from South Africa had sold Mark the recording of the sex we had in the gym. A little narcissistic don't ya think? I was obviously paranoid, a complete fucking mess!

Then one Friday night, I went out with Donna and Michelle to some lame bar in town. It was boring so I just sat there and drank. It was around one o'clock and they were thinking of going to another bar, or getting beers and going back to one of their houses, I don't really remember; I was quite drunk already. I knew the party Mark was working that night was ending early, so I told them to drop me off there. Sometimes if a party ends early the waiters and waitresses will hang out at the bar and have a few drinks.

I was right; the party did end early, and all the workers were around the bar, except Mark. I asked where he was and they told me that he ran out to get a pack of cigarettes and would be right back, so I sat down and had them make me another drink. I preferred vodka to beer; the hangover wasn't as bad. We were all drinking for about a half hour; I didn't know where Mark could be. He specifically told them that if I called, be sure to tell me he was coming back. So I continued to wait, and drink. People started to leave, but I stayed. I was very fucked up now; we had been playing drinking games for I don't even know how long.

At some point I went behind the bar. Mark's uncle, who was bar tending for our little "after party," was showing me how to make the vodka drink that I loved but didn't know how to make. He was about forty-five years old, and I never really spoke to him before this. Mark hated him and always said he was an asshole, so I never made the effort. I didn't realize it, but everyone had gone home. Just he and I were left there, behind the bar, making drinks, and drinking every one we made.

Now the one thing I did know about Frank was that he was a total cheat. That was the reason Mark hated him so much. Here he was, married to Mark's aunt but fucking every hot waitress that was hired. He was hot too, and very sure of himself.

It was the nineties, remember, "grunge" was in style. I had a pair of torn, vintage jeans on that night. I was leaning against the bar to hold myself up, his uncle was behind me, I had my back to him. There was one tear in my jeans that was about five inches below my back pocket, not on my ass, just below it. I remember feeling his uncle's hand slip into the tear and under my panties. Instantly, I became wet. He slid his finger inside me. He started moving his fingers in real slow circles for about a minute. He then whispered in my ear, "Do you want to come upstairs?" I just shook my head yes. There was no thought between his question and my answer. I was a loaded sex addict, with a man's finger inside me. I didn't even know there was an upstairs, or what was up there; I would have done anything he said at that time.

He took me by the hand and led me upstairs. Last thing I remember is kneeling on the floor of his dark office and putting his cock in my mouth, while he lay there naked on his back. The only other thing I remember seeing was cum all over his stomach. I swear on my life, that's all I remember. I completely blacked out. I didn't pass out, but I don't remember if we fucked, or if he went down on me. I don't remember how I got down the stairs or out of the building, where Frank went, if he passed out or left. I just remember Mark's cousin meeting me in the parking lot and driving me home. I don't know if he knew Frank was still there, but if he did, I'll bet he could figure out what happened, knowing how Frank was and seeing how wasted I was. I think I told him I was waiting for Mark, who never showed up, thank God, but I don't remember having a conversation, or even going into my house. I don't remember seeing Mark, or even asking him where he was. I'm pretty sure he was sleeping when I got in, but I'm not positive.

The next morning, when I woke up, Mark had already gone to work, I think.

I'm telling you, I was more wasted that night than I had ever been without passing out. I wish I had passed out. I was gonna kill myself. I didn't know what to do. The only reason I didn't, was because I didn't want Mark to ever find out about it and me not be able to explain what really happened. Not that I was innocent, but I knew he would be devastated, and I had to let him know how it happened. How I was there to see him, how I loved him so much and his uncle seduced me after knowing how loaded I was. Yeah, maybe he was loaded too, but I don't care. I never would have done something that could hurt Mark so badly; I loved him. I hated his uncle. I remember that morning I hoped he died. I remember wishing he killed himself in a car accident on the way home that night. I knew he drove home after drinking that much. He already had three DWIs and was still driving loaded. What a fucking loser. Did I mention he was married to Mark's favorite aunt. Yes, his mother's little sister. And they had a daughter. She was gonna be my flower girl in my wedding next month. What had I done??

I called Donna balling my eyes out. She came over and got me. We drove around for about five hours. I didn't know what to do. Neither did she. She didn't know what to tell me. I was afraid if I told Mark he would kill his uncle. He didn't like him already; he knew how much he cheated on his aunt with the waitresses. I was so scared.

I was scared every day after that. Every day that Mark went to work, I was terrified. I thought each day was gonna be the day that he finds out. I didn't know how, but I feared the worst. I thought that his alcoholic uncle would confess to his wife in some drunken stupor, and then everyone would find out, not only breaking Mark's heart, but humiliating him in front of his whole family. Maybe the bar wasn't completely empty that night. After all, I never found out where the cousin who drove me home came from; he worked that night and he was still there. Were other people there? Were there people walking around with this big secret that was going to ruin my life as soon as they had a few drinks in them? Not knowing was killing me. I know now I should have canceled the wedding that day.

I started to drink more and more. Again, I just wanted to get this wedding over with! I'm having the most beautiful wedding in a big beautiful church, three hundred people, even a horse and carriage ride from the church to the reception, and I want to get it over with. I'll be honest with you, if the invitations hadn't gone out already, I would have found some way to cancel it. I heard later, that young people think if invitations are already out, they feel it's easier to get a divorce than to cancel a wedding. I think that's probably true. I wasn't consciously planning on getting a divorce, but I know now I should have canceled the wedding. I don't know if I would have told about the uncle because that would destroy the family—*No! I would have told Mark about his fucking scum bag of an uncle. Why should I suffer and have to lie again? It was his fault! Why am I trying to protect his family? His uncle should have been kicked out of that family years ago. His wife knew he was a cheat!* I just never wanted Mark to get hurt. What else could I have done?

I wished there was a chance that I could have told Mark and he would have forgiven me. Then we could be married and his aunt would divorce her husband, and we would never have to see him again. But I knew from the last incident that was not possible. If I told Mark, I would lose him forever. I couldn't let that happen. He was my soul mate, and when we first started dating he called me his angel, which was ironic, because I always felt that *he* saved me.

Chapter Eleven

The wedding was perfect. Everyone said so. People called my parents for weeks telling them what a wonderful time they had. I just wish I got to enjoy it as much as they did. I was so frightened, I don't think I took a breath the entire night; I was consumed with fear. Every time someone got up on the stage to make a toast, my heart stopped. I was sure each one was going to be the one to announce what a horrible person I was. No one did, thank God. Finally, it was over. We were married; I was his wife and he was my husband. Now I was safe. He no longer had the option to just "break up" with me.

We had gone through the church "Pre-Cana," which spoke about how this was forever and "what God had joined together, no man can divide." I remember at the Pre-Cana—for those of you who don't know what it is, it's kind of like marriage classes—we were discussing why you were marrying the other person, your fears and your plans as a married couple. I'll *never* forget it; we had to fill out questionnaires separately and one of the questions was, "What is your biggest fear about getting married?" Then we exchanged sheets to read each other's answers and his answer for that was, "If Samantha got sick, or hurt, or left." I balled my eyes out. Tears of joy over how much he loved me, tears of fear if he ever found out, and tears of guilt—how could I have done these horrible things to the love of my life.

When he saw I was crying, he just came over and held me, which as you can imagine, just made me cry harder.

Then, the honeymoon came. We were sitting on the plane, waiting for it to take off. I had to pee, so as usual I got up and said to Mark, quietly, "Excuse me, I gotta pee." I'm a Jersey girl, that's how we talk. No one else heard me. But then in a loud voice, Mark said, "Couldn't you say: 'I have to use the ladies room,' why do you have to be such a pig?" As I walked to the ladies room, I felt very uncomfortable about what Mark had just said. Not angry, and not insulted or embarrassed, I didn't know what it was at first. Then I realized it was fear. What had I gotten myself into?

We finally landed in Jamaica. It was about three in the afternoon and beautiful. I had been afraid of going to Jamaica because I heard of all the fighting and the drugs, but Mark said we'd be fine, so that's where we went on our honeymoon. Thinking back, I really didn't have much say about anything. Remember, how lucky I thought I was when Mark and his dad planned the wedding? I didn't feel so lucky when it was the rest of my life that was being planned for me; the wedding was only the beginning.

We started drinking on the plane. We met another couple who were celebrating their five-year anniversary and started partying on the plane as well. We checked into the hotel and brought our bags up. Mark made himself a drink at the bar in our room while I unpacked—remember, I have OCD and it makes me do things like that. I wouldn't be able to enjoy myself and get nice and toasted if I knew there where unpacked bags back at the room. Yes, *our* bags—packing and unpacking luggage was something else that the woman did.

As soon as I finished, we met our new friends from the plane at the tiki bar on the beach. The water was beautiful; the sand was white and the beach was clean. I was excited again. I don't know if it was the vodka or the beach, but I had forgotten about the fear I felt earlier. I felt like a newlywed and couldn't wait to go back to the room with my *husband*! I loved having a husband; I loved saying, "my husband." I said it the entire week: "Did you meet my husband?" "Did you see where my husband went?" I used it whenever I could; it never got old to me.

We sat at the bar for about two hours. I said I was hungry around six o'clock, although I wasn't; I just wanted to make sure I got sex on the first night of my honeymoon. Remember, I couldn't ask for it, we didn't talk about sex like that. We ate, had a few drinks, and then went back out to the tiki bar for a few more. Our friends weren't there, thank God, because then we would be there all night. Remember, I married a "die-hard" partier. Don't worry, I'm not trying to say that I didn't like to drink till closing too, but when it came to sex or alcohol for me, sex would always win hands down no matter what.

We went up to the room, and I got my sex. It was good too, even without foreplay, or sexy lingerie. I remembered, when we had just gotten engaged, I went out and bought this very expensive, extremely sexy lingerie. It had real silk stockings and garter belts, lacy teddy with matching panties, the heels, the gloves, the works! He was waiting in bed for me one night and to surprise him I came into the bedroom wearing it. He said nothing.

I said, "Well, what do you think?"

He said, "You went through all that and now you just have to take it off. It seems like you wasted your time." Needless to say, after *that* reaction, I didn't waste all that time and money again. We both passed out right after it anyway, so it was good I didn't have to get all undressed. Always looking for a bright side, ya know.

We met our friends for breakfast the next morning and talked about what everyone was going to do that day. They said that they were very hung over and didn't plan on drinking. Not us— hangovers were just a reason to start earlier, you know, "hair of the dog ..."

Before we were gonna party though, Mark had some outdoor activities he wanted to try. Not me, remember, I'm not the outdoors type anymore. He had plans to go scuba diving, parasailing, and fishing. First we went to sign him up for scuba diving. The boat had already left, and you had to have a lesson first. It even *sounded* too dangerous for me. If lessons were needed, forget it! We signed Mark up for lessons on the following day, and for the boat trip out the day after that. I felt bad; he was disappointed. I could tell he thought that you just walk to the end of the pier and jump in, which is exactly what I thought, and I still didn't want to do it. We found out where to sign up for para-sailing, and went there.

As we sat and watched the other people para-sail, Mark begged and pleaded for me to do it too. For those of you who don't know what it is, it's when people are parachuting with a rope connected to a small speed boat that drags them at a forty-five degree angle. As we watched, the people were waving and doing flips while they were floating from the parachute. They really did look like they were having fun floating up there, not too high up either. Mark was so excited to get up there. When we had signed up, there was a sign with the prices that indicated two people could go together. Mark even said we could do it to-gether if that was the only way he could get me to do it. He was saying, "Then you'll have nothing to be afraid of; we'll both be up there, and you can hold on to me." He was begging and plead-ing, saying, "It's our honeymoon, come on, don't you want to try something you've never done before? It'll be so fun! Please, then after this we can do whatever you want."

I started to feel guilty. *No, I remember I started to worry*! I thought if I don't do this with him he is going to be convinced I'm a bore and sorry that he married me. I finally said, "OK, but don't tell me to let go of you. You're not going to be able to do flips and stuff with me hanging on, but I'm not gonna let go." He was very happy. He was so excited. He was like a little kid about to go on a ride at an amusement park; he looked adorable. I was glad I agreed to do it with him.

The boat came back and it was our turn. When we told the driver we were going to go up together, he said we couldn't. He said that to go up in pairs they used a different boat, and that one wasn't running today. He said we could go to the desk to find out when the next time that boat is running. Mark looked so disappointed. I said, "So what, you can still go up!"

He asked, "Will you still do it?" Remember how excited he was that I was going up too. I said, "No, I was only gonna do it with you." He looked so disappointed. I, of course, assumed he was starting to regret marrying me, and that he was picturing the rest of his life doing things like this by himself. I couldn't let him regret marrying me. I was more afraid of that than I was of para-sailing, so I said, "OK, I'll do it too." His face lit up. He became so excited again. He said you go first so you don't change your mind. So, of course I did. The man strapped me in and buckled me up. I was so scared. Then he started cranking out the rope as I lifted into the air. I just kept focus on Mark's smiling face, as the wind rocked me from side to side, until I was so high I couldn't even see him anymore.

When I finally got up there, the wind was so strong it was whipping me around like clothes on a clothes line on a windy day. I was past scared. I held on so tight to the ropes and started screaming for them to bring me back down. I knew something was wrong. I was much higher than those people we had been watching. I could barely see Mark and the driver in the boat. I prayed that they would hear me. I was screaming at the top of my lungs. I figured they couldn't hear me because I didn't feel them start to pull me in.

I started to cry hysterically as the wind was tossing me up and down and back and forth, flipping me around and into the ropes. There were so many ropes going up to the parachute, I thought for sure I was going to be hanged as I kept flipping around them. How come they didn't see me? I couldn't figure out why that man didn't see how high I was. I was directly over the boat at a ninety-degree angle—twice as high as the others. It wasn't right; something was wrong. I could picture the headlines in my mind: "Newlywed Bride Hanged While Para-sailing."

I could tell they couldn't hear me, so I stopped screaming. I just closed my eyes, held on tight to the ropes and prayed. I prayed and prayed for God to watch over me and keep me safe. I knew that God kept me here for a reason because he didn't take me when the car ran me over. Who knows, maybe I needed to write this book and let all you people out there with BDD and sexual addiction know that there is help. Maybe it's to tell you parents that you need to talk to your children more. Tell them how beautiful they are every day and mean it. Find out how they feel about themselves; make sure they know they are important and if something is wrong, get them help! Don't just figure, "Kids at this age are so crazy with boys or girls and their hormones are changing ..." Whatever the reason was, I knew God didn't save me so I could continue drinking and doing stupid things for a guy who I'm not even sure loves me. I was thinking, "*Maybe I'm the one who made the mistake by marrying him!*" Maybe we both made mistakes; maybe we're not soul mates; maybe we aren't even that compatible. That was all I could think about as they began to pull me in. Yes, after the fifteen minutes, which felt like hours, that I was up there, they started to pull me in. Thank you God ... for saving me *again*.

When I got close enough for Mark to see my face, he turned to the driver and said, "I can tell by her face that she didn't like it." As I got into the boat, I said, "That's an understatement." But it was his turn, so I couldn't explain how much I hated it and how I will *never* do it, or anything like it, ever again! I sat down in the boat while he went up. I just happened to look down at my hands, and they were covered in blood. Remember, I told you I was holding onto the ropes so tightly? I hadn't even realized because I was distracted by the fear up there, but my fingernails on both hands had dug in so deeply into my palms that they pierced the skin. Both palms had four bloody holes where my nails had dug into them.

While Mark was up there, I asked the driver, "Wasn't I up higher than everyone else is?"

He said, "Yes, you are very light. How much do you weigh?" I told him one hundred and ten pounds. He said, "Yes, it's probably too windy today for you." He didn't speak great English, so I just dropped it, but I thought to myself, "*Who the fuck is in charge here?*" I wasn't even watching Mark. I was so confused about our relationship, our marriage. Did we make a mistake? I told Mark what happened to me when I was up there, and showed him my hands. He said, "Yeah, I thought you looked very high, but when I asked the driver he said you were fine." Needless to say, after that we went drinking. I got so fucked up the rest of the week, I don't even remember the rest of our honeymoon.

When we got home, I remember praying for answers. I would go to my church and just pray and cry. Now I know it sounds like I was a drunk, which I was, big-time, but you must know that I *never* missed a Sunday mass. No matter how late I was out until or how hung over I was, I always made it to church. I'm not one of those people who thinks I can sin all I want and as long as I go to church I'll be fine in the eyes of God. I don't believe that. I didn't miss a mass because I believed that the power of the Lord inside me was all the strength I had left, and that without it I wouldn't be anything.

I didn't know what to do. I started analyzing every aspect of my marriage and our relationship. It was so hard because everyone, all of our families and friends convinced me that we were such a perfect couple.

Mark and I had a party with all of our friends and relatives there. My mom told me later that she was so happy; she said that every time Mark came into the room my face lit up, and I was always so happy to see him. Was I really? I didn't feel happy; I felt nervous. I didn't know what I was going to do next to disappoint him, or to make him feel embarrassed or ashamed of me. I knew I loved him, but I no longer knew why. I fell in love with him when I was sad and lonely after a bad accident. He took me out and he made me laugh. He didn't always want me around anymore, and I no longer found his jokes very funny. I realized that I had become the butt of all his jokes.

Then one night we went to dinner with his cousins. They were two young guys with their girlfriends, I guess about twenty-one years old. We were just twenty-five and twenty-six so we got along really well. After dinner we were going to a concert in a bar and you had to be twenty-one to get in. We were having silly conversations during dinner, getting a little buzzed. They would tell jokes, mostly sex jokes, and everyone would laugh. They were young, ignorant, unmotivated. I don't even think they worked. Their mother was rich so she just spoiled them and gave them money to go out. I guess she was pretty ignorant too.

Anyway, we had two cars, so after we got the check we still had an hour before the concert. They said, "Good, we'll get good seats." I then said, laughingly, "OK, you four go and save us two seats. We're gonna stop home so my husband can bounce me a few times before the show." Our house was on the way, so it was possible, and we *were* newlyweds. Mark stood up and gave me the dirtiest look. He then turned to his cousins and their girl-friends and said, "You'll have to excuse my wife; I never realized she was such a pig," and then sat back down. I kept my head down so nobody noticed my eyes filled with tears and excused myself to go to the ladies room. When I was in there, I balled my eyes out. There were no windows in there, but if there were, I'd have climbed out and left. I didn't know where I was going, but that was it. I don't think I was ever so humiliated.

Looking back now, if there were windows in that ladies room, we would have split up that night. I'd have left him, done, over, divorce! I always held the car keys in my purse; I would have driven to my parent's, and they would have agreed. Here we were just married, and his younger cousins, who looked up to him, watched him treat me this way. If it were anyone else, I would think, "What a bad example Mark is setting about how to treat women," but I had already heard the way these two talked about women. They weren't any better. After all, their father and Mark's father were brothers. It's a damn shame that shit like this is passed on more easily than kindness, respect or generosity, which both their mothers had.

Anyway, I cleaned myself up and met them at the car. I didn't say another word the whole ride there, and when we got there I "drank my face off" and sat at the bar while they sat at a table. I don't even remember if he asked me why I was acting this way. Probably not, he probably just told his cousins that I was a bad drunk. That's what he would usually say. Little did he know, I wouldn't have to drink so much if I hadn't married him.

Chapter Twelve

About three or four months passed. I don't really remember those months. One thing I am sure of is that I was drinking more than ever. That was usually my escape from situations that made me uncomfortable, and I do remember that after I realized my marriage may have been a mistake, I felt very uncomfortable just waking up each morning. Besides that, I hated my job. No, that's not exactly true; I loved being a nurse, I was a damn good nurse, because sober, I'm a real "people person." I liked working in an office, getting friendly with the "regular" patients. I just hated my boss.

I was working for a doctor who was pure evil. He was greedy; he was a liar; he would even put me down in front of patients *and* my co-workers. Remember I told you I had word-finding difficulties, well, to compensate, I would speak very quickly. I still do. I guess it's the thought that if I use an incorrect word, the people I'm speaking to may not catch it. It wasn't deliberate; I wasn't even aware how fast I spoke. If that *was* my subconscious plan, it didn't work. Everyone always knew when I used a word that didn't fit the conversation, and my co-workers used to make fun of me for it. That evil boss of mine even yelled about it one time in front of a patient. I was passing on an urgent message the office manager told me to give him. I found him in one of the rooms working on a patient. I walked in and gave him the message. He stopped what he was doing, looked at one of the other nurses and asked, "Do you *ever* understand a word she says?" He then looked back at me and yelled, "*Now what are you trying to tell me?*" I just walked away without repeating the message. I was mortified. I went into the bathroom and cried.

When I got home that day, Mark was already at work. When he called me on his break, he could tell I was upset. When I told him what happened at work, he yelled at me too. He said, "When are you gonna grow a fuckin' backbone?" I hung up on him and balled my eyes out, again. I wanted to run away from every-thing—my job, my marriage. What was I doing? I was crying all the time. I was skinny and pale; I hated my life.

Mark called me later to apologize and said, "I just don't un-derstand why you take that shit?" I answered, "We can't all work for our family." He and his father used to argue all the time at work. If I argued with my boss I would have been fired. I now had a mortgage to pay. If I lost my job, I could lose my house, the house where Mark was living for free. He didn't help with the mortgage; he was a fucking child with no idea about responsibil-ity.

Chapter Thirteen

We had gotten a ski vacation as a wedding gift. It was given to us by Mark's friend Tommy and now fiancé Gina. It was a condo in Vermont; the four of us were going for New Years and staying for a nice, long weekend.

I couldn't wait. We had just been to another wedding. One of Mark's cousins knocked up some chick, so the ceremony and the reception were both at the banquet hall. At the reception I had gone up to the bar for a Bloody Mary. I could feel a presence behind me, and when I turned around it was Frank. He then came up to the bar next to me, so close, kind of leaning into me. I had been waiting for this opportunity; no one else was around. I said, "Listen, I don't know what happened that night, whether it was wedding jitters, cold feet, or just too drunk, but whatever it was, it's never going to happen again."

He paused a couple seconds, picked up my drink and handed it to me. He looked me straight in the eyes and said, "I disagree." I just took my drink and walked back to my table.

I was relieved to get the conversation over with but couldn't believe his reply. Was he crazy? Apparently so. I just put it out of my mind and focused on the trip we were planning. Gina and I had become close friends. Not so close that I could tell her anything that had happened with other guys, but close enough that she could tell me she sees how I could get pissed off and hurt at the way Mark treated me sometimes. Also she was able to confide that she even had some doubts about marrying Tommy sometimes. He would get real sloppy drunk and it was a big turn off to her.

It's funny, I liked her so much even though Mark treated her like gold. If he treated me with half the respect he gave her, we wouldn't have half the problems we did. I would think I'd be jealous of a girl like that, but I knew it was all him. She treated him like her fiancé's best friend and nothing more. But he thought she was the perfect girl. She liked the outdoors, camping, rock climbing, probably parasailing! I was sure at times he wished he had married her instead. But you know what Mark, you dumbass, she also loves sex. Tommy went down on her in our bathroom when we had our big party. Put her right up on the vanity and got down on his knees. She was the one who told me we had to have anal sex—she had read about this certain position and it felt so good for both of them. I told her, "No, I can't talk about sex like that to Mark. He calls me a pig and gets very uncomfortable; he didn't even like when I wore hot lingerie."

She got very wide-eyed and said, "You're kidding me." I shook my head no and saw how she felt sorry for me. She knew how wild I was sexually. I had told her stories of the past.

So, we flew to Vermont for our ski trip. I was away from life, finally. No wicked boss, no getting up at 5 a.m. Even Mark was in a really good mood. He was so excited; he and his family had gone skiing twice since I met him, but I never went. The idea of using vacation time from work to go some place colder than home never even entered my mind, but Mark had been skiing all his life, was an excellent skier, and loved it. Remember I told you about Mark's personality, the more dangerous, the better, which was now the opposite for me. I was still anxious about crossing a busy street!

On the ride up there we were listening to the radio. I heard that Sonny Bono had been killed in a skiing accident. I became so upset. I was a few years older than Mark, Tommy and Gina. I grew up in the seventies, so Sonny and Cher were a big part of my childhood. Nobody had cable, or VCRs yet; the shows we watched were *All in the Family, The Love Boat, Fantasy Island,* and *The Sonny and Cher Comedy Hour.* I had the Cher doll; I still have it. I love Cher. Many people have told me I look like her; I don't see it, but I hope they do! Needless to say, I was very sad to hear that Sonny died, and how ironic, he died in a skiing accident, and I'm on my way to my first ski vacation.

I had another one of those feelings like God was nudging me, you know the feeling, you feel it in your gut, like something just isn't right. I began to pray, telling God that I hear him, but I don't know what to do. I just asked him to watch over me. I promised him, I told him that I see the signs and get his message, but I don't know what to do. I was trying to let him know that I didn't need another "boulder!"

We finally arrived and although I was cold, the condo they had rented was beautiful, and we had three days and two nights so I wanted to take it real slow, drag it out as long as we could. My idea of a vacation would be to lock ourselves in the condo, sit in front of the fireplace, and make love all weekend. We unpacked the car. Mark had rented me skis and bought me a ski outfit for Christmas. I felt bad; Mark was so excited and so badly wanted me to love skiing, but I knew it wasn't gonna happen. I did promise him that I would take lessons. I unpacked the suitcases, and we found out where to go for dinner. We had gotten there too late for any skiing the first day, so we went out for a nice dinner. We didn't drink very much—I didn't want any hangover for my skiing lessons the next morning. After dinner we just went back to the condo and got ready for bed. I was nervous for the next morning, and Mark was excited. We had a really nice dinner, and made love that night. I was happy.

We woke up the next morning and got ready for skiing. I was so nervous I didn't eat breakfast, and Mark just had coffee because he said he didn't want to feel full. Even with all my ski clothes on, I was freezing my ass off. Mark had even bought me these little heat pads to put in my mittens. I was always cold, even at home and in the spring and summertime. I figured it was because I was so thin; that's what everyone used to say, "Of course you're cold, you don't have any meat on you. You don't have enough blood in your body either—look how pale you are." My co-workers would say it; my relatives would say it. I would find out later that they were wrong. I wasn't cold because I was too thin; I was cold because I was very sick.

We carried our skis and all that stuff that goes along with it. I haven't skied since, so I don't remember the details. I just remember all those clothes, hats, gloves, carrying all this shit and trying to walk in the snow with all of it. This wasn't a vacation; this was work to me. He dropped me off where the lessons were, a tiny little slope with little girls and old ladies all standing in line, and he got on the chair lift to go to the advanced slopes. They were all labeled by colored signs at the top of each slope, I forget the ranking of them, it was like blue and green were the advanced, or maybe it was black. Yes, that was it, green circles hills were easier, then blue squares were harder, and the black diamond hills were for advanced skiers only.

All I knew is that I was on the little one; "for beginners only" is what my sign said. I had my little lesson. They showed me how to put skis on and take them off, how to hold them, how to use the ski poles, and how to get down this tiny hill. I was able to do it without falling, but I wasn't very steady.

Since the accident, the brain damage had made it so that I wasn't very coordinated. I couldn't really use the poles to help with my balance, and I was freezing. It was quite ironic that before we went, his mother told me, "Just do what I do, sit at the lodge and drink hot cocoa." Mark was always telling me to do things like his mom, for example, when we talked about having children—Mark was just dead set about having them. No matter what, he wanted kids, and I thought I did too, but I was concerned about working that long day and having the energy for all the attention children deserve afterwards. He would always say, "My mother did it and she had two boys. You'll be fine." He always spoke that way too. Whenever we talked about children he always described it like, "You'll be fine," and "You'll work it out," and "You can handle it." Never "We." Isn't that odd? It frightened me. Even when I would call him on it, he would say, "The wife takes care of the kids, the father teaches them how to have fun, how to be tough." My point is how come in this case I couldn't do what his mother did, just sit at the lodge and drink hot cocoa? The one time I want to do exactly what his mother does, he won't let me.

Mark was an excellent skier; he had gone on the "black diamond" while I took my lessons on the beginners slope. When he was finished, he came down and watched. I was a little bit embarrassed; you can imagine how I must have looked. When I was finished, we went to lunch. He said I looked great, and that he "couldn't believe you had never been on a pair of skis before; it looks so natural for you!"

What did he think, I just fell off the freakin' turnip truck or something? For one, it looked *exactly* like I had never been on a pair of skis before, in fact, I was so wobbly, it looked like I never used this pair of legs before!

You know how some couples have nicknames for each other? His cute little nickname for me was "ree-ree," what he thought was cute for retarded, because of my word-finding difficulties after the accident that nearly killed me. Isn't that sweet! What a nasty jerk I had married. I had to be brain damaged to put up with all the abuse for so long and just keep my mouth shut. Anyway, on a pair of skis, I finally looked the part of my cute little "pet-name."

The second reason I knew he was full of shit was because he never complimented any of my talents or achievements. He had a selfish reason for complimenting me, and after lunch I found out what it was.

He said, "Come on, now I'll give you your first lesson of a real hill."

I told him, "The ski instructor told us we had to stay on the green hills." We got on the chair lift, which I was also so afraid of. I don't know how or why, but even though I was hit by a car on the street, ever since that accident, I have been afraid of heights, so riding the chair lift made me dizzy, and I felt like I was going to slide off—I hated it!

On the way up, Mark was telling me to just relax, even if you fell off nothing would happen to you. That didn't help; all I heard from that was that I probably *was* going to fall off.

We were approaching the "green circles" slope, so I said to Mark, "This is the hill I have to ski on; show me how to get off this thing."

He said, "No, I'm gonna take you to the next hill, believe me you'll be fine."

I got so nervous and said, "But the instructor said the green circles only!"

He got annoyed and yelled, "Look, I've been skiing for fifteen years, they have to tell everybody the same thing. I saw how you were skiing; you can do this. Are you gonna listen to him or me?"

We finally got to the top of the mountain, where we had to get off. He said, "I'll go first, just watch me and do the same thing," he got off nice and easy; it looked so simple. When I tried, I looked like "a bull in a China shop." My arms and poles were flying around; I knocked over all the cones, and landed with my legs and skis all tangled up lying in the snow. It was entertaining though; I made Mark and everyone else who saw me laugh their asses off.

We walked over to the top of the hill, and oh my god, I remember exactly that sick feeling just thinking back to this, and it was like fifteen years ago. I was standing there, looking down at how shiny the snow was on this steep hill. Now I may not be an experienced skier, but I know that shiny snow meant that it was packed and very slippery, kind of like a top layer of ice. I was scared. I spoke with a quiet voice because I knew he was going to yell at me, "Mark, I can't do this, it's too slippery."

Mark answered, "Yes you can, stop thinking about what that instructor said; he planted the fear in your mind so you're just afraid because it's not the hill he told you to go on. I'll bet you if there were a sign up here with green circles, you'd be down already."

He was wrong. Just looking down the hill, I was getting dizzy again. I was watching these experts practically *fly* down the hill. I knew I couldn't do it. Even as we were standing there I was sliding around, that's how icy it was. I told him that; I said,

"Look at me, I can't even stand up here without slipping." My voice started shaking as I said that, and my eyes filled with tears, I was so afraid.

When Mark saw I was crying out of fear, he became frustrated and started yelling, "*I can't believe you; you are such a pussy! If you're not even going to try, then start walking down and I'll see you when you get there!*" And off he went. He flew down that hill so fast, it looked like he had wings—it didn't even look like his skis were touching the ground!

I took off my skis and started walking down this steep, icy hill, crying my eyes out. This time I was crying out of fear, sadness, embarrassment, loneliness; I felt so lonely, this was a winding hill with so many trees that I couldn't even see the people at the bottom, and everyone skiing this hill flew by me so quickly they didn't even see me. I was way off to the side so I wouldn't get in their way. With each step, I tried to dig my heel into the snow, but it was so packed with ice that I would slip and fall every third or fourth step. My balance was even worse because I had to hold my skis—you don't realize how heavy they are until you have to carry them down a mountain. I kept on crying harder and harder. I felt like a little kid, falling down in the snow, wiping my runny nose, and my tears with my icy mittens.

After about a half hour, I was still crying, my face felt frost bitten, all my clothes were soaked from falling so much and I didn't even know how far I still had to go. I couldn't see the bottom. I wasn't even crying anymore about the present circumstance that I was in. I knew I would eventually get to the bottom of this mountain. I was crying about the "big picture," the life circumstance I had gotten myself into.

I told you I felt like a child, and I was twenty-six years old. I continued to cry because I kept thinking about *my* future children. How was I going to protect them from Mark? He already told me that he was gonna teach them how to have fun, and how to be "tough."

This wasn't fun for me, just like parasailing wasn't fun for me. What if it's not fun for my children either? If I couldn't say no to him, how could I teach my children to say no to him if they were afraid? He will be their father; you teach children to "obey" their parents. I didn't want to disappoint him; imagine how much more hurtful it would be for his sons to be called a "pussy" and to be told "you better get a backbone" by their father, who I'm sure they were gonna idolize. All the younger boys who knew him wanted to be just like him—his little brother and all his younger cousins tried so hard to please him. He had a very big ego; when he was disappointed in you, you knew it.

I just kept picturing my little boys, or little girls, hanging from the parachute, scared to death just like I was, but not wanting to disappoint their daddy. I think it was walking down that mountain that I decided I wasn't going to have children. If I couldn't protect myself from him, how was I going to protect my children? He already told me each of our roles in parenting.

I finally got down the mountain. It took about an hour and a half. I went back to the room and he was there waiting for me. He told me that tomorrow he was gonna take me shopping. That was his apology. Remember, I was told early in the relationship that he would never apologize, and he never did.

We did go into town the next day. I could tell he felt guilty; we went into the shops and he'd tell me, "Here, try this on; I know you love these sweaters." I would try it on, and he would say, "That looks great, let's get it for you." I, of course being in charge of the money, would say, "No, that's too much money." But he would insist, and buy it for me. That was his apology. He was right, he never said it, but that's how he would show it.

I know a lot of you are maybe thinking that expensive gifts are better than apologies, but not always. Maybe a gift along with an apology is great, but no apology was implying that he was allowed to treat me that way and there would be no consequences.

When we got back from town, he went skiing alone. I stayed in the condo thinking about how and when I was going to tell him that I didn't want to have children. I mean we had talked about it; it was decided from the beginning that we would. We had even picked out names. I knew this could possibly end my marriage, and I wasn't even sure if that was such a bad thing.

When he came back from skiing, we went to dinner and I acted like nothing happened. I had decided I wasn't gonna tell him on vacation; he was having such a good time, why ruin it.

Chapter Fourteen

All I could think about for weeks after we got home, was how I was going to tell him that I didn't want to have children. I knew for sure there was no way I could have children with him. There was no way I would be able to sit back and watch my children take part in sports or activities for the sole purpose of pleasing their father. I knew, just like me, they would do anything to avoid seeing or hearing Mark's disappointment. I knew the pressure our children would feel to "prove how strong" or "how brave" they were, by doing things that they didn't want to do, even doing things that frightened them. I also knew that eventually our marriage would end because of it. I did realize, though, that if my telling him I no longer wanted children would end the marriage now, that as hard as it would be, it would still be easier for everyone than if we got divorced after having children.

You may laugh and think I'm a coward, but I finally told him in a note. I would have told him face to face, but I figured I would get it all out, tell him everything, without him being able to walk out before I was finished. I explained everything in the note— not wanting children, my need to include oral sex in our sex life. There was no way I could tell him all that in person, because even if he didn't walk out, he had a way of cutting me off when he didn't like what I was talking about, and remember, we didn't talk about sex, it made him very uncomfortable. We just did it. I don't remember exactly what the letter said, but I do remember being very careful so that he didn't feel like I was saying he would be a bad father. Here's what I remember:

Dear Mark,

I love you very much and I want us to stay together forever. I know how we have been planning out our future, having children and raising a family ever since we were dating, but lately I have been thinking a lot about having children, and I don't think our schedules would permit us to spend any time as a family. You work nights and weekends, and I work days. You have already told me that you have to sleep during the day, so I would have to drop the baby off at childcare on my way to work, which I would never do, because I wouldn't leave my child with strangers. I thought during the day they would be with you.

I also have wanted to tell you for a long time that I love oral sex. I love to give it and I loved when you went down on me. I don't think that there is any reason for us to go without, just because we are married.

I love you!

That was it. I didn't say how I thought he would intimidate the children. I felt that would only cause a fight. Plus, I really did have a problem not spending any time together as a family. Another thing that I didn't mention was how tired I was. I knew that I would be the one always feeding, bathing, and playing with the children, and I was already tired. I worked fifty hours minimum each week, did the food shopping, paid the bills, and did the laundry. I prepared the meals when he was home for dinner; I even took the garbage out. I didn't have the energy left for the most important job, raising children. I couldn't tell him that, because he would either say, "My mother did it, you could do it too," or something that he used to tell me, "You don't have any stamina." He used to say that as a catalyst, thinking that if he said that, I would try to prove him wrong. It worked in the beginning, but as I recovered more and more from the accident, I was able to recognize those little games he would play with me.

I left the letter for him when I went to work. I guess he read it when he woke up. He didn't call me at work, but when I got home, I saw the opened letter on the kitchen table. By the time he got home from work, I was sleeping, so we didn't talk about it for that entire day. I was so anxious. I wanted so badly to know his reaction to the letter. The next day was Friday, and he happened to have off from work. When I got home he was there watching TV. I went in and said, "So what's your reaction to my note?"

He said, "The sex part is fine. We can do that if you want, but as far as having children, I want children. That's why we got married." I couldn't believe what he just said! I quickly reacted and said, "We did *not* get married just to have children, at least I didn't. I married you because I love you!"

He rolled his eyes and said, "I know, it wasn't the only reason, but we said we were definitely going to have children, and you knew my work schedule." He was right, I did know his schedule; I guess I was one of those many fools who think that things are going to be "magically" better once we got married. That's when I finally told him how tired I was, and I didn't think I could do everything. I was surprised, he must have wanted kids more than I even knew because that's when he said he would help me more around the house, and he didn't want to hear about not having kids ever again.

I should have been ecstatic, right? I was gonna get the sex that I had missed, and he was gonna help me around the house. But I wasn't. He saw that even with all my requests being met, I wasn't as thrilled as I should be. He didn't understand. How could he? I hadn't told him everything. I didn't tell him that I still didn't want to have children because I was afraid he would treat them like he treated me. The sex was important, and I was glad we were bringing oral sex back into our sex life, but having BDD, the compliments were equally as important. In the beginning he would tell me how much he loved me and how beautiful he thought I was. I missed that too. Especially since I worked so hard to keep looking exactly how he wanted me too—which was not easy. I had to stay at 110 pounds. My skin wasn't great so I had to keep any acne break outs hidden. I always had to dress "hip" and sexy. I even asked from time to time, "How do I look?" He'd say, "Fine." When I would ask, "Mark, do you still love me?" He would say, "I married you, didn't I?" I needed more. Whether it was the BDD, insecurity, whatever the reason, I couldn't live without it.

It's funny to look back. We had seen a girl we knew who had her wisdom teeth out. For those of you who have had yours out, or know someone who did, you are pretty scary looking immediately afterwards, and for two or three days while it's healing. Mark knew I needed to have mine out and he said to me after seeing the way she looked, "When you have yours out, could you go stay at your parents' house?" And you know what, I *did*! About a month after that, I got my wisdom teeth out, and I stayed with my parents until all the swelling went down. I think by then I had realized, with or without children, our marriage wasn't gonna work.

That Friday night, after the discussion about the letter, we went out to dinner. We usually did if he was off on a weekend night, and before dinner was even served, he would always call friends to meet us at the bar, or at our house afterwards; it was never just the two of us anymore. Tonight was different. We had planned to have sex, including oral sex, after dinner so no calls were made. It was so fucked up that dinner felt awkward because we knew that afterward, instead of going out, we were going home to have sex! After being together for three years and married for five months, we should be comfortable, even excited to know we were gonna "have sex" as soon as we got home. We weren't.

I don't know if it was because it was going to be oral sex, which we hadn't done in two years, or because it was planned. Spontaneous sex is always better than planned sex. We finished dinner and went home. The oral sex was good; it always had been good, which is why I missed it so much, but the awkwardness took away from it. Besides that, I couldn't stop thinking that in the past I had felt more comfortable with strangers than I did with my own husband. I knew there was something *seriously*

160

wrong with that. The oral sex was foreplay, neither got off; then we had sex. We both got off, but it wasn't fun. It was quiet and almost felt staged. We got dressed, and he called his friends to come over.

I couldn't keep it in. Just because he told me he didn't want to hear it, I was now strong enough to tell him how I felt. It was only a few days after the talk we had, and I told him that I still didn't want to have children. I admitted that I knew our schedules when we planned our future together, but I hadn't thought about it until now. I told him I was gonna feel like a single mother, we wouldn't have any time as a family, and I didn't want to live like that. At least now, when he's working at night, I can go out to bars with friends, or to dinner with my family. Once I had a baby that would all stop for me but not for him; it wasn't fair.

You're not gonna believe his answer. He said, "If you don't want to have kids, then I want a divorce." He got up, and went to work.

Looking back, divorce was inevitable; our marriage didn't have a chance. I was still living with that fear about his uncle every day, and drinking too much to numb myself. His uncle wasn't the only reason; there were many things wrong with our relationship. Mark was a thrill-seeker, while I was very cautious after the accident. He was a "man's man," meaning he liked to hang out with the guys, watch the games, sit around and complain about their wives. I wanted attention from my husband. I wanted to be number one on his list of priorities and that was never gonna happen. I needed to be told he loved me, and I needed the compliments. I needed more.

Another big problem we were having was that the more I recovered from the accident, the less he liked me. He hated that I bought the house, and now he hated that I made more money than him, and he realized how intelligent I was too. Remember, in the beginning, I could hardly speak. I didn't know that many words; my voice was soft from the respirator, and I was timid. Now that I was working, I was less timid because I dealt with many different people every day. My brain was healing, so my vocabulary improved a lot, helping make me more confident. I was no longer the right girl for him. He liked being in charge. He liked having a quiet, obedient wife without the confidence to stick up for herself. That girl was gone for good.

If we were out with his friends from work and I got tired, or was bored, he would mock me and say, "Oh, the princess is tired, or the princess thinks she's too good for this bar." *Well let me tell you now, I am a princess, and you should have been my prince.*

You hear that ladies—each and every one of you—you are a beautiful princess and you should be treated as one. And you guys out there, if you want a princess, act like a prince, compliment her, hold her hand, get the door for her. And ladies, you have to let him. This women's lib shit has gone too far. The pendulum has swung too far the other way; let men treat us like ladies again! If you don't feel like you deserve it, then you're hanging out with the wrong people. Surround yourself with people that you love and who love you back—people who aren't afraid to tell you how amazing you really are—then you'll feel it. Don't accept anything less. Life is too short to spend with the Donna's and the Mark's in the world.

Chapter Fifteen

I now knew that the marriage was over. I started drinking a lot and going out with friends. Donna and I were out one night at a local bar. We were playing pool and met a brother of one of our friends from high school, Jason. He was with a friend of his, Ron, who was pretty hot, but Donna was still with Jerry, living together now, and I was married so it started out as a very innocent night. As the night went on, Ron started flirting with me and I back at him. I was getting pretty wasted, so when they asked if we wanted to go back to their place and play drinking games Donna and I were both into it.

Fast forward: I don't remember how we got here, but I'm lying on the couch and Ron has my top pulled up and bra off, if I was even wearing one, and he was sucking my nipples. I remember it being very casual. He was actually kneeling on the floor fully dressed facing the couch and we were having a conversation, a sexy conversation. Some guys *so* know how to get a girl hot. He was telling me how hot I was, how I had the most beautiful tits he had ever seen. He knew I was married, but figured if I didn't care, why should he? It was so weird; I didn't feel like I was cheating. I know it was partially 'cause I was wasted, but also because I didn't have a sexual relationship with my husband. He didn't speak sexy to me like this; we just would fuck once in awhile.

Donna came around to the couch and saw him sucking my nipple. We both looked up at her and laughed. I think she said she was gonna get going and asked what I wanted to do. Well, I think all three of us knew what I wanted to do! He looked at me and said, "If you want to stay, I'll drive you home in the morning." I said, "OK," looked up at Donna, still with my tits all exposed, hard and wet from his soft, sweet tongue licking them, and said, "I think I'm gonna stay here." Again, we all just laughed.

So Donna left and I think Jason went to sleep. Ron took me to his bedroom and we started fooling around. I wish I could give you more details, but I was so wasted, I don't remember a thing! This sounds like I did something stupid right? But you have to realize *how* stupid this was. I didn't know this guy. I didn't even know Jason that well. They lived in the same town; how did I know this wasn't going to get back to Mark? I didn't. So good for me! I now have another guy to worry Mark will find out about. I was so fucking stupid. I know this sounds a little confusing since I already knew my marriage would end soon. It was confusing to me too, but I just didn't want to hurt Mark's feelings and end the marriage that way.

The next morning, after I got home, I called Donna, crying from guilt, asking her why I kept doing this. I swore I loved Mark and hated what I was doing, and I truly did, but I couldn't stop. I not only hated cheating, I hated not having the control to stop it.

Weeks went by. I tried to stay out of bars. I would go to my parents house or go out with Mark during the week. We would go out together like friends do. Not like a couple. He wouldn't hold my hand or kiss me in public. I was always afraid of running into someone I fucked. Then, my brother asked if I wanted to go out with him and his girlfriend. They were going out with a group of friends to a comedy club, so I said, "Sure" and thought to myself "sounds safe enough," so they picked me up and we went.

I was having fun, getting a good buzz, but I could feel her friend's boyfriend kept looking at me. I had known of him, but never met him. He had been dating a girl I knew growing up. She was a year or two older than me, and he was like five years older than her so he was well into his thirties and so was his girlfriend. I was still around twenty-six, so I just figured he was checking me out because I was younger. His girlfriend looked in her thirties, and was hot so I didn't think much of it.

After the show was over we were discussing where to go. It was only like eleven o'clock so I wasn't ready to go home. Neither were my brother and his girlfriend, so I said, "Let's all go to my house and play pool." I had a pool table in the basement; we stopped on the way to get more liquor. Some of the people went home, but Jim, the guy who was looking at me, said he and his girlfriend were coming over, along with my brother and his girlfriend. I remembered Mark saying he had an early party, so I figured he may be home too.

We got to my house and went into the basement. I ran upstairs; Mark was sleeping already and I woke him up. I told him I had some people downstairs; did he want to come join us? He said no and went back to sleep.

It was just me, my brother, and Kathy, his girlfriend. I asked, "Where's Jim and his girlfriend?" They didn't know but said Jim and his girlfriend had followed them to the house. A few minutes later, Jim came in. My brother and Kathy were already playing a game of pool so I asked him, "Where's your girlfriend?" He said, "She had to go home." Which was weird because she and I were complaining that the night was still so early while we were deciding where to go.

My brother then said, "Come on, let's play doubles." Jim looked at me and said, "You and me?" I said, "Sounds good." I guess we played for about an hour. We were all pretty loaded except Kathy; she was driving and she didn't feel good so she wanted to leave. I said, "No, you can't all leave me here this early. I can't drive anywhere."

Jim said, "I'll stay if you want to keep playing." My brother asked, "Is that alright?" I said, "Yeah, that's great."

Jim and I played two more games of pool and kept drinking. We were standing there talking when all of a sudden he put down his pool stick and pressed me up against the wall and started kissing me really hard. I could feel his hard-on grinding up against me and got so wet. He then dropped down to his knees, undid my jeans, pulled them down and started licking my pussy right there against the wall! He said, "My God you're so wet," slipped off my shoes and peeled my jeans and panties all the way off. He grabbed me and bent me over the pool table, unzipped his pants and slid his huge, hard cock deep inside me.

This was like a fucking fantasy, literally. I *totally* forgot my husband was sleeping upstairs, which shows you what I mean. With sex addiction, like every other addiction, all common sense leaves your brain. All you're thinking about is getting off. Just like other addicts are chasing the "high" or the "buzz" or whatever the addiction is, I was chasing the orgasm, feeling sexy, feeling desired. It felt so good, the rush and the loss of control we had, but I figured I was too drunk to cum. But then, he slid that cock into my ass and we both came. It was so fucking erotic. Thinking back to that night, I don't remember any fear of getting caught. I get turned on all over again from that wild night.

As I was putting my pants back on, I said, "You gotta go." He said, "Don't tell me you didn't love that." I said, "My husband is sleeping upstairs."

His eyes grew so wide and he said, "*What*! You're kidding me?"

I said, "Nope," and went upstairs as he left. I got in bed and went to sleep right beside my husband. When I woke up, he was at work already.

It was Saturday so I just laid around all day, ordered food in and thought about this crazy life I was living. Who was I? I had no idea. I didn't tell anyone about this, not for a while. I wasn't worried about him either. We didn't have friends the same age, and he had a girlfriend he got rid of to come play pool with me. He must have known from the beginning. I swear there is something, some pheromone or chemical that sex addicts give off because men just knew I was "fuckable." Married or not.

Time just passed. I went to work, hated my boss, and tried to stay out of bars. I knew I couldn't trust myself. Then my brother called me and said they were going to a party with some of Kathy's co-workers. One of her friends was leaving so they were giving her a going away party. I said, "Yes, definitely. Where is it?" He said "It's going to be at Jim's house; it's a barbecue. I'll pick you up at seven." I hung up the phone and went back and forth for about a half hour whether or not I should go. I knew his girlfriend was gonna be there so that helped. Not to mention, this was a party so there would be lots of people at his house so nothing could go wrong.

I decided to go. I wanted to get seeing Jim again over with anyway. I didn't want to see him in public and be all nervous. My brother picked me up and I have to admit, I made sure I looked my best. I didn't want him to look at me and say to himself, "What was I thinking?"

We got to his house, walked into the yard and I was right. A bunch of people I didn't know. People who worked there, Jim and his girlfriend, their friends—what a relief! Jim walked over and said hi. He did have a very sinful look in his eyes and asked if he could get me anything. I said, "Yes, a Coors Light please?" He said, "No problem." He got me a beer, opened it, handed it to me and said, "Anything else?" I said, "No, that's it. Thank you." But those god damn eyes ... every time he looked at me I became a little aroused—I was recalling that night in my basement and I knew he was too. I was so glad to get that initial meeting over with. Last I saw him I fucked him on my pool table, kicked him out of my house and went upstairs to my husband. He didn't need to be as respectful as he was.

I was having fun. We were all playing drinking games; I was meeting new people and had finally stopped feeling nervous about being at his house. At around ten o'clock people started to leave. I couldn't believe it. These people were in their 30s, not their 70s, but baby sitters and all, the party was dying early.

I went in the house to use the bathroom. As soon as I came out, he was standing there behind the kitchen door where no one from the outside or the kitchen could see him. He pushed me up against the wall behind the door and started making out with me again. Again he pushed his body up against mine so I could feel his hard cock and know it was there for me. Then we heard people in the kitchen. He told me to go back outside, and he went upstairs. I got back outside and sat down. *"Uh oh, what's gonna happen now?"* I thought to myself. I was a bit drunk, so I wasn't that scared, not to mention that my brother, Jim's girlfriend Kathy, and a bunch of others were still there. About another hour passed. The party picked up and I was having fun again. Jim returned and joined in the drinking game we were playing.

Then a few more people left and my brother said, "We're going back to Kathy's, you want to come?" I said, "Why, this is fun, stay here." He said, "No she's getting cold."

Jim said, "You can stay if you want and I'll drive you home later." I looked at him and again, those eyes. This time I knew they were telling me to stay; that if I stayed something was going to happen. He had already kissed me with everyone there. Even his girlfriend! At this point I had a real good buzz and was *so* hot for him. I said, "OK, if it's no problem."

He said, "None at all."

The only people left were me, Jim, two of his buddies and his girlfriend. We were just sitting around talking, drinking, smoking. Then Jim stands up and says, "OK everyone, I'm tired, you guys gotta get outta here." I looked at him wide-eyed this time. His friends stood up, and I asked, "Could one of you drive me home?" Not even thinking about how drunk they were.

Jim said, "No, I'll drive you home. I told you I would." I looked down at his girlfriend, and she looked pissed off! I walked inside to get my purse and he followed me in. He said, "Go upstairs and wait for me." I said, "What? Are you kidding?" He said, "No, hurry up, I'll get rid of them." So, of course, I went upstairs, found the bedroom, sat down and lit a cigarette.

After about two minutes I heard yelling outside. It was her, his girlfriend. Then I heard him yell back and a car door slam. He came upstairs and said, "See, everyone's gone." I said, "What about your girlfriend?" He said, "She's going home." Then the phone rang; it was her. I heard her yelling. I stood up and said, "Ya know what, just take me home. This isn't a good idea." He tells her to hold on and asks me, "Do you mind if she comes over too, she would love that. She thinks you're hot too. She would love that." Meaning, we would have a threesome.

I said, "No way, just take me home. Really I don't care." He said, "No, forget it then." He got back on the phone and said to her, "Just go home. I'll talk to you tomorrow." And he hung up. I would have been so pissed off if I were her. That would be a little bit too far, even for me.

He laid me down and got on top of me. We started making out and I forgot all about the girlfriend, and my husband. He took off my shirt and bra, then slid my jeans and panties all the way off and went down on me so good. My knees were bent up by my ears; his tongue felt so good on my clit and he had slipped a finger inside me. He licked me 'til I came then got undressed himself and got on top of me. I was still so hot from his tongue I came again as soon as he slid his cock inside me. Actually, the way I remember it, I came a few times just fucking. I couldn't believe it. Usually when I drink that much I have a hard time with multiple orgasms. Not with him. He was good. After he finished—I don't remember where he came or if we used a condom—I think we both fell asleep, or passed out, whatever.

When I woke up it was still real early, like 5 a.m. or maybe even earlier if it's possible, because it was starting to get light outside. I stood up and started getting dressed. I lit a cigarette and that woke him up. He looked at me and asked, "Where you going, come over here," and opened his arms. I put my cigarette in the ash tray and lay back down on top of him. He rolled me over, took off my shirt and slid off my panties—that's as far as I had gotten—and started licking my pussy again. He used his finger to slide the wetness from my pussy down to my ass. Then he started fucking me again in the ass so hard I came so fast, and thankfully so did he.

I don't remember if we went back to sleep and woke up or how we got to this point, but I was sitting on top of him while he was lying down. I don't know if I was sitting on his stomach or perched on his cock but he asked me to pee on him.

I said, "Get out of here!"

He said, "No really, that's so hot."

I said, "No way."

I remember getting off of him and saying, "I really gotta get home. I didn't tell my husband I was staying out all night and I'm afraid my brother's gonna call." I was done. This shit was out of my league ... sex with him and his girlfriend, peeing on him ... eew! It had been hot, but it was over. It was too weird, even for me. He drove me home.

Mark was sleeping and I had to take a shower. Now I felt gross, just the thought of it. While I was in the shower, Mark woke up. He had to go to work. When I got out of the shower I just put on my pajamas and got into bed. He said, "Rough night, huh?" I said, "Yeah," thinking to myself, if he only knew, he'd be so disgusted with what I had done, not because I was his wife, but because he found that shit vulgar—no matter who it was.

That was it. He didn't ask where I went, where I slept. We were roommates.

Chapter Sixteen

I returned to the therapist I had seen after my trip to Florida. I learned in therapy that in the back of my mind, I always knew that Mark and I weren't right for each other. I learned that was the reason for the cheating. I swear to God, I wasn't a cheat. It took me awhile but I did finally learn that I was a sex addict. I was addicted to all the feelings I got from sex, emotional as well as physical, and there is a difference between a cheat and a sex addict. I've known "cheats," and they don't give a "flyin' fuck" about the cheating; they don't feel guilt and are only sorry when they get caught. I remember after cheating, I literally got sick at work. I was dizzy because I couldn't eat, but when I tried to eat I couldn't keep anything down.

That therapist was right, but I refused to listen. Mark and I met at a time when I was just a fraction of a person. I had no business choosing a husband in the condition I was in. I didn't know who I was, how could I possibly know who was compatible to me. Somewhere, subconsciously, the therapist said, I knew I had to break this relationship up, so I sabotaged my marriage by cheating. I was a terrible liar, and the guilt was killing me. I didn't know how to explain all this to Mark. He had a hard time listening to things he didn't want to hear.

The therapist suggested that I bring him in for couple's therapy. After begging and pleading with Mark, he finally agreed. We went to one session; nothing was settled or even discussed in the session except Mark repeating that it was all a waste of time if I still didn't want kids. On the way out, he said, "You're crazy if you think I'll ever do this again."

Looking back, I don't know why I did it in the first place. I knew the marriage was over. There was no way I was having children with this monster and I couldn't even look him straight in the eye anymore after all I'd been doing. We didn't even like each other anymore. To anyone who asked how we were doing, I'd just say, "Fine." I wasn't fooling anyone, not even myself anymore.

In the beginning, I put up with the bullshit because I believed that Mark rescued me from that lonely little world I had lived in after the accident. Don't get me wrong, that was true, but I was no longer that scared little girl who was unable to drive and was going to therapy three times a week. I should have realized that without Mark, I would be just fine. At this point I would be even better. But I begged him to come to therapy with me and he wouldn't.

Mark moved into the guest room of our house. I slept in the bedroom and because of our schedules, we saw very little of each other. I kept going to therapy; I was so depressed. My marriage was over and I hated my job. My boss was such an asshole. He treated me worse than my husband did, but I had a mortgage and a car payment, so I couldn't end my relationship with him. I felt like I was completely empty inside, and too ashamed to talk to my family or friends. Between a failed marriage and a verbally abusive boss, my self-esteem hit rock bottom. Remember, I defined myself by the way the men around me responded to me. Mark said as soon as he found a place to live he'd be gone, like he couldn't wait to go. Meanwhile, my boss constantly criticized and insulted me.

Thinking back, this "doctor," this "professional" man who is supposed to take care of people once told me that I looked like an alien! Can you believe it? I hope he's dead now. No I don't, but I know he will suffer; the energy you send out always comes back. After the way he treated his employees and his patients, his suffering will be worse than death. Death is often calm, quiet and peaceful, with loved ones around you. He doesn't deserve that. I just hope none of his children pay the price for him. You know what I mean, right? Some religions believe that your children have to suffer for your sins. That would suck. He didn't even care that much about them. The only thing he really loved was money. I don't want you to think I hated this doctor just because of a few insults. He used to price his cosmetic procedures according to what the woman was wearing. If a woman came in with a Gucci purse, and wanted a full face of laser done, he would charge six thousand dollars. If another woman, same age, wanted the same procedure but had on old shoes and a no-name purse, he would charge her less. Not to be kind either, only because he knew she couldn't afford it and wouldn't book the procedure. Anyway, work was not a safe place where I got to escape from the troubles at home.

I was so ashamed; I couldn't even go home to visit. I felt so humiliated. How do I tell my family about the horrible things I had done. They would know just by looking at me that something was wrong. If I even tried to explain I knew I would start crying my eyes out. I couldn't bear to go home and see the disappointment on my father's face, or have to listen to my brother tell me that I better be careful because girls who looked like me won't have many proposals. *Which was a bunch of bullshit anyway because by the time I was twenty-five years old three men had already asked me to marry them, and by age thirty, four men had, so there goes your theory!*

I felt very depressed. Of course, like many other times in my life, I tried to numb myself with alcohol. As you all know, this is like trying to extinguish a fire with gasoline. I would wake up each morning on the verge of suicide. I was working in Manhattan now. My greedy boss figured he'd make more money there. The commute sucked, but I had bills and I no longer had Mark's help. The one good thing was I could go out after work, and I didn't have to drive home—I was taking a bus to and from work, which was the easiest and the least expensive way. There was a bar four blocks from the office, near my bus stop. It was a quiet bar with a pool table and a juke box; I used to go there after work.

The bartender started flirting with me the first night I went. He asked me if I was married; I said, "Yes." He then asked, "Happily?" I said yes because I had never seen this guy before, so it was none of his business. He told me his wife hates him and hadn't given him sex in six months; he said the only reason they were together was because they had a daughter who was three years old. As he was giving me free drinks, our conversation became sexual. I confessed to him that I also wasn't getting enough sex, how my husband was so conservative that I was getting myself off every day with a vibrator my husband thought I bought for back pain! I also told him that I kept an extra vibrator in my car so when I would go on long trips I would drive alongside a truck for the driver's reaction when he looked down. I told him how many of them would beg me to pull over and how hard the temptation was many times.

I think I knew something was gonna happen that night when he told me he had a customer he needed to serve but was unable to get off the cooler he was sitting on because everyone would see how turned on he was by me. Just hearing that turned me on. Closing time came; I was wasted. Everyone left as he closed the bar, but he asked me if I wanted to stay and have a few drinks with him. He told me that he lived two hours away, and would stay overnight for four nights in a row, then go home for three nights. We were having a nice time. I was very relaxed around him and he was with me. We were confessing all of our dirty little sex stories to each other and laughing about it. It felt so good to say them out loud and not be judged or worry about who would find out. He didn't even know my name, not to mention that he lived in another state!

He then said to me, "I'm gonna ask you a question; if you don't feel comfortable, just say no and we will keep hanging out, but I have to ask."

I said, "Go ahead, ask." He said, "I want you to stay right where you are, sitting on that barstool, but I want to kneel down in front of you, slide off your pants, and lick you until you cum so many times that you start pulling me by my hair to get my face out from between your legs."

Well, I'm sure you all know that I was physically unable to say "no" to that. I became excited just from his explanation and just nodded in response. He knelt down on the floor in front of me and started to do exactly what he described.

After about twenty minutes, I could tell that the alcohol I drank was going to inhibit me from having an orgasm in this position. I started begging him to fuck me. He stood up, his pants were already undone so he was able to jerk off while he was giving me head. He picked me up, laid me on the pool table, and started fucking me until we both finished. It was about one o'clock in the morning; he sat with me at the bus stop. When it arrived I just got on the bus without a word. I may have said thanks for sitting with me or something, but I didn't say whether I'd be back or not. I couldn't even think that far in advance. I had to get up for work in four hours.

I woke up a few hours later, hung over as hell, but I had to go to work. I didn't really have any regrets about the night before; Mark didn't sleep home most of the time, so I had no guilt. The marriage was over; he just hadn't moved out yet. We no longer shared a bed and very rarely were home at the same time. If we were, the other was sleeping. I figured it was better than sitting home crying—I was sick of that! I would cry in the car; I would cry in the bathroom at work. I felt so horrible all the time.

It was Friday, thank God; for some reason, as bad as I felt about my life, I still felt a little better on Fridays. Probably because I wouldn't have to see my asshole boss for two days and I hadn't seen Mark since the night we went to the therapist.

I made plans to go out with Michelle that night. She had a new boyfriend, and we were going up to his house for a barbecue, and then out drinking. I was crying as I was getting ready that night; I hated the way my life was turning out. I never imagined this; I knew people who had been divorced, but I never heard of someone behaving this way.

I called Donna and asked her if she would pick me up; she was also going up to the barbecue. She said she would, so I made myself a drink as I was getting ready. We arrived at the boy-friend's house and had a few more drinks before dinner. By the time everyone started to eat, I had a good "buzz," and didn't feel like eating, so I just kept on drinking. Was there a name for this behavior, besides "slut?"

After dinner, everyone was talking about, "should we go out, or should we stay in? Where would we go, if we went out?" I was getting pissed off. My marriage ended, although I hadn't told them that. The last they heard was that we went to therapy, but Mark hated it and wasn't going back. But they knew he was sleeping in the guest room, and that I hated my job. I was not in the mood to sit around and watch movies with a happy couple, and Donna, who was still seeing Jerry at the time.

I didn't even have to work the next day, none of us did. If I had known renting movies was a possibility I would *not* have even come up here. I wanted to go to a bar! I think I bitched enough so we finally went to a local pool bar. I was drinking and playing pool; I was pretty good too. I won the table a few times, so now I was playing against a few guys that were in the bar. The one guy bought me a beer, so I sat down next to him when I was finished playing. We started talking. Before I knew it, my hand was on his thigh; what a whore I was. My friends came over to me and said, "Come on, we're leaving." I looked at the guy sitting next to me and asked, "What are you doing?" He said, "I have a pool table at my house, if you want to come over there." I said, "Sure." My friends were already on their way out, so they didn't hear this.

When we got outside, the two guys went to their car. I went over to my friends, and told them I was going to that guy's house to play pool. I hadn't gotten his name yet. They yelled at me, "You are not; you just met him, and you don't even know his name!" I ran over to his car and asked, "What's your name?" He told me, I said, "I'll be right back." I ran back and told them his name. They just insisted, "Get in the car, you're going home!" So I opened the back door to Michelle's car and slid over towards the door on the other side. As everyone else was getting in the car, I slipped out the door, ran to the guy's car, and jumped in. He saw what I did, so he just took off. It was so fun, it felt like an adventure. The car was a two-seater and when I jumped in, I jumped on the passenger's lap, and we peeled out of the parking lot. My friends were pissed; no, they were worried—that was a very stupid thing I did.

He dropped off his friend and we went to his house. The pool table was in the basement; we played pool for a little while, had a few beers, and then went up to the bedroom. You can imagine how loaded I was by this time, so I don't remember the order of events in the bedroom. I'm sure I gave him head, because that was just something I did, I always gave head. *Thank you God for never letting me get any diseases!* One thing I do remember was that he had a huge cock. The condom was even too tight so it would cut of his circulation and he would go limp by the time he got it on. Let this be a lesson to you smaller penis men; it isn't always such a good thing to have a huge cock. Not just this case either, most girls can't give good head to a large penis. My friend Jerry has a huge cock. I never had it, but Donna told me and so many others confirmed it. He *loves* anal sex, but Donna will no longer let him because it hurts too bad. Skill and technique are much more important than size, believe me!

Anyway, I think I passed out while he was struggling with the condom. I do remember being a drunken dumb-ass and saying, "Forget about it, leave it off," meaning the condom, but *thank God* he said, "No, I don't play that game."

How lucky was I?! I would have gone through months of worry, AIDS tests, all the blood tests. I had been through it before. Whenever I would have sex without a condom, or forget whether or not we used one, I would be in a panic for weeks. I also wouldn't have sex with anyone until I found out. In my book, it's murder when you think or know you may be infected and still go on having sex with other people. Even in my situation, when I would have unprotected, drunk sex with strangers, I always made sure I wasn't infected with anything before hooking up again. I know I'm no saint, but I'm pretty proud of that and wish more people were as careful. You can now buy AIDS tests over the counter at pharmacies, and that probably saves a lot of lives. So many people are embarrassed or ashamed to go to their doctor, which is ignorant, but so is having unprotected sex.

I woke up the next morning and called Donna to come pick me up. She did, and I apologized for the night before. I realized they were worried and it was a stupid thing I did. I told her what Mark had said, about how he wanted a divorce if I wouldn't have kids. I hadn't told anyone yet, except for that bartender in New York. She asked me if I was gonna see this guy again. I told her, "No, he asked for my number but I didn't give it to him. I told him I'm afraid he'll call when my husband is home. He still has his key." She and I both laughed, it sounded so crazy. I didn't dare tell her about the bartender.

I continued seeing the bartender two or three nights a week. My boss had kept one office in Jersey City, so we were there half the time and in New York the other half. I didn't want anyone from work to know about the bartender. It was pretty easy because one other nurse lived in the city and the other took the train. My boss had a driver, and he wasn't the type to have a drink after work anyway.

After closing the bar, we started to go to the room upstairs where he slept on a couch. The second night we had sex, I found out he had a "foot fetish." While he was fucking me, he would not only suck my toes, but put all my toes—the entire front of my foot—in his mouth and then when he was ready to get off, he would shove my own foot into my mouth. Yeah, it was weird, but I found it amusing. The sex was great though.

I would go there alone so nobody knew who I was or could tell anybody what I was doing. I never paid for my drinks, and after he closed up he would bring me upstairs to the room he stayed in. He always gave me head first. Sometimes we would sixty-nine, but he knew how much I loved getting head and how long I had gone without it, so he always got me off with his tongue before he started fucking me. He would usually fuck me in the ass, which I loved, and it was great because there was no pregnancy risk. I also had zero self worth at this time so I couldn't care less how he felt about me. I didn't care if he thought I was a whore or not because I knew I was. I didn't worry about disease either. I figured he was safe because he was married and had a healthy child. Looking back that was a stupid assumption. I probably wasn't the only customer he was fucking if he wasn't getting any at home. I just had that constant angel on my shoulder; I never got a disease from any of these men. *Thank you again God*!

I usually didn't go to his bar on Friday's if we were in Manhattan, but then one Thursday when I was there, he said, "Come here tomorrow night. I got someone to cover for me and I want to take you out."

After work, I got changed; I told my co-workers that my girlfriends were meeting me in the city, and I went to his bar. I had a few drinks while waiting for his shift to end, and then he and I went bar-hopping. It was more fun for me that night because he wasn't working. I had his undivided attention, and you remember how important having a man's attention is to me! At one point he even said to me, "Why couldn't I have met you eight years ago?" and then kissed me. Bullshit or not, I was drunk so I bought it, and it felt good. We had a blast. We played pool, we drank, we danced, and then we got a room. Not the best room, but a bed was better than a couch or a pool table to have sex on, plus there were mirrors on the walls which he pointed to while I was riding him and said, "Look at how beautiful you are." And for me, with BDD, that was better than the sex, the room, the alcohol. That was the best part of the entire night.

We woke up the next morning pretty late. He was working that night, so he asked me, "It's Saturday night, why don't you come in with a friend tonight?" I told him I'd think about it. I wasn't sure I wanted anyone to know about him. I went home to my empty house.

This beautiful house that I loved so much was quiet, and now seemed so sad. I didn't even tell my tenants what was going on or how Mark was moving out. I was too embarrassed. I checked my messages. Michelle had called asking what I was doing that night. I figured I'd call her and see if she wanted to go into the city. I figured she would understand since she was fucking one of her married bosses before she met her boyfriend. I called her back, and she was excited. She was as sick of the local bars as I was.

On the way in, I told her about the bartender. She didn't care. She said, "He sounds like an asshole though; why doesn't he just divorce his wife?" I said, "I don't know, that's his problem. I'm not looking to get into a relationship with him; he's just free drinks after work and good sex during a bad time for me."

When we got there, we were drinking and playing pool with some guys that were regulars. Neil—that was the guy I was fucking—had introduced me to them when I first started going there, so I knew them and felt comfortable drinking with them. Michelle felt comfortable too, as a matter of fact, she hooked up with one of them. It was pretty cool. Michelle worked right outside the city, and would meet me there after work on the days I worked in the city.

This lasted about a month. Then one day, after I worked in Jersey, Michelle called me from Ken's apartment. Ken was the guy she hooked up with. They were a "couple" now. She told me that Neil's wife is pregnant. He was full of shit about his wife hating him; she just wasn't giving him a lot of sex because she was six months pregnant. I felt like shit. It was bad enough knowing he had a child, but I had assumed his wife was fucking around the same way he was. Apparently I was wrong again. Michelle went on to say, "If you keep seeing him, don't call me anymore!—and hung up." *This from a girl who was banging her happily married boss*! Don't you wish you had friends like me?! Another reason I always hung out with guys: my girlfriends were shit!

I went to the bar two more times and pretended like I didn't know anything. I was glad Michelle and Ken didn't go there anymore. The last time I was there, we were having sex on the usual couch. He was on top and my hands were around his back. I was just about to finish when he smacked me across the face and yelled, "Watch the nails!" I guess in the heat of the moment, I scratched him with my nails and he was afraid his wife would see it. I didn't get up, I didn't hit him back, I didn't even say anything. I hit bottom. *This* was rock, fucking bottom. When he finished, I got dressed, went home, and never went back. I was glad that it happened. I hated myself for continuing to have sex with him after finding out his wife was pregnant, but I couldn't stop myself. My addiction to sex was growing stronger and stronger. I couldn't control it. Thank God I had just a smidgen of self respect left. I wasn't going to let this low-life hit me. I guess that was what it took to get me away from the losers, a smack across the face. If you remember, that's what got me away from Mike, too. He was the first guy who hit me; Neil was the last.

I continued going to bars alone, just not that one. I was ashamed of myself, embarrassed by the person I had become. I was going to local bars so I could take a taxi both ways. I have to give myself credit, no matter how desperate I had become, I was always sure not to drive myself out drinking. I knew that if I was going to a bar, or a party, I was going to be too drunk to drive. I never had just one drink or just two beers. Some people drive themselves out, take a cab home and leave their cars there overnight. I think that's too risky, because the sober you is making the plans, but the drunk you, who still has the keys, has to make the decision at the end of the night. Too often a person who is too drunk to drive feels like they're "fine to drive."

I wish I could say that I always was this responsible and never drove while I was drunk, but this attitude didn't start until I bought my first house. I do remember when I was younger, we would alternate weekends. Each weekend someone was the "Designated Driver." Unfortunately, this did not require us to stay sober; we just had to be the one to risk the DWI that weekend. After I bought the house, when I was told that if I got into an accident or God forbid worse—hurt somebody while I was driving drunk—they could sue me and take my house. I really loved my house. Apparently I cared more about the house than I did my own safety. How stupid you are when you're young.

Chapter Seventeen

I stuck with my decision even after divorcing Mark. I'm not having children. I have puppies. I think it's one of the best decisions I ever made. I love them as much as I would love a human child, but there is less fear with puppies. To those of you who are parents, I would not give you advice, so don't think that is what I'm doing. I am just sharing a realization with you. Your kids are going to drink at some point, no matter what. Let them know that they can call you for a ride if they've been drinking and they won't get punished. Looking back, my parents would have come to get me if I had called, but I never did. We never had this conversation and I assumed I would have been punished. So instead, I drove drunk. I got rides from strangers, I hitchhiked; I slept at the homes of people I didn't know.

Also, let your children know that there *is* a higher power. Whoever, whatever you believe in, it doesn't matter. Just make sure they know that they aren't alone in this journey. It's too scary a world to let them think they're on their own. I always knew that I was loved by God. I always felt God's love within me, guiding me. Obviously, I didn't always follow, but never blamed God or felt abandoned when things went wrong or got crazy. I knew I made very bad decisions. Remember I was drinking too much too often and alcohol made it difficult to recognize the signs that God was sending me. I knew my life had gotten off track and didn't know what to do about it. My bad decisions brought on such bad circumstances.

Somehow, with all the partying I did, all the lost weekends, I would say ninety percent of the time I would make it to church. Now, I'm not one of those preachers who thinks if you don't go to church you're going to hell, or anything crazy like that. I just always thought that with everything he had given me, the least I could give was an hour each week to say, "Thank You."

When I was younger, I didn't listen to even a word the priest would say. I would just talk to God throughout the entire mass, without a drop of guilt. If you open yourself up to your higher power, again, whoever or whatever you believe it to be, you will feel it. If you allow yourself to stop resisting and stop second guessing, just allow yourself to give into the flow, the energy of your higher power will guide you along on your journey. I know it's not easy, the ego can be very powerful. That's what the second guessing is—the ego wants control. My point is, if these rules hadn't been instilled in me by my parents, my life would have either ended or been ruined a very long time ago. Thanks again Mom and Dad, I love you.

I know I said that after I got my house I didn't drink and drive anymore, but to keep this journal truthful, there was one time I did drive drunk. I don't even know if I was legally drunk, but if it had been up to me I would not have driven. Mark and I were at a Christening. It was during the time he was in the guest room, but it was a mutual friend of ours, and everyone was invited, husbands and wives, lots of people we both knew. The Christening was at a nearby restaurant, and the friend of ours who was hosting invited everyone back to her house when it was over to continue partying.

Mark walked up to me and said, "I don't want you going to the party after this."

I asked, "Why? Diane invited me too." He said, "I want to have fun, and I won't if you're there." I got very scared and said, "But you drove me here, how will I get home?" He was annoyed and said, as he shoved the keys in my purse, "It's five blocks away; you'll be fine."

So I drove home, and wouldn't you know it, I got pulled over by a DWI officer for stopping in front of the stop sign instead of behind it. When she came over to my window, she smelled the alcohol right away. She asked, "Have you been drinking?" I said, "Yes, I was just at a Christening, and I had a few drinks." She had me get out of the car and called for back-up because she was a rookie. She asked me to sit on the curb while we waited, so I did. When the second car came, he had me do all the DWI testing. I walked the line and did the hand tricks to my nose. I did them all with ease. He asked me to stay on the curb while he went over to his car to check my information. Luckily, he finds out my uncle is a police sergeant in the next town over.

As I sat there, I thought to myself what an overprotective guardian angel I have. I drive after drinking *one time*, and she sends a cop out after me. Around five minutes later, the cop came back. He said to me, "Listen, you passed the tests fine, but given the amount of alcohol I smell on you, I wouldn't feel safe knowing you're out on the road tonight. I could either give you a breathalyzer test, or I could call your uncle to come pick you up."

Immediately I answered, "You can call my uncle." My uncle and I were, and still are, very close. My aunt and uncle came right away. They didn't judge me at all; they didn't say anything about it. My uncle drove me home, and my aunt drove my car home for me. I asked if they would please not say anything to my parents. I didn't want them to worry, thinking I drink and drive all the time. He said, "It's your business, you tell them if you want them to know." He is awesome, my uncle, and not just for getting me out of that mess. Our families are very close. I did end up telling my parents a year or two later. They felt sorry for me more than anything. You see, it turns out my family is very awesome and I was always lucky to have them. Everyone makes mistakes, especially parents. There are no instructions given; you have to learn as you go along. That's another reason I never want children. They're too easy to mess up.

Then one Saturday evening I didn't feel like going out. My mom and I went to T.G.I. Fridays" for dinner and to talk about my divorce; she wanted to take me out and cheer me up. She knew about the married bartender I was screwin'; I told her everything. She was great. I know I told you we never spoke about anything having to do with sex, but I had to talk about it and she was a great listener. While we were there, I had a drink, a vodka and tonic. I don't know if you've ever had that there, but it's huge! By the time I got home I felt like going out. My mom was tired and didn't like bars, but she wouldn't let me go out alone. I called Donna. She said that she and Jerry were going to a new bar in town and asked if I wanted to join them, so I did.

They picked me up, and when we got there a band was playing; one of Jerry's friends, "David," was there. I knew him from town; he played in little league baseball with my brother, and my dad was their coach. We were all sitting at the bar. He and I were talking and laughing; for the first time in a long time I was having *fun!* We were talking and drinking, listening to the band. Before we knew it, Donna and Jerry were leaving. They asked if I was ready to go; I said, "No, not yet," and looked at David. He said, "I can drive you home when they close if you want." I smiled and said, "Yeah, let's stay, thank you!" We said goodbye to Donna and Jerry and continued talking.

We drank and talked for another hour or two. I got pretty drunk. At one point, I leaned forward to reach the ashtray, to put out my cigarette. As I sat back down, I turned my head towards him and gave him a long, hard kiss with a sexy slip of the tongue! What a lady, huh! He didn't mind, thank God; we both laughed and kept on drinking. A few minutes later, the bar had "last call." He asked me if I wanted to come over. I said, "Sure, do you have a pool table?" He said, "No, why?" I muttered to him, "Because tomorrow when Donna asks, I'm gonna tell her I went back to your house to play pool." We both laughed, and he said, "Donna and Jerry both know I don't have a pool table."

I laughingly replied, "That's OK, Donna will know what I mean when I talk to her. Going to your house to play pool just sounds a lot less 'trashy' than admitting what we're really gonna do!" His eyes got wide as he smiled, grabbed his keys and said, "Let's go then!"

We went back to his house. It was actually his father's

house, which he was watching while his family was on vacation. We went right downstairs to the basement. It started by *him* dropping to his knees and pleasuring *me* orally! He was very "skilled" and sexually selfless the entire night. He was all about pleasuring me! This was a nice change. I have had many one night stands with men I met in a bar. Most weren't even worth explaining, so I haven't mentioned them. You can imagine how they went, a typical one night stand. We'd go to his apartment, house or hotel room; I start giving him head, and when he's good and hard, we have sex. The drunker they were, the longer it took. When they were finished, it was over. I didn't have an orgasm most of the time because I was too drunk. Sometimes I faked it just to make them finish, but unfortunately, many men have no idea when a woman has an orgasm and just assume she did because he did—such idiots. I would then get dressed and they would drive me home.

By the way, for all of you who still believe that being gay is a "choice" people have. I can assure you it's not. If I could have "chosen" to be gay I *so* would have. Guys had treated me like shit my whole life; I would have loved to be attracted to women. Unfortunately for me, I was all about the cock!

Many one night stands would happen on vacation weekends down the shore. One makes me laugh every time I think about it. I had hooked up with this really *hot* Puerto Rican guy, Thomas or Robert or something like that. When he first approached me, he said, "Hey Barbie," because I had long blond hair I guess, and kept calling me that and making blond jokes. To get back at him, I called him "Jose" because he was Puerto Rican, so it was very funny, we spent the night having sex at his beach house calling each other and responding to "Jose" and "Barbie." I can't remember what his real name actually was, and I'd bet he wouldn't know mine either! I don't even remember if the sex was good or not; I was loaded.

Chapter Eighteen

There was beauty in taking taxis to bars; besides not drinking and driving, I wasn't without a car the next day if I left in someone else's car. Yes, I know, I was very stupid. Not only did I leave with strangers most of the time, but I got in the car with them when they were drunk. Again, I do know how stupid I was, but I have two things to say in my defense. I would usually ask, and each one would say they were "fine" to drive. I know I shouldn't have believed them, but by that point I was so drunk that everyone around me *seemed* sober.

As far as all the sex, I truly was, didn't know it at the time, but learned later that I had become a "sex addict" by the age twelve. So by this point in my story, I was so far gone that I was unable to control what I was doing when it came to sex. That's not an excuse; that's a sickness. Just like a junkie or an alcoholic. I wasn't hurting anyone but myself.

Most of the time we used condoms, and like I said, the times that we didn't, I would get a test for AIDS immediately afterwards. Needless to say, the test was negative every time. I am *blessed* and *thankful* to God to be alive and healthy today.

Back to David, the sexy, skilled, selfless lover I began to talk about in the previous chapter. When we woke up, it went back to the routine of all the times before. I said, "I gotta go, will you drive me home?" He drove me home, and we were both silent the whole ride home.

When he stopped in front of my house, I complained, "I have to be at a baby shower in two hours." Smiling sympathetically, he joked, "Better you than me!" As I was getting out of his car I sarcastically said, "Thanks!" He just smiled and winked as I shut the car door. I went inside dreading this shower but I had to start getting ready. I made myself a Bloody Mary because my cousin was picking me up for the shower, and I wouldn't have to drive. I felt better, but of course there was no alcohol at the shower, so within an hour I felt like death again.

When I got home, I planned to take two aspirin and sleep my blues away. Not only was the house depressing now that Mark and I were getting divorced, but Sunday nights were always rough. I was usually regretting my actions of the weekend, and dreading going in to work the next day to see that monster I worked for. Before I fell asleep, Donna called me. As soon as I got on the phone, we both started laughing at what a slut I was. I didn't even ask her if she spoke to David, because as I explained earlier, she liked to put me down and I didn't need to hear any more criticism, not that night. I was pretty hard on myself as it was. But surprisingly she volunteered the information; and it wasn't bad! She said teasingly, "David called," and started laughing.

I said, "Oh no, whatever he said, he's lying!" She said, "No, he thanked us! Then he asked, 'Who are you gonna hook me up with next time, a super model?'" I told her I didn't understand. She explained that he meant the last time they hooked him up, it was with a girl who he thought was pretty, but that he thought I was even hotter than she was. In other words, he thought their hook-ups kept getting better and better. Of course you know that made my whole night. It totally changed the way I felt. I was happy. I made something to eat and put a movie on.

Chapter Nineteen

Monday morning came. As some of you "drinkers" know, Monday blues are bad enough, but after drinking the entire weekend, the depression caused by the alcohol added to the Monday blues makes you just want to die. You hate life; you hate yourself—at least I did.

The week went by and Friday night came. We were having a fiftieth birthday party for my dad at a restaurant that my family went to for most holidays. I was pretty excited for that. All my cousins, aunts and uncles were gonna be there, and when we all got together, we ate good food, and drank a whole lot of alcohol.

My uncle is a lawyer. Whatever you think about lawyers, reverse it. He is the most kind and generous man; he would pick up the tab *every* time. Most of us got drunk on expensive wine those nights that we would never be able to afford on our own! It was fun. I have a huge family, and everyone is real close. We always lived within ten minutes of each other. Even when my parents moved to Virginia, a couple years later, not only did I follow them there, but two of my uncles also bought houses there, keeping us as close as we were in Jersey.

After dinner, everyone was having dessert. I wasn't; I never ate dessert because I would save my calories for alcohol. I knew how much sugar and calories were in drinking, and I didn't want to get fat, so I never got dessert, but I did always drink—a lot! I told my cousins that I was going to call a cab to take me to the bar, and for them to meet me when they were done. They asked me to wait, but a band that I liked was playing at ten o'clock, and I wanted to get a seat at the bar.

When I got there, it was packed. There weren't any bar seats left; I even had to squeeze my way up to the bar just to get a drink. As I stood there waiting to order a drink, I saw David, the guy I had the "one night stand" with the weekend before. It looked like he was with a girl; I was trying not to stare, but I wanted to see if he was really with someone. The bar was so packed—standing room only—so it was hard to tell.

I got my drink and lost sight of them, so I just watched the band. I forget the name of the band, but they were really good. They sounded just like whoever they played, mostly covering bands which were popular at the time—Pearl Jam, Stone Temple Pilots—this was the music I was listening to at the time. It was the '90s, so most of us were listening to Grunge, which shows that I wasn't myself. I am a girl from the '70s and I *love* '70s music, '60s too, mostly folk; always have and always will. Another indication that I was "off" is that I would listen to it *really* loud.

Even friends could tell I wasn't myself. I pulled up to Donna's house one day and Jerry said, "That's Samantha who just pulled up with that music blaring!" Donna said, "No way, she hates when people do that!" I do hate when people do that, but it *was* me. I didn't realize until about six months later, when I was back to my softer '60s and '70s music, that I was trying to drown out my thoughts with the loud music. I guess subconsciously I thought that deafeningly loud music would quiet the voices in my head that kept reminding me how pathetic I was. All I could think about was what a disaster my life had become. I had become a whore, possibly an alcoholic, unable to stay married for more than eight months. I felt embarrassed, humiliated, and ashamed.

So for those of you who listen to *really* loud music—you know, so loud it doesn't even sound good—surround yourself with silence for a little while. Listen to your thoughts. Find out what it is that you're trying to drown out and then deal with it.

Remember, once you bring a problem out into the light it becomes so much smaller than when you are holding it in.

As I stood there, drinking and watching the band, I felt someone tap me on the shoulder. I turned around, and it was him. He said, "Hey, what's up?" He was alone, but I didn't know if the girl was in the ladies room, or if she was just a friend, or even if he was there with her. After all, the place was packed. Turns out, he was alone. We started talking, and then my brother and all my cousins arrived. It was good; he and my brother hadn't seen each other in a while, so they started talking. My cousins told me that it was too crowded and they were all going back to my brother's apartment. They had just stopped in to ask if I wanted to go too. I said to David, "We're all going back to Paulie's apartment, do you want to come?"

He said, "Yeah, sounds good." I was happy.

When we got to my brother's place, David and I sat together. We were talking and laughing, but I felt a little bit uncomfortable because Joey was also there.

Remember "Joey" from middle school? I talked a little bit with him and he said, "I heard your marriage didn't work out." I said, "Yeah, what about you, are you with anyone?" He said, "No," and then made an insulting remark about David. I got annoyed and said, "Be nice, he's really cool," and walked away. I didn't talk to him again. I guess at some point he realized there was something going on between David and me, and he just went to sleep in my brother's room.

I spent the whole time there with David. I forget the conversation, but somehow we decided that I was going to go home with him, this time back to his house. Well, it was his grandfather's house, but it was where he lived. His grandfather was a doctor and worked all the time. David had finished his time in the army, and hadn't decided where he wanted to live, so he stayed and helped out at his grandfather's house in the meantime.

I must admit, I don't remember that night; I was pretty smashed. I do remember waking up and having sex in the morning, again and again. It was really great It was the first time we were having sex without any alcohol. Finally, we decided we needed some food. He went and got Chinese food for us. We just laid around for hours eating Chinese food, talking, kissing and having sex. No TV, no cell phones, no interruptions, just us. It was so beautiful. I can remember going into the kitchen to get a drink of water. As I filled the glass, I looked out the window above the sink. It was a cold but sunny day in the fall. I stood there staring out the window; I *loved* the silence and the still-ness surrounding me. For the first time in a long time, I felt at peace and comfortable just being myself. I was calm and in the moment; I felt happy, like all my problems had disappeared.

I went back into the living room where we were lying on the floor, talking and eating our Chinese food. I was so comfortable with him. I normally wouldn't eat in front of a guy I just met, but I ate the Chinese food. Not only that, I told him *everything* I had done. It was like purging my conscience; I didn't hold any-thing back. I told him about all the crazy sex stories, how guilty I felt but wasn't able to stop. I told him that I just figured I wasn't the marrying type. I told him how much I loved Mark and would never do anything to deliberately hurt him, but I couldn't stop myself. I even confessed to him that I fucked around with Mark's uncle. I cried as I told him because I thought for sure he would lose any respect he had for me. But he didn't. Instead, he hugged me and said, "I already knew; Jerry told me. You have to be care-ful; Donna tells Jerry *everything* you tell her."

He told me about himself and his family, how he went into the army because he wasn't serious about school. He would sign up for college courses and not show up. He said his dad was a hippie and didn't want his son going in the army where he could end up going off to war. It was everything his father was against, and sadly, he did end up going to war—Desert Storm. He said once he was sent overseas, his mother and grandmother would just cry every day. They had no way of contacting him. No way of knowing if he was alive or dead or hurt.

He told me he was over there for Christmas and all the guys were receiving packages, letters and food, everyone but him. He said he felt so sad and so alone as he watched his friends open their packages. Apparently everything his family and friends had sent him was held up for some reason, and he received it all a month after Christmas. How sad is that? I remember tears pouring down my face as he told me that story. We were talking about our favorite things too. Favorite TV shows, what music we liked, what songs were our favorites. Then we got to movies. I told him my favorite movie of all times was definitely "Grease." I remember I was around eight years old when I saw it in the movies. I was so captivated by that movie, I hadn't touched my popcorn or soda, and I *loved* movie theater pop corn. I even bought the book with my allowance; yes, there was a "Grease" book. I got the Olivia Newton-John Barbie, and I got the "album" too—remember those? As soon as VCRs came out, I bought the movie. I don't think I ever liked another movie quite that much!

Then something incredible happened. I think it was just a small part of God's plan for me. Either way, I was amazed. He told me his favorite movie was "The Outlaw Josey Wales." I said, "*I knew that!*" He said, "What do you mean you knew that?" I said, "I have no idea, but I knew that was your favorite movie. Let me think."

Then finally, it came to me. I said to him, "Your father sent that movie to you while you were in the army." He looked stunned and said, "How the hell did you know that?!" I told him, "I was the cashier at the video store he ordered it from. He told me when he ordered it that it was his son's favorite movie, and he was away in the army. He sounded so proud of you." We were both pretty amazed.

It was about two o'clock in the afternoon now and he said, "You're not gonna believe this, but I have a date tonight." We were both so hung over. Now it was my turn to say it, and I did, "Better you than me."

We both laughed. He told me they had dated twice; they didn't have sex yet and it wasn't serious. Some time passed and I don't know how or where I finally got the courage up to ask him, but I did. I said, "Can I ask a favor?" He said, "Sure." I said, "I promise I won't get mad or sad if you say no; and then I asked, "Could you cancel your date tonight and come out with me?"

He said, "I thought you felt like death and were gonna stay home tonight?"

I answered, "No, I feel better now, and I'm sure once I have a Bloody Mary I'll feel just fine." He said, "OK, where do you want to go?" I said, "T.G.I. Fridays." He said, "Sounds good." I was *so* happy.

About an hour passed, and I said, "You better call that girl soon if you're going to cancel your date." He said, "I know, I just *hate* doing this. It's not easy for me to do; I don't want to hurt her feelings." I said, "She's gonna be a lot more upset if you call her after she has already showered and gotten ready for your date."

He said, "You're right, but I can't do it in front of you; I'll feel very self-conscious." He took the phone and went upstairs. About five minutes later he came back down. He looked all disheveled. He yelled, "*I hated doing that*!!" I said, "I know, I'm sorry."

We showered; then I went back to my house to get dressed, and we went to T.G.I. Fridays. We ate there, and had a few drinks, then went back to the bar where we met. We left early, went back to his house and had *great* sex all night. The next day, I got up early. I had to go home and get ready for church. I told him I had a really nice weekend; he took my number and I left.

You know what I prayed for when I got to church, right? Yes, I prayed that he would call me to go out again, and he did. That Wednesday he called me at work. I had given him my work number because Mark was still living in the guest room. We made plans to go to T.G.I. Fridays—remember, they serve *really* big drinks there and we would get hammered. It became a Wednesday night tradition for us.

We had become a couple quickly. After Mark moved out, David would stay at my house most of the week. It was only about four months before he moved in with me.

Another tradition that got started was "Porn Sunday." Yes, I continued to go to church on Sunday, and he would come with me even though he wasn't Catholic. The porn started after we got home from church.

Some of you "Old School Catholics" may be thinking that it was sacrilegious or something, but it wasn't; we were in love.

We were a couple in a monogamous relationship expressing our love for each other. We only named our lovemaking on Sundays "Porn Sunday" because I would dress up in sexy, or slutty lingerie and we would watch porn while we had all kinds of crazy sex.

I don't see anything wrong with that, and I'd bet that if you were able to ask Jesus he'd be fine with it too! If God wanted sex to be used for procreation only, he wouldn't have made it feel so good.

Chapter Twenty

About six months went by. David and I were *very* happy together. We were probably partying a little bit too much, and thank God David noticed it, because partying too much was what I always did. I'm an extremist; I don't do anything in moderation, and drinking was how I dealt with my demons. I couldn't face them sober, and I wasn't ready to face them. We would go out both Friday and Saturday nights, Wednesday night, and usually get "lit" after the "Love Fest" on Porn Sunday.

Then, one Sunday, David and I were both feeling like death, too sick even to have our traditional sexy Sunday, and David suggested that we try to stop drinking. He said that he was going to stop and it would be easier if we did it together. By this time, my hangovers were getting so bad on weekends that I couldn't eat or get out of bed. I think I even got alcohol poisoning once because I was sick for about four days after one night of drinking. Needless to say, I was all for not drinking anymore. Unfortunately, that was easier said than done.

So we stopped drinking "cold turkey." When weekends would come, both of us would get very cranky—me more than him usually. A few times I even said we should just cut back, not drink so much, instead of stopping altogether. David got nervous; he would tell me that he was afraid I was an alcoholic, but I knew I wasn't. I don't know how I knew, because all alcoholics deny their addiction at first, but I was sure. Maybe it was because I never really liked the taste of alcohol, or maybe it was because if someone would offer me a glass of wine or a beer on a day that I wasn't planning on getting drunk, I would refuse it—even if everyone else was drinking.

It didn't matter though; David was worried. I guess my biggest argument was, "What about weddings? We don't dance, and weddings are boring if you're not drinking. Everyone drinks at weddings." Finally he said it like this, "We have both been drinking for eighteen years; let's quit for eighteen months and see how we feel. If you want to start again, fine, and if I want to, I will too."

It sounded like a great plan, and we decided to try it out. He had gotten books about alcohol and what symptoms of withdrawal we might be feeling. One of the books he got was called *How to Stop Drinking Without AA*. This was where I first learned about the "Psychic Change." The books helped because we *were* going through withdrawal and had no idea what to about it. If you think about it, I had been drinking at least two nights a week for about eighteen years, so my body had to react somehow. That was the reason for the bad moods we were both having.

I later learned that my withdrawal was worse than his because I was emotionally dependent. I wasn't emotionally dependent on the alcohol; I was dependent on the ability it had to hide the way I felt about myself. When I would drink, I wouldn't think about what I looked like. I wouldn't feel slutty or guilty for fucking around. I wouldn't remember all the stupid things I said or did on past drunken occasions, the people I hurt, the lies I told. Thoughts of the past that would haunt me when I was sober were erased with alcohol.

David was different. He partied to have fun. When he was in the army, he would party with his friends, go home with a different girl each night and feel no unbearable guilt. He wasn't hiding from the past inside a bottle like I was. That's why it was harder for me—not because I liked alcohol more. David *loved* Guiness beer; I hated the taste of beer and of everything else I drank.

I think I drank vodka so much because it had no taste; I drank solely to get drunk. You can imagine how frustrating it was for David; here I was showing *all* the signs of alcoholism: denial, finding excuses to drink, and being bitchy to him on the weekends because I wasn't drinking. I had all the signs, but I knew for sure, that wasn't my problem.

After a few months without drinking it got easier. Our bodies got used to going without alcohol on the weekends, so the moodiness stopped.

Then after about six months, we found another addiction to fill our weekends. We joined "swing clubs." I know many of you may not know how a swing club is run. It's a lot less sleazy than you may think, or at least how I thought it was. When you get there, you have to prove that you are a married couple. You both need to show picture I.D. showing the same last name and the same address. Finally, if you wanted to drink, you have to bring your own alcohol and leave it with their bartender so they could monitor your drinking. I'm sure not all swing clubs were like this. I'd find out later that they are not, but this one was really nice. The place was clean; there was a stage where women could get up and strip for their husbands. There was a big dance floor where people could dirty dance. There were about thirty TVs up in each corner with porn on every one, and the clientele were from middle to upper middle class areas. They were teachers, lawyers, nurses. There was nothing trashy there. Admission was fifty dollars per person so I guess that helped keep the place to a certain standard.

David and I remained sober. Not only because we had stopped drinking, but we were afraid to lower our inhibitions while in such a seductive setting. Before we even decided to go, we made rules for ourselves as a couple. We were only going to hook up with other couples. It sounds obvious, but some couples would split up and mingle on their own. The other rule was, we would never "swap," we would only "soft-swap." This meant that there was no actual "intercourse," and no oral sex. For example, I could give a guy a hand job, and David could get a hand job from another wife, but no blow jobs. It was kind of like a "no exchange of bodily fluids" rule. We still loved having sex with each other, which was usually all that we'd do at the club; it was just very hot having sex with people all around us who were also having sex. There was a huge room with mirrors on all four walls, so we could all watch each other—very hot and a floor made of mattresses. We *always* brought own sheet, but they gave out sheets to whoever didn't bring one.

It was during this phase that I learned I was a sex addict. Realizing, at such a young age, that sex was the only way I could feel beautiful was the beginning of my sex addiction, and now it was at its peek.

David loved sex as much as I did. Crazy sex too; I would give him head in front of the camera in the bank lobby at two o'clock in the morning. We would have sex on the train late at night in Hoboken. But this was even hotter than anything we had done before. One night, at the swing club, there were nine of us connected by tits, tongues and cocks; even with maintaining our rules ... it was hot, we had some *wild* times.

While all this was going on, we remained sober. I got up each morning, put on my scrubs and went to work. After we quit drinking I learned that I had an anxiety disorder, a chemical imbalance that could possibly have been caused by the accident or all the drinking, or maybe it was just something I would go through no matter what I did. I later learned that sex addicts do have trouble socializing—weird, I know, almost like an oxymoron.

It was easy to socialize at the swing club. I figured nobody there could judge me; they were into the same crazy sex I was— "birds of a feather," ya know. It was the events with "regular" people, like weddings and stuff, where I had problems—*especially* if David's family was going to be there, like at his cousin's wedding or his grandfather's funeral. I felt that everyone could see right through me. It's narcissistic, but I would feel like everyone there was judging me, talking about me.

Looking back, it really was "off the wall" *crazy* for me to think that at their father's funeral, David's dad and his aunts and uncles weren't grieving the loss of their father, but judging me and wondering why David would be with someone like me! Anyhow, I was put on Ativan by my doctor, and it worked. My anxiety was decreased so much, I was no longer intimidated by that asshole boss of mine, so my work was better and he promoted me to head nurse. That cheap fucker gave me a box of business cards that had my name with "Head Nurse" under it, but no raise. I literally worked myself sick for that monster.

One morning, I woke up, and I couldn't talk. My tongue lay paralyzed on the floor of my mouth. I couldn't speak clearly; I couldn't drink water without dribbling down my chin. David had to go to work, but my mother came over and took me to the doctor. We found out that my thyroid had bottomed out. There is usually thyroid hormone in every cell in the body, but mine wasn't making any. Again, it could have been from the accident, the drinking, or just genetic; whatever the underlying cause, working fifty hours a week without stopping to eat lunch didn't help. I was put on medication for thyroid replacement. I know it's very common; I'm sure many of you have this same disease or at least know someone with it. It's not as easy to fix as these doctors think. There I was, still feeling tired, sleeping 14-16 hours a day, gaining weight but eating nearly nothing and losing my hair—which are all signs of thyroid disease. These doctors would say I was fine, *such idiots*. One of them even said, "These aren't diet pills you know." Thinking that I was only concerned about the weight gain. I swear I nearly punched him in the face. Finally, my fourth doctor, thank God, changed my medication and I began to feel better.

Finally, I could deal with all the stresses of life even without alcohol. I didn't miss drinking a bit. I replaced it with sex and was much happier all the time. I even liked myself a little better. I figured out that I was only drinking because I hadn't liked myself very much. I didn't like the way I looked; I allowed other people to treat me badly and knew what they thought of me, but it took sobriety for me to finally realize that they didn't really know me. I was much better than the person everyone thought I was.

I think that's what kept me going, I knew I was a good person. I was with David now and he knew I was a good person. He also thought I was beautiful and sexy, and when I was with him I *felt* beautiful and sexy. All of my sexual needs were being met by him. He would buy me sexy lingerie, and of course, he was the one who found the swing clubs for us. He knew I liked my sex to be a little crazier than most girls, and he loved that about me. Even though I felt better about myself, others still felt the same way about me, and it still hurt. David played hockey and one of his teammates said to him, "So you're with Samantha now; I think everyone has had a piece of her." David answered, "Well it's just gonna be me from now on."

That hurt me so bad; that guy who shot off his mouth never even had a "piece" of me. I think we made out in middle school or something, but he *never* got sex or a blow job, he never even got more than a kiss from me! *Where the fuck do you get off talking about me that way?* I felt such hate for that guy. That was early on in our relationship. What if David cared what people like you thought? What if after hearing that, David had stopped seeing me? I never would have known what happened. That's what I mean folks: *please, please*, don't gossip! You can really ruin someone's life with *one* sentence. And half the time it's not even the truth!

David didn't even tell me about that incident until five years after it had happened. I forget how it came up, but I remember everything else. We were out to dinner; it was before we even ordered, and it ruined my entire evening. That's how much it still hurt. It obviously didn't affect David's feelings for me in any way, but over five years later it still hurt my feelings bad enough to ruin an evening out with David.

When David realized how hurt I was, he felt bad for telling me. He said he knew not to tell me when it first happened because it would be too hurtful for me to hear, but thought that enough time had passed and I was strong enough not to be hurt by that type of ignorance. That was one of the things I loved and still love about David, he *always* protected not only me, but my feelings as well.

I know that some men can be pigs and want their wife or girlfriend to act like a "porn star" in the bedroom, even if the woman isn't comfortable with some of it. David wasn't like that. David introduced me to the swing clubs, not only because he knew I would love the excitement of it, but he also thought it would help with my dysmorphia. I had told him all about it. He didn't understand at first, because he would tell me I was beautiful all the time. But eventually he realized that I had to believe it, not just hear it. Don't get me wrong, it was great to hear all the time, but I guess if you don't feel beautiful, words can't change it. I know, it's such a fucked up disease I had; I feel so blessed he didn't just say, "This is too much work!" and take off! Instead, he was always looking for ways to help me. He thought that going to swing clubs might help with the way I felt about myself. And it did, temporarily.

I'm not trying to say he didn't enjoy the swing clubs too, but he thought that if I saw how many men wanted to be with me when we went to the swing clubs, it would convince me that I couldn't be ugly. He knew how I needed men to want me in order to feel beautiful, and he knew at swing clubs a lot of men would want to be with me—and they did.

Not only men either. One night a girl came up to me and said, "My friend over there thinks you are really beautiful. Is there any chance you would hook up with her?" Now let's face it ladies, we have all fantasized about being with other women; well, here I had the perfect opportunity to live out that fantasy. I had on lace panties, a push-up bra, and matching thigh highs. I was thinking this was gonna be a show for the men. After all, that was the main reason I was doing it, for their attention. So I laid down on the mattress. She took off my bra and started licking my nipples, then kissed down to my belly. I was very turned on. She slipped off my panties and started licking my already wet pussy. There were about nine guys standing around us who were also becoming aroused. My eyes were shut, but I could peek through my lashes at how hard they all were and how they were touching themselves. It got me even hotter. I felt like all of these men were having me; I was the source of their excitement and I loved it.

One night a man said to me, "You know you are the most beautiful woman here." Whether he meant it or not wasn't important; it made me feel *really* good. He then asked, "I don't suppose your husband is willing to swap?" I said, "No, we just soft swap." He then told me, "I couldn't soft swap with you. I would want you too bad and would be afraid I'd lose control." Again, *that* made me feel really good about myself.

Sounds kind of creepy now, but that was exactly what I needed to feel beautiful. It was too late to get the feeling that I was beautiful from my father; I was an adult now. Girls who get that from their fathers start when they are babies. But my dad is so great, once he realized how important it was to me to be beautiful in his eyes, and even now, he not only tells me I'm beautiful all the time, but he makes me feel beautiful by the way he speaks to me. I can really feel how much he loves me. Also, when he tells me I'm beautiful, it makes me feel so much better than when these other men did.

This was what I had wanted for so many years but didn't know how to ask for it. So all you fathers out there, *please* learn from me. This is the main reason I am publishing these journals, so that no child, *ever*, has to hit bottom so many times before finally realizing how amazing they are.

Chapter Twenty-one

When David and I first started dating, I was coming out of a broken marriage and was very sad. I remember telling David, after we told each other we loved one another, that I loved him so much, but could never get married again. It was way too painful, and I couldn't risk the possibility of going through that again. I knew I was putting the cart before the horse. The relationship was still new and we hadn't even discussed marriage, but I was twenty-nine and he was thirty, so I didn't want to waste his time if he was looking for a wife. You see, he had never been married and I knew if I hadn't, I would eventually want to be.

He answered honestly and said, "Well, at this point I am in no position, financially, to get married, but I do think that someday I would like to get married. Who knows, if you still feel the same I guess I'll have to make a decision, but I'll cross that bridge when I get to it."

That was it. We never talked about it again until about a year later. I was madly in love with him, and I had changed my mind. I didn't know how to tell him, so when a friend of ours got engaged, I said jokingly, "Wow, he must love her more than you love me. You never asked me to marry you."

He answered, reminding me, "That's because way back in

the beginning you told me you never wanted to get married again!"

I quietly said, "So I changed my mind." A few months later, on New Year's Eve, as we were just getting ready to leave for dinner, he called me into the living room. He started kissing me in front of our Christmas tree, telling me he loved me.

I remember I felt so good the way he was kissing me and holding me, but at the same time I knew something was going to happen but had *no idea* what. He then got down on one knee with a *beautiful ring* in his hand and said to me, "I will love you my whole life, you and no other. Will you marry me?"

That proposal was from the movie *Braveheart*, and he knew I thought that it was so loving and romantic in the movie. It was even more romantic when it was said to me! What a wonderful, beautiful, shocking surprise it was; I was so happy, so excited. I, of course, said "yes." I ran next door where my aunt and uncle were having a New Year's Eve party and showed the ring to my family. My parents and my entire family were there; it was a perfect night. I don't think I stopped smiling all night.

We made all the plans together, except the dress of course. My mom and I picked out my dress. I wore white again; it was David's first wedding and I thought it was appropriate. Not to mention, we were getting married at the reception hall because I couldn't get married in a church—at least not a Catholic church like I did the first time. Even though my first marriage only lasted eight months, it hadn't been annulled; you can only get married again in a Catholic church if the first marriage is annulled. It's a stupid rule, made by the church to make money, not by God. I didn't care; I knew that God brought us together and wouldn't care where we got married.

The wedding was beautiful: not too big, not too small, just perfect—I know I sound like Goldilocks, but it *was* perfect. We had a patriotic theme with small American flags on each table because everyone was still in shock from 9/11. I even painted my toenails like little flags and we played "Proud to be an American" for a tribute to everyone we lost and their families as well. We lived in New Jersey, across the river from New York City.

Many of us saw the disaster, but no one could believe it.

We went on our honeymoon for ten days. It was nice to stay in a big, beautiful hotel room with room service and nobody there to bother us. Remember David and I had been making love for two years now. We were having crazy sex in crazy places, so that wasn't the big deal. We still weren't drinking, but we allowed ourselves to drink on our wedding night. We got too hammered to make love, and both decided it wasn't worth the hangover the next morning so we didn't drink any more on the honeymoon. We went to an island where there really wasn't much to do that didn't include drinking, so when we weren't having sex, there wasn't a whole lot else to do.

It was just the two of us there, which was great, but even at home, we were always alone together. Most of my friends—remember those wonderful people?—dropped me when I stopped drinking. We are still close with Jennifer and Nicole, but we didn't live near each other anymore so our friendship stayed strong with phone calls, cards and letters.

A few months after the wedding, I became very depressed. Many people told me that brides often suffer the post wedding blues. It's similar to postpartum depression, which is when a woman becomes very depressed after giving birth. They say that sometimes after all the joy of planning the wedding, picking out dresses, music, and honeymoons, a bride becomes sad that it's finished. I doubted that, because I was so happy to be married to David. I loved taking his name, being called "Mrs. Barrett," and working part time instead of full-time because I went onto his benefits plan. As far as missing the planning, David and I did everything in like two days, so I don't think it was that either. Whatever it was, it was terrible. I couldn't stand going to work anymore; my evil boss put out too much negativity for me to handle. Between his lying to patients and my fights with the god-awful office manager, I couldn't stand the thought of going there anymore.

Another thing was Donna. This girl who was supposedly my "best" friend for eight years decided to start snapping at me for no reason and being a total bitch without telling me why. When

I called her, or if we went on walks, I would feel nervous and didn't know what to say. I would tiptoe around her and watch what I said; it was hardly a friendship at all by now. Once on one of our walks I asked, "Is everything OK?"

She said, "No, you always ask how me and Jerry are doing, like you're looking for something wrong."

I said, "I promise I'm not. I'm sorry if it sounds that way." Then, like a month later, she's still being a fucking bitch to me, so I ask, "Are you sure everything's all right?" She now answers, "You always make everything about you. Whatever we talk about, you always bring it back to yourself." I forget what I said, but I'm sure I apologized even though I shouldn't have. This is why I was depressed. I kept on apologizing to this bitch for things I hadn't done. This pathetic female had too many goddamn rules. I can't talk about her, and I can't talk about myself ... What am I allowed to talk about?! That was it; that was what bothered me. I was kissing her ass and had lost self-respect. I remember that I'd think about her every day, wondering why she was mad and David would say, "Don't worry about it, it's her problem. She treated you like shit anyway; you don't need her." He was right, and I finally figured out it wasn't that I wanted her friendship, I wanted—I needed—to get my self-respect back.

Then one day, after I realized what was bothering me, I needed to tell her everything that I thought about her. I had to stop apologizing and defend myself. It was night time and we didn't talk on the phone anymore, so I started writing everything down in a letter because I didn't want to forget anything. I would rather confront her about it in person, but how would I arrange that? Ironically, as I started writing, out of the blue, she called me. She wanted to go for a walk. Now I know there is no such thing as coincidence so I thought this was a gift from God. I wanted to talk to her in person because I knew when she was lying or when she was nervous by her face and her body language. Even on the phone would be better than a letter, but she was always such a wicked bitch on the phone that I knew I would end up telling her off and hanging up on her. So, of course, when she asked to go for a walk I said yes, come on over.

I asked her what her problem was. I told her that her attitude towards me had been very cold for over a year now, but I never knew why. After David and I had gotten together—and remember, David and her boyfriend, now husband, Jerry, were good friends—she had just changed her attitude toward me. I worried that maybe Jerry was not the person I thought he was. Maybe he told Donna about the time he tried to seduce me in my basement, and just maybe, he turned the tables in his fictional way of telling his stories. He was known for making shit up and embellishing stories, so maybe he told her what happened, but made me the one who approached him, and he the one who stopped it. I wouldn't be surprised.

I told Donna, in this confrontation, how I was so upset when she told Jerry about what happened with me and Mark's uncle. Her response to that was that she was so worried about me because I was drinking so much that she had to talk to someone about it. You may be thinking that she really may have been worried, and that was indeed the reason for her to tell her boyfriend about my secret—my secret that she promised she wouldn't share with anyone. Unfortunately, I know for a fact that this was not the reason why she told him. She had told me once that Jerry loved when she would come over to my house, because when she got home she was all hot and wanting sex. She used to get all turned on by my sex stories I would tell her, and then go home and use them as foreplay

That's why she told him about Mark's uncle! It's bullshit that she was worried about me; she never cared about anyone but herself!

She had the nerve to tell me that she had been angry since I started dating Mark, that's right, Mark! That was over three years earlier, but she said that I put him first—that I would only go out with her the nights that Mark was off. Isn't that the fuckin' pot calling the kettle black! I couldn't believe it. She has been mad at me, this long, for something she had done, *even worse* by the way, to me—and I had just accepted it. I didn't say anything; I just listened to her demented reasoning and idiotic excuses. She's got to be kidding me!

Finally, when she was through telling me what a rotten friend I was, I told her, "After my accident, all of our friends used to ask me if something happened between you and me in Florida. They wondered why you never visited me when I was home from the hospital. I just told them that you had a new boyfriend, and that was it. They couldn't believe that I wasn't pissed off, or hurt, but I just wasn't!"

Do you know how she responded to that? This cold bitch said, "Who asked you that?" Like I was making it up or something! I said, "That doesn't matter!" I wasn't gonna tell her so she could bitch at them. I said, "Believe me, a lot of people wondered; we used to be together every day, then you don't visit me when I can't walk, can't drive. Everyone wondered, except me, until now, why didn't you ever visit me?!"

She responded, "What did you expect me to do, come over to sit there and play Sega with you?" I answered, "That's all everyone else did!"

At one point, she started to cry. I was glad, because at least that showed she was at least a little bit human. Maybe she was feeling guilty or a little ashamed; I know I would cry if I knew I hurt one of my close friends. Then she said, "I don't know why I'm crying; it must be PMS." So that took away any trace of caring or human emotion! I didn't care though. I wasn't looking for any apology; I didn't need one. I felt good. I got it out. I really want you to understand that.

Writing this feels *so good* for that same reason—just getting it out! If you are carrying any guilt, or anger, or hurt feelings from something you or someone else said or did, *just let it out!* Yes, it will be difficult, but trust me, you will be so happy that you did it as soon as it's over. Even if you did something that you think might cost you a friendship, it's worth it. It's probably ruining your life, as most of this was ruining mine. Not to mention, a true friendship can survive anything.

It took me eight years to realize that the relationship I had with Donna was hardly a friendship. I must have known down deep that she wasn't worth anything, otherwise I wouldn't have fucked that guy she was seeing. I never did and never will do that to any other person, friend or not. Bad Karma ... don't need it. Life goes by too quickly. You have to enjoy every single second of it—all the good it has. If there is something you are holding in that is interfering with your happiness, please, just let it out. Try writing it in a journal first. Don't just write what happened, write why it happened, how you felt when it happened, how you still feel about it, why you think you feel that way still. Sometimes that is enough; it was for me in many cases.

I just had to forgive myself, and that couldn't happen until I remembered that God had already forgiven me. So when you write it down, also write, *God has forgiven me already*, and I give myself permission to forgive myself. Remember too, you are only human. So many of us have such high expectations of ourselves; we feel we need to be perfect in every relationship: the best daughter, the perfect wife, the nicest person. We aren't, and we will never be.

Another pressure that I have always put on myself is actually quite comical now that I'm thinking about it. It's a bit narcissistic too, and I'm sure I am not the only one who does it. In our minds, we tend to exaggerate the impact we have on other people's lives. If I was promiscuous on a weekend, and slept with a guy I didn't even know, I was sure that the whole town was talking about it during breakfast with their families—not the wars going on in the world, not the birth of their new niece or nephew; they were talking about what or who Samantha Barrett did that weekend, right? Again, probably not; we may be the center of *our* Universe, but everyone else is the center of their own Universe too! I'm sure some of you do this too, and we really have to stop. Not because it's wrong, but because it's self-torture! *If* we're gonna make things up, they should at least be happy, fun fantasies.

There are so many wonderful things going on in life to think about—real things too. Like for me, I have two dogs, and the hundreds of adorable things they do each day are so funny; they are the type of things that when you think about them you can't help but laugh out loud! Even if I'm alone sitting in traffic or sitting alone in the waiting room at a doctor's office, it makes me laugh to think about them. I don't care if I look like the crazy girl laughing all alone ... I *am* the crazy girl, but I don't care because I'm also a really cool chick! Don't worry about what others think of you. Once you stop trying to please others and be yourself, flying your "freak flag" if ya got one, life can be really great!

OK, back to what I was talking about. I was sad, and I didn't know why. That is actually how I got my first puppy; my mom bought her for me as a surprise Christmas present to cheer me up. My mother is so great; she believes a puppy can heal anything. When my mom has the blues or feels anxious, she doesn't take any medications. She goes to a puppy store or the shelter and just holds the puppies. She lets them run around outside to get some exercise, and rubs their bellies. She's really an awesome lady, my mom. If I did that, I would have like four hundred dogs. It's very hard for me to go to the shelter if I'm not bringing home a dog. My husband won't even let me go because he knows that.

My mom was right; the puppy did keep me happy at home, but so did my new husband. It was whenever I had to leave the house that I became very anxious. Finally, my husband took me to a doctor and I started taking anti-depressants. They worked for the most part; I was able to go to work and function, but still, I was sick of dealing with assholes. I wanted to start a new life with no Donna, no evil boss, and no ex-husband. So I did. David and I took a vacation to see the house my parents bought in Virginia, and while we were there, we bought a house just twenty minutes away from theirs. When we got back, I gave notice to my boss, and six weeks later, we moved to Virginia. *Now I was happy*!

We rented out our house in New Jersey, so I didn't have to work. For about two months David and I just fixed up our new, beautiful home. It was really great being home together, but then life caught up with us, and David had to get a job. I missed him so much. I had gotten used to having him home every day. I never left the house because I didn't want to leave my puppy home all alone. I figured she would be so scared in this new place all alone. Finally, Dave said to me in a light, but worried voice, "You have to leave the house once in a while; it's not healthy to stay in all the time."

I told him that I didn't want to leave my baby alone, so he said I could get another dog to keep her company. Of course, I went to the shelter the next morning and brought her home a sister. Everything was perfect. I was in beautiful, sunny Virginia; I had two beautiful puppies; I didn't have to work, and I was married to the man of my dreams!

Chapter Twenty-two

Perfect goes away.

After about five months, some dark clouds began to form over the paradise I had been living in. It all started because I felt guilty. David started his job. He got up each morning, and worked 8 to 5 Monday through Friday, while I stayed home. Yes, I took care of the housework, the laundry, the meals, and the food shopping. If it were twenty years earlier I would have felt like I was doing exactly what I was supposed to be doing, but it was 2003 and women were supposed to work now. What made it worse, I think, was that I loved being a housewife; it didn't feel like work to me, even though as many of you know, it's a *lot* of work. I always wanted to be a housewife, but unfortunately, I was born too late. The economy had already been altered so that most households depended on two incomes.

I never understood how "women's liberation," the move-ment of women who protested that they wanted to work outside the house, had become so widespread. I could see maybe one or two women here and there wanting to work, but enough to mess up the economy so badly that women like me, and many others, who wanted to stay home were no longer able to. I know many women disagree with me, and I suppose there were other factors which changed the economy so that women had to work. I know many think that women's liberation gained "power" for women, but whatever power women gained from the "women's lib movement," the option to stay home and raise our children went away. I, personally, wouldn't have made the trade, and I wonder if women knew back then about the economic changes and the effects on the "family unit" that followed "women's liberation," would they still have wanted it? In other words, "If they had it to do over again, would they?"

If so, how selfish of them; the "family unit" as we all knew it has been dissolved, strangers are raising most of our children, and fifty percent of all couples are getting divorced. Even men have changed. Even men who earn enough money to support a household want to marry women who are also successful. Many of them aren't looking for a woman who is going to be a good home maker and loving mother, they want a woman who is able to contribute financially. It makes me sick, and it reflects on the children in society. Do you see some of these kids? They're gonna make some pretty interesting adults. Let's just all pray that they don't reproduce.

Out of my guilt of staying home, I told my husband that I would start taking care of the lawn as well. I went and bought a lawn mower and a weed trimmer and attempted to take care of the lawn. I was five-foot-three and weighed 120 pounds. Needless to say, I wasn't able to do it. I sadly told my husband about my failure that night when he came home from work, but, as usual, he was very understanding. He told me that he really didn't think I would like doing the lawn work, and he didn't even like the idea very much himself. He was a little bit old fashioned as well and didn't want to see his wife pushing a lawn mower in the Virginia heat.

I loved him so much that I told him I didn't want him working eight hours each day and then working outside taking care of the lawn on the weekends. He finally said that we were in a position financially where we could hire someone to come and take care of the lawn. I was *very* happy. I told him I would start asking how much they were. I used to walk over two miles each day around my community and see many of the landscapers at work, so I figured I would ask them as I was walking along.

I had asked about five of them, young and old, no special qualities, and each told me the same answer, "I'm sorry, I'm not taking on new customers." Finally, one guy, a younger one, told me, "Yes, I can put you on my route. I'll meet you at your house when I finish this job." I finished my walk and went home to wait for him. While I was waiting, I was watching television and maybe did some housework. I didn't do any fixing up. What I mean is I was *not* attracted to him at all. He seemed like a kid. Not to mention, I wasn't looking; I was in love with my husband and my life.

When he arrived, I let him in. He had already evaluated the front yard, so I was bringing him through to the back. I offered him a drink of water and he accepted. While he was in the kitchen, he complimented the house, saw our wedding picture and asked how long we had been married. I told him and he responded by telling me he had been married for four years. He told me they had two small boys and showed me pictures of his family. I felt more at ease knowing he was happily married with children. I figured there was no chance he would approach me in any way.

I know, I sound naive. I, of all people, should know better, but it all seemed very innocent, and it was—until we were drunk. When David and I had been fixing up our new house, I started drinking again. I figured it was harmless. We were home together; we didn't go out to bars or anything, and I was just drinking white wine spritzers while I painted because it was so boring and monotonous. David didn't; he stayed alcohol free and worried about my drinking.

So back to the "lawn guy"—now that I knew he was "safe," you know, happily married with children, I figured I could offer him a "real" drink. I was having one; it was rude not to offer, so I did, and he accepted. I showed him my wedding book. I told him how I hadn't been going to bars or anything and asked him what places were good. He told me about one that was nearby, so I asked him to call his wife and ask her if she wanted to meet up with my husband and me for dinner. He said, "No way, we have no one to watch the kids; I don't think she'd want to."

I was so excited at this point. I had someone to drink with again, and I wasn't gonna give up that easily. I said, "OK, then how about you and I go to the bar now, and when my husband gets out of work, he'll meet me there, and you can go home." He said that was OK with him.

I was getting so excited to be going out. I called my husband and told him that I hired a landscaper and that he told me of a good restaurant/bar that was nearby. I told him that the landscaper was going to take me there. It was about 3:30 p.m. and I wanted him to come there after work. He sounded very apprehensive and a little annoyed. He asked me if I started drinking already and I answered childishly, "Yeah, so?"

He said, "You sound like it. You sound giddy 'cause you get to go to a bar. Are you sure it's safe to go out drinking alone with this guy you just met?" Again, like a spoiled brat, I answered, "Yes, he's fine! Are you gonna meet me?" Feeling like he didn't have a choice, he answered, "Yes, call me when you get there to let me know where it is and how I should dress." I happily said, "OK, I'll call you, I love you, bye!"

I told the guy—I forget his name—that I would be right out. I went to my room and got changed out of my walking clothes and fixed up my make-up in about two minutes—the fastest I'd ever gotten ready in my life! I said good-bye to my puppies, and off we went. A little buzzed already, I jumped into his pick-up without thinking twice. What a dumb-ass I was.

When we got to the bar, I ordered a vodka gimlet. I figured this was my first time out in a while, and I didn't know when the next time would be, so I better make it worth it! I don't know what he was drinking and didn't care either; this afternoon was all about me having fun. I probably had like four or five and was *wasted* in the first hour. He started telling me, "You'd better call your husband soon; I gotta get going."

I kept giving him different reasons why I should wait, like, "he's not home yet," or "he's gonna shower first when he gets home." Just talking about it is making me really sick. I was such a fucking asshole to put my husband through that. He had no idea where I was. Here I told him I was going out with a "lawn guy," one who didn't have a name, who could have been a rapist or some serial killer, and I don't call for nine hours. Last thing I remember about that night was fucking this "lawn guy" like the white trash whore that I had become. I was riding him in the front seat of his pick-up truck parked in the parking lot of a bowling alley.

I woke up the next morning and wanted to die. I never lied to my husband and had no intention of starting. I saw an empty six-pack of beer which indicated that I had forced David to drink. My strong, brilliant husband who hadn't had a drink in such a long time, and didn't want one either, finished a six-pack and a pint of scotch while waiting up worrying about his loser, lush of a wife. I sat on the couch crying, waiting until he woke up. I didn't know what was going to happen. Was he gonna leave me? Was he gonna make me leave? I was so scared.

Finally, he woke up and came into the living room. He sat down and asked, "So, do you have anything you want to tell me?" I just nodded. I started crying again and got up to go sit on his lap. He put his hands on my waist so that if he didn't like what I said he could lift me right off. I held on tight with my arms around his neck, still crying, unable to speak.

He said, "You fucked him, didn't you?" Crying even harder I nodded my head. He pushed me off his lap and stood up. He asked if I knew what I put him through? I swore I was sorry and that it would never happen again. I said I would never, ever have another drink if he would stay with me.

He said, "You know I thought you were dead, right! Out with some landscaper that you just met. You didn't even know his name. You know young women disappear from this area every day; how could you be so stupid?" I just kept repeating, "I'm sorry, I was drunk, it's not an excuse, I just wasn't thinking. It will *never* happen again, *please* don't leave me."

My wonderful, amazing, incredible husband said, "I'm not leaving you. I was so worried that something happened to you; I couldn't even picture myself living without you. I love you. He gave me a great big hug and kiss and said he had to go to work. I just stayed home feeling so undeserving of having a man like this and thanking God for sending me this wonderful man who loves me, and promising God that I would never do anything like that again.

Chapter Twenty-three

Unfortunately, like any addiction, promises aren't enough to prevent it from happening again. As any addict reading this could probably predict, it did happen again. A couple more times, too. I was a happily married woman who always wore my *beautiful* wedding and engagement rings. I was so proud to be married to David. I would always brag about, "My *husband* says this ..." or "My *husband* did that...." It didn't matter. Sex addiction is a disease that controls your actions; you become powerless against it.

I am covered in tattoos. About eighty percent of my body is covered with *beautiful* pictures. Pictures of life and pictures of nature. Birds, butterflies, flowers and, of course, Christ, the creator of *all* life! I love my tattoos. I don't know if body dysmorphia has anything to do with my initial desire to get tattoos. Perhaps, like my make-up, I may have initially used ink to take the focus off my face, but even when I began to get healthy, I continued to get more and more tattoos, perhaps for the opposite reason. I now loved myself and didn't mind if people looked at me. I liked the way I looked, and I thanked the Lord for giving me a healthy body full of life. I display my love for life with my tattoos.

Yes, often it is misunderstood. "Old school" folks often assume I am a certain type of person because I have tattoos. Many are surprised that I am a Christian who attends church each week; I no longer drink alcohol or use any non-prescription drugs. I don't even smoke cigarettes or ride motorcycles, but for some reason, people assume I do all these things just because I have tattoos.

If there is one thing we can give up, all of us humans, it's "labeling" each other. Don't assume that people who have tattoos are bikers; more importantly, don't assume that bikers are not good people. Some of the nicest people I know ride motorcycles. Somewhere in time, I guess, maybe when the ego began to develop or maybe from the beginning, humans felt the need to label one another. As it continued, we began to recognize the "labels" as fact. People are now identified by the label that society sticks on them instead of by getting to know them and learning about who they really are. What a terrible loss for everyone.

People can be so interesting. There are billions of people in the world and each one is an individual. Just as we have learned, and teach our children, not to stereotype people according to their gender or nationality—both of which were decided by God at the time of conception—we *cannot* categorize people according to a label that was made from a judgment by another human! We would get along so much better if we didn't. More people would simply smile at one another, which in turn would make us all happier and healthier. It's true. My mother recently read that smiling causes your brain to release chemicals which make you feel better. I swear it's true! Even if it's a fake smile, if you're sad and force a smile just for the release of the endorphins, it works.

I understand our fears of the unknown, including fear of people we don't know. Fear is necessary; it was given to us for self-protection. But protecting yourself is very different than removing yourself. It is possible to meet and interact with other humans in ways that are safe. Obviously, nowadays, you don't want to go into a person's home that you have just met. You shouldn't even get into a person's car who you don't know that well. There are other options. I'm telling you, watch an old movie, one from the forties or the fifties. When you see the way neighbors and people on the train and co-workers interact, it makes me sad at how distant we have become from one another.

OK, I got a little side-tracked. Back to how it happened again and the significance of telling you about the tattoos. I was getting a tattoo on my hip, beside my belly button. I met with the artist, and we discussed the picture and its placement. There was no flirting from either side. The position I had to be in had to stretch out the skin tight on my belly. My jeans were unbuttoned and unzipped so the material could be folded back to expose the area that would be tattooed. My panties were up and intact. I was lying on a sort of padded weight bench; he was on an adjustable stool on wheels.

He was sitting perpendicular to my body. It was the only way he could reach this area without laying across my chest or my knees; so still, no sexual undertones at all! He started tattooing. I had tattoos before, and I have a really high pain tolerance so there was no surprise. There were a couple of areas along the bottom of the drawing that caused his elbow to rest between my legs—over the jeans and panties—so still, not a sexual advance. Between the pressure of his elbow and the vibration of the tattoo machine, I began to get excited.

I knew I could have an orgasm from this and wanted to badly. I didn't see any harm in it because I was able to be still about it; he was looking down at his work and the motor of the tattoo machine was so loud it easily covered any heavy breathing. Even though the rise and fall of my belly indicated heavy breathing, I was getting a tattoo. Most people breathe heavier when a needle is being dragged across their body, and I figured he wouldn't notice what was happening. I was wrong. Before I knew it, the tattoo gun was on the desk; his face was pressed against mine in an open mouth kiss, and his hand was between my legs with his finger inside me until I had the wild orgasm that had been building for about forty minutes. I returned the favor by dropping to a squat position and sucking him off.

I was in a sexual trance. I wasn't thinking about anything except my orgasm and possibly another one I sometimes would get while giving head in a squatting position. I hadn't gotten my second orgasm but was still in a hazy state of mind. When we were through, I got back on the table and my bandage was applied. Not a word was said, not from either of us. I felt like a really backward whore as I paid cash to the man I just gave head too, but I did sign a contract prior to beginning which designated the price of the tattoo. I didn't hesitate to pay him. I was humiliated enough already. I felt as though I brought it on myself, and I did get off so why shouldn't I pay for a tattoo that, thank God, turned out beautiful.

I got in my car to drive home. I began to feel sick. The sexual "high" was gone and the guilt was overwhelming. What was this going to do to David, to my marriage? I had to tell him because I felt that honesty was the only redeeming quality I had left, not to mention, if I started lying I would definitely lose him forever.

When I got home, David was there. He was excited to see me and right away asked, "Let me see it! What did you decide to get?" When I had gone for the tattoo, I hadn't told him what I was getting. I wanted it to be a surprise. Nice surprise right? I didn't say anything, and I guess I had a sorry expression on my face. My husband saw my face and asked, "What's the matter, don't you like it?" I started to pull the bandage off the tattoo to show him and said, "Yes, I like it, but I have something to tell you." I began to tell him what happened. Surprisingly to me, he didn't get too upset.

As I was telling him what happened, I assured him that I wasn't attracted to the artist at all, and that because of the excitement caused by the vibration, I didn't feel any pain from the needle. It completely distracted from the burning that occurs with getting a tattoo. He understood! I was *so happy*! He did ask, "Did you do anything to him?" I became very nervous, and my voice got low. I answered, "Yes."

"Did you fuck him?" my husband yelled. "No, I swear. I didn't fuck him, I gave him head, that's it. I felt like I had to return the favor—he did get me off." My husband then said, "OK you little whore, I want you to tell me exactly how it happened, in detail, and do it to me the same way."

I actually became frightened. My husband seemed like a different man. He *never* called me names, and sex was always so fun and loving between us. I did exactly what he said. It was the coldest sex we'd ever had. I wasn't about to complain. I was just happy that he didn't leave. I did, however, see a part of him that I never knew existed. Later that day he asked me, "Listen, I know that there was nothing going on between you and the artist, but since it's so soon after the last time, *please* don't let it happen again. At least until I feel secure in our relationship again."

I said, "Yes, I promise not only that, but that it will *never ever* happen again. Even when you do feel secure, I will never let anyone except you ever touch me again!" I meant that too, with every part of me. I never wanted to touch another man besides my beautiful husband. Hopelessly, he said, "Well, let's just say for now until I feel better. Then we'll see what happens."

I got scared. I said, "What do you mean?" I don't want to be with anyone else!" He said, "I know you don't, but I think it might be too much for you to say never again. Just like alcoholics, you have to make short-term promises to yourself. Like people that belong to Alcoholics Anonymous, they stop drinking one day at a time." I wasn't going to argue, so I said, "OK, I'll do anything you say; I love you."

Of course, like most addicts, I was sure I could say "forever" and actually stick to my promise. I was also still in denial. There was no way you could compare me to an alcoholic. Those people are sick. There is no way I'm addicted to sex, I just like getting off—that's what I thought. Who doesn't like having orgasms? But he was very forgiving, so I was in no position to argue. All I knew was that I was very blessed and lucky. However you might judge my actions, I say *blessed* because having a husband like this was obviously a gift from God.

The tattoo I got was part of a set. It was a bird, a "Phoenix." I planned on getting one on each side. I have an art "theme" going throughout my body and as each vision came to me, I went and got it done. Well, at this point, only half was done. I still have Obsessive Compulsive Disorder, so this wasn't going to sit well with me for long. I figured I would wait until some time passed before I asked David if I could go get the other side done.

About five days after the first side was tattooed, I couldn't stand it anymore. I had to ask, and, of course, my husband was fine with it. He just asked, "You remember our agreement, right?" I said, "Yes, my love, and it will *never* happen again!" We kissed goodbye, and I went to the tattoo shop.

I sat there waiting a little while until the artist finished the person he was working on. As I sat there looking around the shop and remembering what happened, I couldn't believe what I had done! That would never happen again, I thought. I must have lost my mind! To risk everything I have and love about my marriage and my life for an *orgasm*! One ten second feeling of passion that my husband gives me whenever I want! What was I thinking? That must have been it; I must have lost my mind.

Finally, my artist finished and called me in. I explained to him laughingly that this was just going to be a tattoo this time, nothing else. I explained how I told my husband and promised it wouldn't happen again. He was surprised that I had told my husband and that he understood.

He saw the first tattoo had healed beautifully, and started on the other side. About fifteen minutes into it the same thing began to happen. Once the elbow rested on my body, everything else followed exactly like the first time. I couldn't believe it.

Afterwards, as I sat in my car, I thought about it and began to believe maybe I was sick. I didn't want to do it, but I couldn't stop it from happening. It was like the part of the mind that controls my body and its actions shuts off as soon as I get excited. What was I gonna do? Is there any chance that my husband would forgive me *again*? I was terrified.

This time I was crying the whole way home. I was sure David was gonna leave me this time; I knew something was wrong with me. What kind of person does the things that I was doing? My husband heard the garage door open and greeted me at the door. He saw that I was crying and asked very sweetly, "What's the matter baby, are you OK?" I cried harder and just hugged him without answering.

He grabbed me by shoulders and pushed me away yelling, "Did you blow that guy again?" I just kept crying. He knew, and I was so disgusted with myself, I couldn't bear to say it out loud.

He yelled, "I can't believe you! I only asked you to wait. You couldn't even do that for me, you whore! I hate you! I just kept hugging him and crying, telling him how sorry I was. When he stopped yelling, I moved my hands down his waist to his belt. I undid the buckle while he was still quiet. I unbuttoned and un- zipped his jeans. He wasn't yelling anymore so I knew he was more relaxed and thought maybe if I sucked his cock this hor- rible fight would end like it did last time.

As I started to pull down his jeans he stopped me. He put his hands on my shoulders and pushed me away from him. He yelled, "No, I don't even want you touching me. Stay away from me." He buckled his pants grabbed his keys and started to leave. I was balling my eyes out. I was so scared. I told him I didn't even want to do it, told him I know there's something wrong with me and promised I'd get help.

He turned around. "What do you mean you think something is wrong with you?" he asked.

I said, "I don't know, maybe I *am* a sex addict. While I was waiting to be tattooed today, I was thinking back and couldn't believe what I had done. Even before he started tattooing me, I told him that nothing was gonna happen. I told him you knew. I lost control, I couldn't stop it."

He turned and came back in. He put his keys down and put his arms around me. He asked, "Who are you going to go to?" I said, "I don't know." I grabbed the phone book and started looking for a counselor. I found many Christian counselors. By this time I had already been disappointed by four doctors, so I thought I would try a Christian counselor. I mean, I am a Chris- tian and do believe that God is ultimately the one who is going to help me no matter which doctor I see. So I called.

I saw him for over a year. He was incredible. Christian coun- selors are *very* different from the others. They show you how to open up and let God in to fix the problem. Many other doctors think they *are* God and try to fix it themselves. He helped me with my body dysmorphia by showing me how to change the way I see myself, and sent me to a psychiatrist that gave me Lu- vox for my OCD and Xanax for my depression and anxiety. I knew that I had started having sex because it made me feel pretty for that short period of time. Now that I didn't feel ugly, I figured the problem was solved. Unfortunately, what I hadn't realized was that I had become addicted to the sex. No problem, right? I'm a married woman. My husband and I are very sexually active. Who cares if I'm a sex-addict?

I was right. It was no problem being a sex addict—for about three months. Then, one night, David and I went to a bar. We had been there before; it was like a club with live music and a dance floor. It also had a pool table, which was all we did while we drank—we played pool.

This night there was a guy there who was also playing pool. He was younger, about twenty-five; his name was Steve. While we played, Steve would talk to me—not flirt, just tell me about his divorce and how he missed his daughter. But as the night went on and we all continued drinking, he started telling me how beautiful I was, how jealous he was of my husband, and even though I thought my BDD was gone, I could have listened to this all night.

David would say to me, "This kid is annoying, why doesn't he find a single girl to talk to?" I would answer, "Don't worry, he just got divorced and he misses his daughter." The flirting got even more intense as the night went on. If David was at the bar or in the men's room, the flirting went further. When I would bend over to make a shot, Steve would get behind me to show me how to line it up and let me know how hot I made him by pressing himself into my ass. I could feel his hard cock through his jeans and also became aroused; I felt guilty and excited at the same time. I physically could not tell him to stop; it felt too good. I was very happy that David was there, otherwise I would be in trouble.

I may have been in trouble anyway. After finishing a game between just David and me, I went to the ladies room. Steve followed me in. I started to tell him he had to get out when he pushed me against the wall and started kissing me. He pressed his body into mine, grinding up against me. I could feel how hard he was. It was hot; I was so turned on. I heard someone trying to come in and it kind of brought me back to my senses. I said, "We can't do this; I'm married; my husband is here." He said, "Tell me you don't want me and I'll leave you alone."

I couldn't say it. I couldn't even pretend; he could tell how much I wanted him. Thank God someone knocked on the door. I just opened it and walked out; he followed me. The woman coming in must have figured we were a couple fooling around or arguing, but I didn't care; I didn't even look at her. I just walked straight back towards David.

David said, "I'm tired, do ya want to get going?" Now, I was one of those people that never wants to get going—not until last call lights come on and they're throwing us out. Steve had come back to the pool table and overheard me saying to David, "No, I don't want to leave yet."

David said, "OK, one more game." We argued a little bit as we played—no yelling, just me saying how I wanted to stay. I even went up and got another drink.

Then, after hearing the conversation, Steve said, "I can drive you home later if you want to stay." David looked at him and then looked at me. I said, "OK," and asked David, " Can I do that?" David gave me a dirty look, stepped closer to me and whispered, "Are you fucking kidding me?"

At this point, I was drunk and said, "Why not, they're closing in an hour; I'll come right home." He said angrily, "Fine, you wanna stay that bad, then stay." We finished the game; David hadn't said a word. Finally he said, "OK, I'm leaving; you're really not gonna come home with me?"

I went over and put my arms around him. I knew he was mad. I said, "I'll be home soon; I love you, don't be mad." He kissed me good-bye and said, "Come on, walk me out to the car." I remember I was so drunk I followed him out with the pool stick in my hand. He said, "I don't trust this guy; he's been hanging on you all night. He wants to fuck you, ya know." I lied, I said, "I don't think so, I think he's just lonely, besides, I don't wanna fuck him, so it doesn't really matter." He then said, kind of relinquishing all hope of changing my mind, "All right then, I'll see you later." And he left. I went back in the bar, returned to my drink, and with the pool stick still in my hand, asked, "Who's playing?"

Steve said, "I'll play you." As we played, he continued to rub up against me each time I bent over to shoot. I drank my guilt away, and when the game was over, we left and got into his car. He started kissing me; we were making out and he pulled up my shirt to expose my breasts, caressing them and saying, "You have the most beautiful breasts I've ever seen." He moved down to licking my nipples, getting me so hot.

Before long, he said, "Let's go to my house." I said, "I can't." He then slid his hand down my pants and said, "My God, you're so wet; I want to be inside you. Come on, I know you want me inside you, I can feel it; I'm gonna make you come so hard."

That was it. I was almost there already; I couldn't resist—I felt I needed him inside me. I agreed, and we went back to his place and had sex. I passed out afterward; about four o'clock in the morning I woke up. I couldn't believe it, what had I done. I started shaking him, "Wake-up, wake-up, you have to take me home!" He got up, got dressed and we got in the car. I dropped my head into my hands and said, "I can't believe I did this." He said, "I'm sorry, I really thought you wanted to; it felt like you did."

I didn't respond. All I could think about was that this may have cost me my marriage; there is no way David can forgive this. When I got home, his bags were packed. Our wedding picture had been taken down and was resting up against his suitcase.

He told me he couldn't take it anymore. He loved me very much, but it was too painful. I had a meltdown. I begged and pleaded for him to stay. I asked him to lock me in the house from the outside. I told him I wouldn't go anywhere without him. He said, "That's no way to live; you'll just end up resenting me." I promised I wouldn't, but he wouldn't go for it.

Finally I said, "We'll find a treatment center with doctors that only treat sexual addictions." He answered, "Doctors don't work; we've tried so many." I cried, "No, I mean a hospital, I'll sign myself into a rehabilitation center or a psychiatric center. There must be treatment for this. It's a real disease." He asked, "You would be willing to do that? You would go live at a hospital?" I said, "Yes, if it would save our marriage, I would do anything!"

He called the psychiatrist I was seeing and asked if there were any hospitals he recommended for this. They didn't know of any. We finally found one online. My husband drove me there. It took four hours to get there, so it was about midnight when we arrived. It didn't look like a nice surrounding neighborhood. After we walked in the door my husband said, "I can't leave you here; it doesn't seem safe." The patients were sleeping so nobody was around, and the lights were all dim. There was just one older security guard sitting at the desk. He gave me paperwork to fill out. It seemed dingy and unkempt. David said, "Come on, I won't move out; I forgive you. I love you, and I don't want to leave you here." I said, "No, I will do anything to get better. Just think how wonderful it's going to be when you don't have to worry anymore. I have to stay. I'll be OK."

He helped me fill out the paperwork; we hugged and kissed goodbye, both of us crying as he left.

Chapter Twenty-four

A woman security guard asked for a urine sample. After I gave it to her, she searched me to make sure I had no drugs or alcohol on me. The first security guard took my purse and all personal items I had brought with me. I realized that this must be a rehab mostly for drug addicts, but they said on the phone that they treat sex addicts too. They treated us all the same. I wasn't allowed to bring my vitamins in with me. I had to give my medications to the pharmacist; there were no locks on the doors to the rooms, or the bathrooms, and there were cameras up in the corners of each room. All the monitors were at the nurses' station, which was in the center of the bottom floor. I went to bed about two o'clock in the morning and was woken up about once every hour to take my blood pressure, temperature, and pulse. Something told me I was in the wrong place.

They had given me a schedule the night before so I had an idea about the routine. They banged on everyone's door about 7 a.m. Everyone had to be in the cafeteria for breakfast by 8 a.m. The first group meeting began at 9 a.m. There were meetings all day. They lasted about forty-five minutes each with some breaks in between. Every meeting was about how we weren't going to use drugs or alcohol, and what we were going to replace them with in our lives. Discussions about how we got money for our "Drug Of Choice," how the money for drugs affected our household income, our jobs, our health—pretty much *nothing* that applied to my situation.

Finally, I went to this girl "Kelly." She had been assigned to my "case." I was told to report to her each day or whenever I had a question or a problem. Well I reported to her after the *tenth* meeting on the first day. I told her, "I don't belong here. I am a sex addict, not a drug addict, not an alcoholic, and that is all they are talking about! My insurance didn't cover this, so I paid $3500 on my credit card because I wanted to save my marriage. This is a waste of time and money for me."

This snooty little bitch had the nerve to say to me, "OK, every time they use the work drugs or alcohol, in your mind, replace it with the word 'sex' instead. Don't discuss your problem out loud, because when addicts are in withdrawal their libido is very high and if you discuss your experiences in group you are going to make it very hard for them to focus on their recovery. So just know in your mind what you are here for, but don't voice it out loud in group or meetings."

She then closed my folder because she was done with me. I didn't say anything. I just got up and went to my room. I was stunned! I had just spent $3500—money which I didn't really have— to check into a hospital that doesn't treat my illness, and I am not allowed to discuss my problem in any of the meetings. Not to mention, I was just informed that I am surrounded by twenty-five men and twenty-five women whose sex drives were higher than mine at this time. *Too fucking ironic to believe, don't ya think?*

I knew I had to save my marriage, so I stayed. After three days, I was moved upstairs, which were the exact same rooms, but without the cameras. I was also allowed phone calls now, so I called David and cried as soon as I heard his voice. I told him everything about what Kelly said but told him that it didn't matter. I told him that just being away from him made me realize that I can't live without him, and I won't *ever* do anything to jeopardize our relationship again.

That's when this wonderful man of mine told me, "I'm not going anywhere. I love you so much and I will stay with you no matter what." I was crying so uncontrollably, listening to his sweet, loving voice and kind words, that I was unable to speak. He kept asking, "Are you OK? If you want to come home you can. I will come get you whenever you want."

Finally I was able to speak. I said, "No, I want to stay. I'm gonna try and do what Kelly said. Sex is my addiction and I can't risk not getting better. I heard the puppies in the background and couldn't stand it. We said "I love you" and "I miss you" to each other, and then I hung up the phone and ran to my room crying.

I was so homesick I just stayed there crying and skipped the next meeting. My roommate came in and said, "Oh, there you are. You didn't go to the meeting." That's how it was there—everyone had a roommate. The rooms alternated two guys, two girls, no locks—a great place for a sex addict, surrounded by guys with crazy-high libidos, right? What a joke.

Needless to say, couples were forming left and right. People were fucking in the rooms during meetings. Guys were getting blow jobs in bathrooms in the hallways. Someone on the phone either made a mistake, or lied to us. This was no place where a sex addict could get help. This was probably one of the *worst* places a sex addict who's trying to get healed should be. All I knew was that I had to make it through. Just eight days and I'd be out of there. I'd be back home with my husband and my puppies and my marriage would be saved. No more fear for David, and I would be able to trust myself. Hell, if I could remain faithful in this "fuck-fest," I could be faithful anywhere!

As it turned out, I couldn't. I didn't make it through the eight days.

One of the counselors there—I don't think he was a real "counselor," but I don't know what his official title was. I only know he was the one—or one of the ones that seduced me. There was this other patient too, but the counselor was by far the worst because he was there to help me.

There were counselors that the patients had to meet with each day who kept track of our progress, like Kelly. There were also counselors and therapists that spoke at the meetings. Finally, there were psychologists and psychiatrists that we also had to meet with once in a while because we were all medicated, so we had to be under the care of a doctor. These doctors, by the way, were the biggest jokes I had ever met. At the time, I had been a nurse for twelve years and I couldn't believe these men were doctors. This must be where doctors end up when they can't make it in the real world, caring for a bunch of junkies and medicating them so much that they walk around like zombies all day drooling on themselves. I remember most of them passed out during the meetings, practically sliding off their chairs! It was so pathetic.

I swear, if I didn't think my staying there was saving my marriage I would have punched my "doctor" right in the face on my second day there. His "diagnosis" for me was, "Maybe you're just not the marrying type." You fucking asshole! I wonder how many people's lives were ruined because they listened to you. How many naive people end up worse from you fuckers just because you have an M.D. after your name.

Anyway, one of the counselors *loved* my tattoos. One day when we were all lined up like cattle waiting for our pills—it is just like in the movies; you have to take it right there where they can watch that you really swallow it, and finish the little paper cup of water they give you. While I was leaning against the wall in the hallway, waiting my turn, the "counselor" waved me over. I had met with him before; he was very nice, helpful, let us all know that he was available if we were having any problems. I liked him, so I walked over. He was squatting down, leaning against the wall so I sat down in front of him. He smiled at me. He was not bad looking, had a kind face and a nice smile. He was a tall black guy in good shape, probably in his early forties.

He said, "I just read your chart." And with a concerned look he asked, "How did this happen?" So I told him pretty much what I've told you reading this, but the short version.

He was very professional, didn't make any rude or sexual comments. In fact, he told me to be careful around there and to go to him if anyone bothered me. I thanked him as he was getting up. He was the speaker at the next meeting. They finally called me up, so I took my medications and went to the meeting. The meetings that he spoke at were my favorite. He was an excellent speaker, very honest. He was a recovered cocaine addict and most of the addicts there could relate to what he had been through. He made them feel like if he was able to do it, they could too. Even though I wasn't a drug addict or alcoholic, I could see how helpful he was to those that were. He was very positive. I finally found something good in this "cuckoo's nest." I'm not exaggerating either; it was a scary fucking place. There was one man in there, probably in his twenties, who smoked embalming fluid, you know, the liquid they put in dead people so they don't decompose before the viewing. This poor soul was dying from the outside inward I was told. I still couldn't smell from my brain injury, but the others complained how he stunk. His hair all fell out. His skin was peeling off, and slowly his organs would start dying. It was so sad and just added to my crying spells every time I thought about him. I didn't even understand what he was doing there. I thought for sure there were better places he could be during the little time he had left in his life, places where real doctors could take care of him and keep him comfortable. There was no way these clowns were helping this poor kid. God bless him.

Each day, one of the many meetings would have my new friend, my favorite speaker, to brighten up my long, boring, sad, homesick day. When he would walk in, he would look at me and smile, and because I was so miserable, I couldn't even muster up a fake smile so I'd just wink back at him. Then one day, the third or fourth day I think, while we were all waiting in the hallway for our pills, he came over to talk to me. He said in a very low voice, "If I tell you something, you promise not to get offended?" I said, "Sure, you can tell me anything." I was so curious, and a little nervous. Remember, I can't smell, so I was afraid he was going to tell me that I stunk or something. They took my perfume when I was admitted because it has alcohol in it, so perfume wasn't allowed. I was afraid that maybe I forgot to use deodorant or something. I wouldn't be offended, I'd be humiliated! He leaned a little closer and said, "I am dying to see the rest of your tattoos!"

I was so relieved! I said, "Sure, anytime." I didn't do it right there because my tattoos go from the back of my neck, down to my toes and all around my entire body. He said, "OK, but it will have to be in my office or your room because I could get in trouble." I said, "You just tell me when and where. No problem." Remember, this guy hadn't made any sexual advances towards me *and* he worked there so I wasn't suspicious at all. Plus, you could hear in his talks that he had really hit bottom and didn't want anyone else to go through what he had been through. He really made you feel like whatever you were there for, whether it was drugs or alcohol, sobriety and healthy living were better.

The next morning, when I went to speak to Kelly, she had a box for me. It was already opened and rummaged through, but we had been told they would do that. It was a stuffed animal puppy which looked just like one of my puppies, and a card from David telling me how much he missed me and how much he loved me. In the card were pictures of him and the puppies. I lost it right there at her desk. I dropped my head into my hands and balled my eyes out while cold, heartless Kelly sat there with her arms folded, not saying a word. Finally, I stopped crying enough to speak. I lifted my head looked at her and said, "Do you see why I checked myself in here? I will do *anything* to save my marriage; if I lose him I'll die."

A meeting was about to begin, so we all grabbed chairs and sat in a circle outside on the patio. Some patients had left and some new ones came just about every other day. When the meeting was over, I went to have a cigarette under one of the umbrellas at a table. One of the new patients came over to me and asked, "Do you mind if I sit?" I said, "No." It was round patio furniture, room for five people, what did I care?

He started speaking to me. It was just like every other conversation started in this place, "Is this your first time here?" or "So, what are you in for?" and "What was your drug of choice?" Before long, we were talking; he was married too, had two kids so, of course, I thought I was safe. Apparently I don't learn my lessons too quickly. Anyhow, thinking I was safe, and he was being honest with me about his addiction, I told him the truth. I told him the real reason why I was there and what I was told to say in meetings. You know this led to us exchanging our wasted, wild sex stories which got both of us so hot. I told him about all my crazy "sex-capades" and how sex never meant much to me at all, nothing more than kissing anyway, how sex and love were so separate in my brain, and he responded by saying, "You are the only girl I ever met who thinks that. I have always felt that way and it's the reason why all my marriages have failed. I can't believe it; I finally meet the girl of my dreams in a rehab."

That was it for me. As you know, whenever some guy told me I was beautiful or sexy or that they can't stop thinking about me, it was a turn on. That feeling of being desired by a man—not just any man, there has to be some chemistry—was guaranteed to get me excited. I was afraid of this guy; I thought I might be in trouble and it turns out, I was.

We had to go out to the patio to smoke, and that night we were both sitting outside. He saw me and moved his chair over, really close. He reached his hand over the arm, slid it down my pants and got me off with his finger. It was so hot. He then un-zipped his pants to show me how hard he was. I started jerk-ing him off and he whispered, "Put it in your mouth." I looked around to see if any one else was there. I then leaned over and started giving him head. It was too obvious what we were doing; every time we heard foot steps I would have to sit up. The work-ers made rounds every few minutes and hook-ups weren't al-lowed. Our chairs weren't even supposed to be touching. I went back to using my hand and he finished that way. Great supervi-sion, right!? I was so fucked up. I would cry from guilt before go-ing to sleep and never wanted to leave my room because I didn't trust myself. I knew I wasn't going to miss anything by staying in my room. The meetings weren't helping me at all; this place was only making me worse. I tried sleeping in one day, but they had a sign-in sheet at every meeting. A female worker came in my room and told me I had to get dressed and go to the next meeting.

The following day I was on my way to a meeting in the downstairs hallway when I saw my new friend, the counselor or whatever he was, coming towards me. He was smiling as usual and asked me, "What are you up to?" I said, "Nothing, I was just going to get a cup of coffee. The next meeting is in ten minutes." Again, his voice got very low and he seemed almost shy when he said, "I'm free right now; if you feel like it we can go to your room and you can show me those tattoos." I said, "Yeah, let's go."

"First, you go," he said. "Make sure your roommate's not there." The rules in this rehab were no guys were allowed in a girl's room, and no girls were allowed in guy's rooms. Not just patients either, even employees of the rehab, but they weren't that aware of what was going on. Remember all the sex I told you the patients were having, and now this.

I went upstairs to my room. She wasn't there; I guess she was on her way to the next meeting like I was. Roommates never seemed to get very close. I was there for just eight days and had four different roommates. I went to go tell him she was gone, but he was waiting right at the top of the stairs. I could wave him in right from my door.

He came in and said, "Are you sure you're OK with this, be-cause if you're not, you don't have to show me." I said, "Are you kidding me? You know why I'm in this place; I told you my story. Showing you my body is nothing to me." As I spoke I pulled my tee-shirt off over my head. I turned around and lifted my hair so he could see the back of my neck where it began. I then let go of my hair and pushed the back of my pants down an inch or two. I didn't have to pull them all the way down, I don't have any work done on my ass—the art work on my back stops at the small of my back. I then turned around to face him. Again I lifted my hair because the design goes from my hands up to my shoulders, then down my chest just above both breasts, meet-ing in the center between my breasts, forming a "V" shape down my cleavage. I then have a four-inch thick body band around my entire waist. I lowered the front of my pants about five inches to show a v-shaped bouquet of purple flowers with green stems on my pubic bone. There is no trace of hair there to distract from the art. It was all removed permanently with a laser years ago. Ian—that was his name—seemed to be shocked. I re-fastened my pants while he just stared at my body. I don't think he had realized how much work I actually had done. He just stared at me with his hand over his mouth. Finally, he spoke. He said, "You are the bomb! I have never seen a body like yours." Then he asked, while staring at my breasts, "Are those real?" I laughed and said, "No, real breasts never turn out this perfect." We both laughed. He walked towards me with his hands out saying, "I can't believe this body; you're killing me."

I said, "You want to touch them? Go ahead." He put his hand over his eyes and said, "I can't believe this is happening." He took his hand down and put both hands together kind of in prayer position and asked, "Are you sure you're OK with this?" I said, "Yeah, go ahead, I'm fine."

Meanwhile, to all of you reading this, why am I in this place? Because I'm not fine and he should have known that! I didn't realize this until a year after it happened. For that entire year I blamed myself for what happened. I felt that I had made the first move, when really, he should *never* have asked to see the rest of my tattoos; not to mention, he knew that he was breaking the rules just by being in my room.

He put his hands on my breasts, and I became *so* excited. He leaned over and kissed me, sliding his tongue into my mouth, getting me even hotter. He was a big man, way over six feet and I'm five-foot-three. He put both hands on my ass, lifted me up wrapping my legs around his waist. My pants were still on, but he began to grind his hard cock against me. I was so turned on and getting very wet. My legs were wrapped around him, and I kept pressing my heels into his ass for a harder grind. I thought maybe I could get off just from that. I was aching for it and he could tell. He threw me on the bed and got on top of me. He started grinding against me again. I don't know if being thrown on the bed did it, but suddenly I came to my senses. I said, "Stop, stop, I can't do this. This is exactly what got me here. I have to stop." Thankfully, he immediately got off me. He got off the bed and so did I. I said, "I'm sorry, but I can't do this." He said, "No I'm sorry. I can't believe this, I'm so sorry. I've never done this before. Are you OK?" I said, "Yes, I'm fine."

He seemed very upset and concerned at what just happened, so I tried to break the tension. I laughed and said, "I guess it's true what they say about black guys." He looked confused and asked, "What do you mean?" I didn't answer. I just smiled and looked down between his legs. Then he got it! He started laughing and said, "Oh, you've never been with a black guy before?" I said, "No, but I've heard all about you and now I know it's true." We both laughed. He said, "You have the most perfect body. I don't know how I'm gonna get you off my mind. You know the best part of my day is when I walk in to speak, I look at you and you wink at me. I love that!"

Isn't it funny how gestures can be taken so differently than how they are intended. Was he taking my "hello" wink as an "I want to fuck you" wink? It's possible. He sat on the bed and put his head down into his hands and stayed quiet. I said, "Are you OK?" He picked up his head, looked me right in the eyes and said, "I'm gonna ask you something and if you don't want to do it, that's fine. I will never ask you again, OK?" I said, "OK," and he put his hand in his pocket and pulled out a key. He held it up to show me and said, "Do you see this key? This is a key to my office. *Nobody* else has this key; therefore, nobody else can get into my office. Everyone's in the meeting right now; we can go down separately and no one will ever know. Do you want to come with me?" I collapsed onto the chair and kept repeating, "No, no, no, I can't do this! This is what got me here! No, it could cost me my marriage, I can't do it!"

He said, "Just answer this one question. Do you want to do it? If there was no way this could hurt your husband or your marriage, would you do it?" I said, "It doesn't matter; there is *always* a risk of getting caught!" He held up the key again and said, "No one else has a key. There is no risk." I said, "Someone might see me coming out of your office; there is *always* a risk. If I get kicked out of here for having sex with you, that's it. My husband will leave and I will never get him back. Whether you believe it or not, he is my life. My sexual addiction is a disease; it has nothing to do with him. I'd die if he left me. You realize what you are doing to me is just like bringing 'crack' or alcohol to one of those people downstairs (downstairs was where all of the addicts of hard-core drugs like heroin, crack, or cocaine would stay). You were an addict, remember how hard it was, right?"

I could tell he felt really bad. He said, "I know, I know you're right. You just don't understand."

I said, "No, believe me, I understand." It was quiet for a minute. I was still all hot and wet, so my sick, sex-addicted mind started racing. Finally I said, "How about this, we'll go into the bathroom and I'll give you head. I'm not gonna finish; I'm just gonna give you a little sample so when you're in bed tonight you can jerk off remembering how good it felt."

He said, "Jesus, where did you come from? I have never met a girl like you ever before!" I stared into his eyes and said, "You're gonna expect me to believe that you have never done this with a patient before?!" He laughed and confessed, "No, there was one girl a few years ago, but she was nothing like you. You are the bomb!"

We went into the bathroom; he dropped his pants, then his boxers. I took it in my hand and started jerking it. I said, "Now remember, *I am not going to finish*! I'll suck you for about twenty or thirty seconds. I'll go as deep as I can, but I won't finish."

To tell you the truth, I was sure this guy was getting laid all over the place, he knew exactly what to say and was well rehearsed. So even if I didn't get caught, I didn't want to have to explain to my husband how I ended up with Herpes, or God forbid, kill my husband with AIDS. I'm sure many of you are judging me, thinking I'm evil, but I'm not; I was sick. That's why I can tell you what I believe to be one hundred percent fact, that God, my guardian angel, or one of the many other angels that I pray to—I don't know which, but some blessed energy—was sent down to stop me when we were on that bed and gave me the strength to stop it. As you know from past events, I, alone, did not have the power to do that on my own.

So I gave him what I promised and stopped. He begged for me to keep going each time I stopped. Thirty seconds turned into three minutes; then finally, I stopped, stood up and walked out. Not only walked out of the bathroom, but out into the hallway. No one was there, so I called to him, "It's OK!"

He followed me and cried out, "You're killing me, you don't understand!" I grabbed his arm to stop him from going down the stairs. I said, "You don't think I understand?!" I reached down and touched myself. I was soaked. I slid my hand back out and touched his lips to show him how much I really *did* understand. To let him know how difficult it was for me not to bend over in that bathroom and have him slide his cock inside me.

He licked his lips and said, "My God, you taste like peaches! I'm gonna be licking my lips all night." I said, "So you see, I do understand!" He said, "Yes, I know you do; I'm sorry for making it so hard. Are you sure you're OK with this? You're not gonna feel like you have to tell your husband, right?"

I said, "Yes, I'm fine." We went downstairs and smoked a cigarette together. The meeting was just letting out, so everyone was going outside to smoke. How obvious, right? I'll bet some people were suspicious. Both of us were "missing" for about a half hour, and then we're sitting together smoking! Come on now, these people were addicts; they weren't retarded.

I think one of the reasons why I came out of that place worse was because that counselor confused me. Initially, when he and I had spoken, before anything happened, he questioned why I told my husband each time I was unfaithful. I told him that I thought that was the only thing I could do to make the situation less horrible. You always hear people who are hurt by infidelity saying, "And to make it worse, you lied to me." I just figured I didn't want to cheat on him, *and* lie to him. I was sick; I couldn't refuse sex offers; I wasn't having an affair. Not to mention, I couldn't look him in the eyes each morning if I had lied to him. I'm not a liar. I wouldn't be able to live with myself; I barely could already. I believed that David was still with me because he knew sex addiction was a disease that I was struggling with, and he knew I wanted to get better. Lying is a choice; there is no excuse for that. He would have no reason to forgive or trust me *ever* again.

After I explained that to him, this counselor, this person who is here to help me, said, "Don't you realize you are being selfish? You're hurting him worse to make yourself feel better.

You are just telling him to get it off your mind. You even said *I* couldn't live with myself; you were only thinking about yourself when you confessed."

I knew that wasn't true; I mean, I knew I wasn't telling David just to make myself feel better. My God, it killed me every time I had to tell him, to look into his eyes and see the pain I was causing him. It was the last thing I wanted to do. I didn't know though, maybe Ian was right. Maybe I put David through all that pain so I didn't have to live with the lie. I was very confused.

Now, with hind sight being 20/20, I can see that this man, this counselor, was "preparing" me because he had something in mind already. He was convincing me that "confessing" was a selfish, hurtful thing to do to my husband, because he knew even in the beginning of the week, when we first met, that he was planning to fuck me; and when he did, he didn't want me telling anyone! It worked. He had me all guilty and confused. I felt like I couldn't tell David about the blow job for two reasons now. First, I was now questioning myself, what if Ian was right and I was being selfish by telling him, but more importantly, I came here to get better. This was my last chance to save my marriage.

After our meeting, later that day, he told me he wanted me to think about going into his office for the rest of the night. His schedule was like nine to five or nine to six, so when he was leaving he kept begging, "Let's meet in my office. Don't answer me now, please, think about it! No one will know. All night tonight, that's what I want you to think about and give me your answer in the morning."

For any of you that have ever been to rehab, for anything, you know you are given journals to write in and workbooks to do for the next day's groups and meetings. Kind of "homework" you're supposed to work on when you are in your room at night. There are no televisions or radios there. After I was home, but not until weeks later, I realized for him to tell me to think only about being with him for the rest of the night, that this alone should have told me that this "counselor" was not about me getting help *at all*! I know it should have been obvious while I was there, but I was not able to see things clearly. They had stopped giving me my Xanax; they didn't have the Luvox to give me for my OCD, so besides the chemicals in my brain being all off balance, I missed my husband and feared I was going to lose him forever. I was homesick and missed my puppies. With all of this going on, I was easy prey. As foolish as it seems in hindsight, at the time I had no doubt that the goal of all the workers there was to get me better.

The next morning, he came up to me in the hallway and asked me, "Did you think about it?" I said, "Yes." I really hadn't though. The thing with my sex addiction was that it was always very "spontaneous." It was hard for me to resist in the moment, but after I'm away from the person, I feel guilty and think only about my husband. I go over it and over it in my head, wondering why I'm doing the things I'm doing. My thoughts that night were not only filled with guilt about my husband, but also with fear. I was afraid that this guy set me up. They made me sign a form upon admission saying that I wouldn't have sex with anyone in the rehab center the entire time I was there. I thought maybe I was being set up or something; I became paranoid. I thought it was like a test to see if I was offered sex, would I take it or not. I didn't know. This was my first time in a rehabilitation center; I didn't know if they tested you to see if you were improving. I know that sounds crazy, but you really start to lose your mind when you're locked up in a place like that!

He didn't take "no" for an answer. He repeatedly asked, "But why? No one could catch us. If you're OK with what happened yesterday, then why not?" Little did he know I was *not* OK with what happened yesterday. I cried in my room all night thinking about whether or not I was going to tell David about the blow job or not!

People were all around us in the hallway—some employees, some patients. Meetings were starting; some patients were just going to the cafeteria. I think he was nervous, so he said, "Come with me." We went upstairs where only patient rooms were. No meetings or groups were ever upstairs. No one was up there, so he led me to this bathroom that I didn't even know was there. It was kind of hidden down a narrow corridor behind the laundry room; he even had to use his key to open the door.

As I look back on it, I'm amazed by the extremes men will go to, the risks they'll take for sex. He put his hands on my shoulders and looked me straight in the eyes. He said, "I could not get you off mind last night. I could taste you; I could picture your body, please, please, please let's do this."

I paused, like I was thinking about it, but like I said, my decision had been made the night before not to go through with it for so many reasons; but the thought of losing David for good was enough. It was *always* enough. In past situations I had been caught up in the heat of the moment. If I had this much time to think about it, I *never* would have cheated and wouldn't be in this place. My problem now was that I was afraid to say "no" to him—afraid of his reaction. What if he threatened to lie and say that I seduced him and got me kicked out? Who would they believe? He worked there for so long and I was just another addict to them; addicts are known to be liars! Finally I just said, "OK, I'll do what I did yesterday, but that's it."

He accepted that only after realizing it was that or nothing. He was already hard. I started going down on him for only about ten seconds when we heard someone in the laundry room. It was just someone starting their laundry, but it scared the hell out of me. I stopped and stood up.

He said, "It's OK, they're just starting their laundry."

I said, "No, I'm done, I'm out of here! That's it, what if they try to come in here?"

He said, "They can't; it's locked."

I said, "So they'll knock."

He said, "Just don't answer, they'll leave."

I got pissed off and said, "Yeah, they'll leave and get someone with a key!"

He pulled up his pants and said, "You're right, that's why we should go into my office!"

I couldn't believe it. It wasn't even funny anymore. A few minutes had passed and it sounded like the person had gone, so I just slipped out the door and went downstairs. I finally got down to the smoking area and collapsed into a chair. That scared me so much, I was done. No office, no more bathrooms; I had three days left and then I was home free! I was just going to go to meetings and spend the rest of the time in my room. After only about a minute, he followed and sat down next to me.

He asked, "Are you OK?"

I said, "Yes, I'm fine. I'm not leaving this seat, though."

I guess he realized how much that scared me; maybe it scared him a little too.

He said, "No, I'm not asking you to go anywhere; I just want to make sure you're OK."

I could tell that now he was afraid that he fucked up, which he did, but that I wasn't gonna tell.

I said reassuringly, "Yes, I'm fine."

He persisted, "You're not gonna tell your husband, right?"

I said, "No way. I told you, the only reason I am here is so he wouldn't leave. If I told him this, he would definitely leave."

He agreed and said, "Good, because you really didn't do anything wrong. I'm sorry I made it so hard for you, but you held out. You should be proud of yourself; you are actually better. Had you ever before been able to resist someone who was so persistent?"

I couldn't even answer him because I was so stunned by the bullshit he was trying to sell me! He was trying to make it sound like I was healed! Didn't he realize that sucking him off twice during the "recovery" is not really "healed"? I didn't care what he thought. He knew I was done with him.

The weekend came, and ironically, one of the meeting's speakers was a *sexologist*! Hello! How come *she* wasn't assigned to me? There is a sexologist employed here, and this whole week passed by without introducing me to her? I *am* in the fucking "Cuckoos Nest!" After the meeting, I went up to her and said, "Hi, I was admitted here for sexual addiction. Is there any way I could meet with you?" She seemed surprised and repeated, "You are here with an addiction to sex?" I said, "Yes." She asked, "How long have you been here?" I told her, "Seven days, and I go home tomorrow."

She then caught me off guard and asked, "Have you had sex

with anyone here?" See, even she knew this place was the worst place for a sex addict to be! I had to lie and say, "No." As she collected her briefcase and her keys she said to me, "When you get out of here, find a sexologist, and find out where there are meetings in the town you live in. Most towns have meetings for sex addicts just like they have Alcoholics Anonymous meetings. Find yourself a good sexologist first, and they'll tell you where the meetings are."

I said, "OK, I will; thank you." I was *pissed*! I felt I was lied to and ripped off. They told me and my husband over the phone that I was going to get good treatment at this place, and I paid $3500 for nothing. No, it was less than nothing; I actually ended up worse because now, for the first time, I had to lie to my husband. I couldn't wait to get out of that place.

Chapter Twenty-five

Finally, it was time to go home. My husband would be there soon to pick me up. I was so nervous. Yes, looking back, I was excited to go home, but nervous to see my husband. I was afraid that my eyes would give me away. I had never lied to him before, and he always knew how I was feeling just by looking at me. He knew when I was sad, scared, happy, angry. I should only look happy to see him, relieved to be healed when he got there. Instead I was afraid to see him, wondering will he see the guilt in my face, the fear; will he recognize a lie?

As soon as he pulled up, I grabbed my stuff and started walking out. He got out of his car, came in, took the bags from me and said, "Let me get those." I just wanted to grab him and hug him and never let go. Already, I couldn't look him in the eyes. I felt as soon as he looked at me he would know something bad happened. People were standing around us, so as he took my bags we kissed and hugged each other tightly but just for a second. The people around us were friends that I had made in this short, but significant experience. Some were women I had connected with and shared stories with, stories I "wasn't allowed" to share in group. Some were "smoking buddies," but not *that* one. I guess they were waiting to meet my husband, who was all I talked about the entire week, and to say good-bye. I must have seemed so cold to them; I just wanted to get out of there. I hugged a couple of the women and waved as I practically ran out the door.

The car ride home was unusually quiet. Not uncomfortably quiet—we were always comfortable around each other—just unusual after being apart for so long. I guess it was because I'm usually telling stories of my day, true stories, just the long version of simple, everyday events. It started after my accident; my word-finding difficulty makes me describe things in length because I can't think of the word that applies. It's hard to explain, but for example: One time I was telling my mother, while we were trying to pick out wallpaper that, "I don't want the kind that makes you feel like there are bars all around the room." What I meant to say was, "I don't like stripes."

Then David said, "Is everything OK? You're so quiet." I answered, "Yes, but I feel weird. I feel like I was in a different world for eight days, and now I have to re-learn how to live in this world. I have nothing to say, I feel like I fell out of life for a week."

He tried to reassure me and said, "Well that's to be expected, you kind of did. Be patient, give yourself time." My God, he is so good to me. He then said, "How about some Starbucks; that might make you feel better." He knew I loved Starbucks and we would sometimes get it as a treat or for a special occasion. So we stopped for Starbucks, and I did start to feel a little bit "normal," or at least more like myself; I doubt if I ever felt "normal." I just felt so good being close to him and couldn't wait to see my puppies.

The ride went pretty quickly. It was so comforting when we drove into our neighborhood. The beautiful fall trees, the neatly manicured front lawns, and then our house. Just seeing it made me feel so happy. I thought to myself, "Everything is gonna be just fine." How could I ever do anything to jeopardize losing this beautiful, brilliant man or this loving, cozy home or this life we've made together? For once in a very long time, I was *sure* of myself. I was *sure* I was going to be in control of my actions. Then, when I walked into the house and saw that the puppies were just as happy to see me as I was to see them, I began to cry. I was so happy I started to quietly pray. I thanked God for letting me come back home, for the unconditional love from my husband, my dogs; my home even felt warmer, cozier.

For about a week, everything was quiet. We found a sexologist like they recommended, but I was hesitant to go to meetings. My husband was disappointed that I wasn't following the instructions given to me by the rehab, the instructions from "Kelly," who sent a set of instructions home with me that listed "do's" and "don'ts" about how to recover from a sex addiction. I knew that Kelly didn't know "jack-shit" on how to treat this disease—forcing me to lie in group and hold back the reason I was there. I just wanted to put that whole week behind me and meet with the sexologist individually. I explained to my husband that all of the meetings in our town were co-ed. I didn't think it was too safe for a bunch of sex addicts to sit around talking about all of their wild sex stories. I could see the meeting turning into an orgy. I think then he understood. He was just afraid, and who could blame him? I was no longer afraid. I knew I was madly in love with my husband. I loved my life; I was under the care of a sexologist, and there was no way I was ever going to be unfaithful again.

My sexologist was the one who told me that even though I was consenting to it, all the sex I had with Joey at such an early age was a form of molestation. She told me that even though your body is developed enough to have sex, emotionally your mind is not able to handle a sexual relationship. I learned from her in only three visits that this was what started the sexual addiction. Perhaps, since I had body dysmorphia and used sex to feel beautiful, I had become addicted within the first few months of having sex. Nevertheless, she explained, that with or without the body dysmorphia, being sexually active at such a young age will always lead to issues with sex—whether it's addiction or something else.

It was all starting to make sense now. I began to understand the reasons why it didn't matter to me, as I was growing up, whether the sex was good or not, why I didn't care whether I had an orgasm or not. I didn't even care if it was abusive sex; men would grab me by my hair, spank me so hard they'd leave hand prints, or fulfill any crazy fetish they had—as long as I was getting male attention, I would let them.

Chapter Twenty-six

I was a sex addict; I went to a rehabilitation center, and now I'm seeing a sexologist. Happy ending, right? But wait, what about the lie? Oh, *that* lie, the "lie of omission." The first lie I "never" told my husband. That was killing me. Everyday, every minute, it's all I could think about. I tried to get it out. I told my mom, but that didn't help; she told me to report the man who seduced me. I then told my sexologist; she said the same thing my mother did. She told me to call and report him. I told her I couldn't risk David finding out. She said, "But what if he does this to another girl, and she commits suicide because of it? You have to tell on him." I still said, "No, I can't risk it."

Not only was I lying to my husband now, but I was also responsible for the potential suicide of some made-up girl. Thank you for that doctor! I couldn't handle any of it; I went back to drinking. David was so afraid, but I convinced him, "I can drink now and we don't have to worry!" After all, I went to rehab for sex, not alcohol. I begged David to go out. We hadn't gone out all month except a couple times during the week to a restaurant or the movies. I wanted to drink; I needed to drink. I couldn't stand living with this lie. They had stopped my Xanax in the rehab and when I went back to my psychiatrist I told him I didn't want to go back on it. I thought maybe taking away my anxiety, *completely*, wasn't a good thing. I was drinking which lowers your inhibitions. Add Xanax and you're not afraid of anything; not even the things you're supposed to be afraid of, like losing your husband and going home with someone you just met. I wanted to go to a bar, drink and play pool; I needed distractions. I couldn't turn off my brain on my own, and all I could think about was that lie.

David agreed to go out on one condition: he didn't want to go back to that same bar, but I begged him. I wanted to play pool and we didn't know any other pool bar. He finally agreed, but was anxious; he said, "I hope that asshole isn't there." I was happy. I was going out with my husband and I wasn't going to think about anything. I was just gonna have fun.

The first night out at the bar, guess who was waiting for me when I went to the ladies room? You got it, Steve, he gave me a big hug and said, "I missed you so much, I couldn't stop thinking about you." Nothing happened. I told him that I almost lost my husband that night. I explained that I had gone to a rehab for sex addiction. I told him I loved my husband and nothing like that night could ever happen again. I figured I was "fixed"; I was back in control of my life, right?

Steve stayed away from us that night, although once in a while I would see him when I went up for a drink. We would smile at one another, but I didn't run into him in the ladies room again and David and I left together before last call.

A few days later we had a big hurricane hit us. David's work closed, power was out, computers were down. For three days our entire city was dark. The food in our refrigerator went bad; trees fell all around our subdivision; even some of our trees came down, but thank God, we had no property damage like some of our neighbors. It was a good distraction for me; we needed candles at night, and we had to find places that were open to get food during the day. My mind was always busy. The air conditioner wasn't working so we had to use fans to cool off. We were told not to drink the water, so we made sure all of us, including the dogs, drank bottled water. All these distractions were great; my brain was too busy to think about that lie.

Then, after three days, everything came back up—first the phones, then the power, then the cable. It was Friday so David still didn't have to go to work the next day. He went to Home Depot; he was always going to Home Depot, he's such a great handyman and can fix anything. While he was gone I took a nice hot shower. I hadn't had hot water in three days and I thought it would be great. Unfortunately, my mind was free again, but I didn't start thinking about the lie, even worse, I started thinking about Steve. When I got out of the shower I called him. He told me they were having a party to celebrate everything being back on and the storm being over, and asked me to come. I figured there was no threat now; I had seen him already and nothing happened, I said, "OK, I'll come, what time?"

I started getting ready. I was blow drying my hair and putting on make-up when David got back. He asked, "Where are you going?" I answered nonchalantly, "Steve is having an after storm party." He said, "You've gotta be kidding me. I've been stuck in this house for three days too, don't you think I want to get out?" I innocently said, knowing what his response was gonna be, "You're invited too, we'll both go."

"I can't believe you," he said. "You know I'm not going to that douche bag's house, and you're going anyway?" he yelled.

I'm disgusted with myself as I write this. I was excited to go, without David. David knew how broken I was; he knew that I was just a shell of the person he had fallen in love with. Steve thought I was perfect, he didn't know me; he didn't know me *at all*, and looking back, that's probably what I liked most about him. I wasn't running away from David, I was running away from the monster I had become.

As I was getting dressed, I assured David, "You have nothing to be afraid of, lots of people are gonna be there; I already saw him at the bar and nothing happened." He asked, "But what am I gonna do?"

"I told you, we're both invited," I said as I grabbed my keys and kissed him goodbye. Thinking back to that afternoon, I kept very busy as we spoke. I couldn't even look at him. Somewhere in that fucked-up brain of mine, I must have known I was breaking the heart of the man I loved, my best friend, and I couldn't bear to watch the hurt I was causing him. *I was a coward; I should have at least had the guts to look in his eyes and see the pain that I was responsible for!*

As I walked out the door, I heard him despairingly say, "I can't believe you're going." After hearing that, something clicked in my head, the excitement vanished, my heart broke. What was I doing? I *wasn't* in control, of anything; I needed alcohol to quiet my thoughts; I was abandoning my husband, who I loved, to go to a guy's house where there were gonna be a bunch of people I neither knew nor cared about. I was even starting to believe the lie that I had gone to a rehabilitation center for sex addiction and had gotten better, when in actuality what I feared was happening while I was in the hospital, was true: I didn't get better, I got worse, so much worse! Now I have to drink to quiet my mind because the lie keeps on repeating over and over and I can't stop it. I am still a sex addict and *that's* why I wanted to go back to that same bar, *that's* why I had to go to this party and leave my husband behind. I realized my addiction that was still in control. I *never* had control at all, I faked it, even to myself. Let's face it, if I wasn't sick, we would have just found another hang out.

As far as being "friends" with Steve, that was impossible after what had happened. That's like an alcoholic just having a glass of wine with dinner. It's undoubtedly going to end disastrously—and it did.

I remember driving that evening to Steve's house. I had just pulled out of my sub-division onto the main road and I kept hearing David's words. I felt so horrible, I wanted to turn around and go back home and go out to a nice dinner with him, or anywhere where it would be just the two of us, but I couldn't do it. I mean I *physically* could not turn the car around—no bullshit here, that is how strong my addiction was. There was another turn off up ahead where my mind and my heart were both telling me to turn around. I remember I intended to turn off, but went right past it. There was a gas station ahead that I *did* turn into. I parked the car and just started crying my eyes out. I prayed; I couldn't understand what was happening. Now I knew for sure something was wrong with me. I was no longer in control, but I didn't know what *was* at that point. I didn't think it was my sex addiction at the time because I wasn't planning on fooling around with him. I was just going there to hang out; other people were there. We couldn't just go into the bedroom; it was *his* party. It was like I was possessed by something, some evil force stronger than myself making me go to this place *I didn't even want to go anymore*!

When I got there, they were all there sitting around watching a game, football I think. I don't give a shit about football—I hate sports. I had no idea why I was going, but I went and as soon as I walked in, I looked around at everyone and wished I was home with David. But I was still unable to walk out.

People are disgusted by addicts, and rightfully so for the pain we cause the people who love us; but I just want you all to know, all of you family members of addicts, that we are suffering too. It's a scary feeling not to have control over your own body, your actions, your life. Imagine, *physically* not being able to turn the car around. Every decision, every action, it's all controlled by the addiction. For me, the addiction was not only wanting sex from a man, it was how I defined myself. I only *saw* myself, *judged* myself, *liked* or *disliked* myself through a man's reaction to me. Without it, I was nothing and *that's* why I had to go to that party, because around David, I felt ashamed, I was a disappointment, I could see it in his eyes, I could hear it in his voice, and he had every right to feel that way. At this party I could reinvent myself. I knew Steve already liked me, and nobody else there knew me.

Before I sat down, I went into the kitchen to make a drink. I wanted to make a Gimlet, but there was no ice and no limes, so I drank warm vodka. I didn't care; I needed to numb my brain. I couldn't stop thinking about David, but still couldn't leave. I was pathetic. After one drink, I felt more comfortable. I was sitting next to Steve pretending to watch the game. He wasn't paying much attention to me, but now I had two drinks in me and could change that. I leaned over putting my head on his shoulder and my hand on his thigh. He looked at me and said, "I thought we had to just be friends." I said, "We are friends."

"Friends with benefits?" he asked. Right then I remember thinking, *my God, he is so young. What am I doing here?* I kept on drinking; I had to turn off my thoughts completely.

I don't remember the sequence of events, but we *did* end up in the bedroom. Once again, I was too wasted to remember the night, but of course, like any other "lush," I passed out afterwards. I woke up and my first thought was David. What was I gonna do; what was I gonna say? There were no excuses. I didn't even have the addiction to blame, remember, in David's mind, "I was all better." He didn't know I was actually worse than before I went to rehab and it was just a matter of time until this would happen. I just grabbed my shit and left. As I drove home I prayed and I cried. I knew I didn't deserve David; he had no reason to forgive me or stay with me; he deserved *so* much better; this wasn't *me*. What happened God? I asked. Help me get back, back to the person I was, back to the life I loved.

When I walked in, David was standing there in the living room, suitcases by his side. I even saw our wedding picture had been taken down and was leaning up against one of his bags. He just looked at me, stoically, and asked, "I thought you were better? What about the hospital and the sexologist?" That's when it finally came out. I had to confess, I said, "It didn't work." I told him the whole story; we were both crying. I never saw him so angry.

He yelled, "I hate you! You ruined my life and I never want to see you again!" I was crying so hard I wanted to die. I couldn't even hold myself up; I collapsed to the floor.

I begged him, "Please let's call Dr. Stanley!" Dr. Stanley was the sexologist.

David said, "It's Saturday; she's closed."

I said, "I know but this is an emergency. If you leave me right now, I'm gonna die. She has to see us; it's an emergency."

He said, "What's this 'us' shit? I don't have to see her."

I said, "No you have to come with me; we have to find a way to cure me of this. I hate doing it; I want to be better. If not, I don't want to live anymore. I'll never forgive myself if I lose you!" I called her emergency line and she met me at her office. Hesitantly, David came with me. She admitted to David that I did tell *her* about the employee and that I had been taken advantage of. At this time he wanted to know why I didn't report him. I told him, "Because I was afraid of losing you," and he said, "Well you can report him now." Then we got back to whether he was going to stay or not.

He was adamant about leaving. He said, "She's obviously hopeless!" The doctor disagreed and suggested that the rehab facility had not been a place for me to get help. She did say, "For now, you need to separate. David needs time to get over the anger and remember that you are sick and that you didn't do it intentionally to hurt him. But that takes time."

OK, for all of you readers with faith, here is a *great* example of "Divine Intervention." David said, "See, this isn't fair. She's fucked up and now I have to move out of my own house, away from my dogs, and into my parent's depressing beach house." Then the doctor asked, "Isn't there any place you can go Samantha?"

I said, "Yes, my mother is down here for the hurricane; I can go stay with her." Now, you may be saying to yourself, "So what, a storm, what's so divine about that?" My father hadn't retired yet, so my parents only came down once in awhile. There was now a hurricane threat for my parent's area of Virginia, so my mom came down to wait it out. The Divine Intervention is that the hurricane passed right over—no storm, no damage done. The storm stayed out to sea and didn't even make it on land. The only thing the storm threat did was give *me* a place to stay.

Like a typical addict, the first evening, I was restless. I called Steve that night and asked if he wanted to pick up some liquor and come to my mother's house. She has a big, beautiful, screened in patio with lawn furniture and a pool. I wasn't planning on fucking him, but I needed a distraction and some alcohol. He agreed, I gave him directions and we hung up the phone. *Looking back, that may have been the worst idea I ever had.* My mother asked, "Was that David?" "No," I said, it was Steve, the guy from the bar. He's gonna come over, maybe go swimming."

She became furious. *"No way, you call him back and tell him he is not welcome here. I won't let you do this to David."*

"Fine, I'll tell him to pick me up."

She said, "You are here trying to fix your marriage, what are you thinking?" I thought about David. I began to miss him. I called him and told him my plans to go out with Steve. I assured him we were going out as friends. I could hear the despondence in his voice, "OK, have fun," he said, and hung up. I started to cry as I thought about him and what I was putting him through; it finally hit me. I called Steve and told him not to come. Then, right away, I called David and told him I changed my mind and wasn't going out. He sounded surprised, and for the first time, in a long time, he sounded happy—happy *and* hopeful. I had my psychic change. I went inside to my mother and apologized. I was crying uncontrollably; I didn't know what was wrong with me. I loved David more than anything else in the world. My mother and I sat and talked and cried, there was no doubt that I loved David and wanted to stay married, and I was going to do whatever it took to make that happen.

The next night, David took me out on a "dinner-date," as advised by the doctor. He dropped me back off at my mom's, and we kissed good night. We would talk on the phone each day while he was at work. My mother and I would talk and pray. We watched Joel Osteen—he is the *best* Christian preacher I've ever heard. I swear, for those three days, it felt like he was speaking directly to me. He was giving me all the answers I was unable to find in the rehab or from any of the doctors. He was saying how we need to forgive ourselves as quickly as we forgive others. We are all sinners and just because we do bad things, doesn't mean we're bad people—and so much more. Then on the third morning I woke up and called David. I asked him if I could come home and he said, "I was hoping you would say that. I miss you so much."

He came to get me and we hugged and I cried. I never wanted to let go. It was a beautiful, sunny day, so we went for a ride on my dad's golf cart. I couldn't get close enough to him. I was nestled up underneath his arm, happier than I've ever been and thanking God for getting me back, back to myself and back where I belonged with the love of my life. We were together for good this time, and *nothing* was going to get between us.

I looked up at David, into his beautiful, eyes and with tears of happiness running down my face, I asked, "Why did you stay with me? After all of the pain I put you through, what kept you from leaving?"

He answered, "I knew you were in there somewhere."

Printed in Great Britain
by Amazon